Critical Theories of Globalization

Also by Chamsy el-Ojeili

CONFRONTING GLOBALIZATION: Humanity, Justice and the Renewal of Politics

FROM LEFT COMMUNISM TO POSTMODERNISM: Reconsidering Emancipatory Discourse

Also by Patrick Hayden

AMERICA'S WAR ON TERROR

CONFRONTING GLOBALIZATION: Humanity, Justice and the Renewal of Politics

COSMOPOLITAN GLOBAL POLITICS

JOHN RAWLS: Towards a Just World Order

THE PHILOSOPHY OF HUMAN RIGHTS

Critical Theories of Globalization

Chamsy el-Ojeili
Department of Sociology, Victoria University of Wellington, New Zealand

Patrick Hayden
School of International Relations, University of St Andrews, UK

First published 2006 by
PALGRAVE MACMILLAN
Houndmills, Basingstoke, Hampshire RG21 6XS and
175 Fifth Avenue, New York, N. Y. 10010
Companies and representatives throughout the world

PALGRAVE MACMILLAN is the global academic imprint of the Palgrave Macmillan division of St. Martin's Press, LLC and of Palgrave Macmillan Ltd. Macmillan® is a registered trademark in the United States, United Kingdom and other countries. Palgrave is a registered trademark in the European Union and other countries.

ISBN-13: 978–1–4039–8638–2   hardback
ISBN-10: 1–4039–8638–X   hardback
ISBN-13: 978–1–4039–8639–9   paperback
ISBN-13: 1–4039–8639–8   paperback

This book is printed on paper suitable for recycling and made from fully managed and sustained forest sources.

A catalogue record for this book is available from the British Library.
A catalogue record for this book is available from the Library of Congress.

10   9   8   7   6   5   4   3   2   1
15   14 13 12 11 10 09 08 07 06

Printed and bound in Great Britain by
Antony Rowe Ltd, Chippenham and Eastbourne

Contents

List of Boxes

Acknowledgments

We would like to thank our editors, Jennifer Nelson and Philippa Grand, and publisher, Alison Howson, for their help and support, the anonymous readers who made useful suggestions for improving the manuscript, and Shiranthi Fonseka for her valuable research assistance. Thanks also to our students, who helped us to clarify some of the ideas in the book. We owe an enormous debt of gratitude to our families for their love and encouragement; this book is dedicated to them.

The authors and publisher acknowledge the use of the Adbusters advertisement courtesy of www.adbusters.org.

Introduction

Said Arojomand (2004: 341) argues that in the period after the collapse of communism (1989–91) 'globalization' pushed 'postmodernism' aside as 'the social scientific master trend of a new era', or as Featherstone and Lash (quoted in Rosenberg, 2000: 2) put it, as 'the central thematic for social theory'. More widely, globalization has been, for more than a decade, a major concern not only in academic but also in government, business, and popular discourse. Zygmunt Bauman (1999a: 1) captures the ubiquity of the concept and raises, at the same time, doubts about its deployment: '"Globalization" is on everybody's lips; a fad word fast turning into a shibboleth, a magic incantation, a pass-key meant to unlock the gates to all present and future mysteries. For some, "globalization" is what we are bound to do if we wish to be happy; for others "globalization" is the cause of our unhappiness'. Here Bauman gestures both to the manner in which globalization is often taken as a process beyond the scope of human control and also to the tendency to appeal to globalization as an explanation for everything. For this reason, discussion around globalization often resolves into a set of unspecific and unquestioned observations: the nation-state is losing power; a new global culture is appearing; there is no alternative to the 'golden straightjacket' (Friedman, 1999) of global capitalism, and so on.

While it seems to us that the debate around globalization is far from exhausting itself it is just as evident that, at the very least, in popular discussions the discourse of globalization works all-too-often as mystification. Thus, casual use of the term 'globalization' frequently substitutes for proper elucidation and critical analysis of a host of complex issues, and in doing so obscures the variety of complex, uneven, and interrelated forces and processes that characterize world interconnectedness.

1

A central aim of this book is to 'demystify' globalization by introducing central issues, unravelling with as much clarity as possible key debates, illustrating with examples, and rubbing competing positions against each other in order to provide an overview of the critical theoretical and substantive field of debate around globalization. This field is, we believe, rich and valuable, illustrating Gregor McLennan's (2000) argument about an emerging 'new positivity' in the social sciences, which seeks to forge a stronger consensus about the state of the world today and put this understanding to 'progressive and effective use in the public realm'. This 'new positivity' is not an anti-intellectual trend that imagines it might jettison theory for straightforward empirical description of 'the facts of the matter' or the 'real world'. In this, we follow the contention – advanced by the theorists associated with the Frankfurt School – that there is no coming naked to apprehension (as the novelist Alexander Trocchi (1966: 9) put it), that theorizing is inescapable, and that 'the facts of the matter' are never something that can be separated from conceptualization or from politics. In this vein, there is some disagreement over the meaning to be attached to the empirical evidence used to support various claims about the effects of globalization. While some may argue that the 'facts speak for themselves', we believe that the available data must be reflected upon within a larger frame of concepts, interpretations, and socio-historical events. Ultimately, evidence about globalization is formed, sustained and contested within particular social, political, and economic contexts, and claims about this evidence must be assessed in light of this. Therefore, a new positivity implies the attempt to connect theoretical innovation and elucidation with substantive issues in the public realm – a return, in many ways, to the sorts of theorizing engaged in by the classical social and political theorists of modernity, such as Karl Marx, Max Weber, and Émile Durkheim. In particular, the theoretical lenses employed in these chapters are provided broadly by critical theory, which we shall discuss in Chapter 1. We will note here, though, that critical theory today is a diverse terrain, providing a rich set of interpretative tools that have varying implications for the understanding of globalization. Therefore, we adopt a pluralistic approach to critical theory, embracing the different specialisms of the various types of critical theory while recognizing their common interests grounded in the possibility of social critique and transformation. For this reason the title of the present book refers to critical *theories* rather than to 'the' critical theory of globalization.

The book proceeds as follows. Chapter 1 begins by introducing critical theory and discussing the different ways it has been employed. We then set out the major theoretical responses to globalization before turning to analyze globalization in history. This analysis is important to understanding the specificity of contemporary globalization. The following section examines some of the main theories of social change, in order to illuminate the connection between globalization and the dimensions of societal change thought to accompany globalizing transformations. This leads, in the final section, to a discussion of the notions of 'development' and 'modernity' as prominent ways of conceptualizing global social change.

Though we deny that the economic, the political, and the cultural dimensions can be unproblematically separated, we use these broad divisions as the basis for Chapters 2, 3, and 4, respectively. In Chapter 2, we explore the economic dimensions of globalization. We begin with the important shift in economic common sense, from Keynesian to neoliberal precepts about states and markets. For many critics, institutions such as the World Bank, the International Monetary Fund, and the World Trade Organization are key contemporary carriers of neoliberal ideology, and we discuss these institutions next. We move on, then, to examine the explosion of global finance in recent decades, and then look at multinational corporations as key agents of economic globalization. Considerations of stratification and inequality involving class, poverty, and work follow, as contemporary globalization is seen as issuing in significant alterations in these terms. Globalization is associated as well with new technology, such as digitalization, the Internet, satellites, and so forth, and these are discussed in the penultimate section of Chapter 2. Last, we examine changes in cities and the growth of slums as manifestations of economic globalization.

In Chapter 3, we begin by examining arguments that posit a recent decline in the power of nation-states. The argument often put forward is that the power of multinational corporations, new organizations above and below the level of the state, and new challenges such as the environment and global human rights, have reduced the capacity of states to act strictly in accordance with their own narrow interests. Others have argued that rather than going into decline, the state's role has been transformed in line with a pluralization in governance reflecting, for instance, the impact of an emerging global civil society. One significant argument growing out of this debate is that such changes in state capacities and roles means a corresponding malaise in democratic politics, the central consideration in our final section for this chapter.

Chapter 4 explores cultural globalization. We begin by looking at the global expansion of the power and reach of the cultural industries. One prominent argument – the cultural imperialism thesis – is that the largely Western cultural industries are pushing us in the direction of cultural homogenization. After considering counter-arguments to this thesis, we focus on the issue of identity and ask whether this is changing under the pressures of growing world interconnectedness. We then explore the argument that today's world is faced not with growing sameness but with clashes of incommensurable worlds or civilizations. To explore this further, the chapter closes with reflections on nationalism, ethnicity, and fundamentalism.

Chapter 5 analyzes the anti- or alternative globalization movement. We start by placing this movement in the context of research on social movements in general. The anti- or alternative globalization movement is characterized by a great deal of differentiation, and we next explore some of the different forces and arguments within the movement, some of the different organizations, mobilizations, and theorists contained within the broad label of alternative globalization. We then consider some of the novel modes of action and organizational forms of this movement, which challenge traditional hierarchical models of progressive social change. The chapter also looks at some of the dilemmas facing alternative globalization as a social movement. In conclusion, we briefly consider whether we have with this movement a contemporary restatement of critical theory's utopian dimension, that is, its compelling vision for reconfiguring existing political practices and social institutions.

1
Theorizing Globalization: Introducing the Challenge

Introduction

The purpose of this chapter is to provide critical tools for, and background to, the chapters ahead. Part of this involves examining globalization's historical dimension, which is vital in thinking about the specificity of the contemporary globalizing moment. In theoretical terms, we want to argue for the utility of critical theory as a way of approaching globalization, and critical theories of social change and analyses of modernity and development, which are linked in a number of crucial ways to discussions of globalization, are helpful in understanding the complexity of globalizing transformations. Above all, we insist on the inescapability of theorizing, and maintain that the imaginative and lively variety of critical theoretical approaches canvassed here shed significant light on globalization.

Critical theory

In this section we introduce critical theory, the theoretical paradigm that informs the investigation of globalization in this book. Critical theory today is a very broad theoretical orientation that includes a variety of different approaches and perspectives, with often contrasting analyses of contemporary phenomena. Despite this diversity there are two primary ways of identifying and defining critical theory and its concerns. The first and perhaps most widely recognized version of critical theory is that associated with the body of work developed by members of 'the Frankfurt School' or the Institute for Social Research, established in Frankfurt, Germany in 1923. 'Critical theory' (which is distinguished from 'traditional theory' – see Box 1.1) is a phrase originally coined by thinkers (including Theodor Adorno, Max Horkheimer, Herbert Marcuse, Leo Lowenthal, Franz Neumann, and Jürgen Habermas) of the Frankfurt School, whose research spanned a wide range of areas such as art and music, political economy, technology, the public sphere, and the rise of fascism. As Held (2004a) points out, however, the term 'school' may connote too unified an image of what was in fact a variety of concerns, approaches, and projects. Nonetheless, the Frankfurt theorists did possess a certain unity of purpose – namely, the attempt to move society towards rational institutions 'which would ensure a true, free and just life' (Held, 2004a: 15) – which gave the 'school' its distinct character.

The Frankfurt School theorists were heavily influenced by the philosophies of Kant, Hegel, and especially Marx, but theirs was a critical, unorthodox Marxist orientation that came to reject the determinism of socialist orthodoxy. Frequently, then, the Frankfurt theorists made a move from political economy to the realm of culture – art, psyche, and leisure, for instance – viewing culture both as a site of integration into

---

Box 1.1   Horkheimer on 'Traditional' Theory

The sciences of man and society have attempted to follow the lead of the natural sciences with their great successes. ... The assiduous collecting of facts in all the disciplines dealing with social life, the gathering of great masses of detail in connection with problems, the empirical inquiries, through careful questionnaires and other means ... all this adds up to a pattern which is, outwardly, much like the rest of life in a society dominated by industrial production techniques. ... Beyond doubt, such work is a moment in the continuous transformation and development of the material foundation of that society. But the conception of theory was absolutized, as though it were grounded in the inner nature of knowledge as such or justified in some other ahistorical way, and thus it became a reified, ideological category. As a matter of fact, the fruitfulness of newly discovered factual connections for the renewal of existent knowledge, and the application of such knowledge to the facts, do not derive from purely logical or methodological sources but can rather be understood only in the context of real social processes. ... In traditional theoretical thinking, the genesis of particular objective facts, the practical application of the conceptual systems by which it grasps the facts, and the role of such systems in action, are all taken to be external to the theoretical thinking itself. This alienation, which finds expression in philosophical terminology as the separation of value and research, knowledge and action, and other polarities, protects the savant from the tensions we have indicated and provides an assured framework for his activity.

Source: Horkheimer (1995: 190–1, 194, 208)

the social order and a place in which one could still hear the faint heart-beat of utopia. This is a tendency counter to that of orthodox Marxism, which relegated cultural questions to superstructural or derivative status *vis-à-vis* the economy. In particular, the Frankfurt School theorists challenged orthodox Marxism's dogmatic adherence to historical materialism and its positivist views of economics, politics and science, advocating instead a self-reflective version of 'immanent critique'. Immanent critique is a philosophical approach according to which theory and its prescriptions for social transformation are regarded as inseparable from the historical, social, and material contexts of their own genesis. In other words, immanent critique involves critically questioning the norms and values found within existing social arrangements and institutions, in order to expose contradictions and tensions between ideas and practices which often lead to unacknowledged forms of oppression. Once such contradictions and tensions are exposed, historically possible opportunities for emancipation and social change can then be identified and put into practice.

It is important to keep in mind that the Frankfurt School theorists had witnessed not only the defeat of the post-First World War socialist uprisings in Germany in particular and across Europe more generally, but also the rise of fascism in Spain, Italy and Germany, totalitarianism in the Soviet Union, and, in Adorno, Horkheimer, and Marcuse's exile in America, a new form of domination centred around mass culture and consumption (Anderson, 1976). For these theorists, there was nothing 'self-evident' about history and society, and progressive revolutionary struggle was neither automatic nor inevitable; this position ran counter to the optimism of socialist orthodoxy, which considered socialism an inevitable development out of capitalism.

These thinkers engaged in imaginative and speculative endeavours, seeing such theorizing as important in going beyond appearances and the givenness or 'naturalness' of facts. As Marcuse (1973: 145) argued, 'the real field of knowledge is not the given facts about things as they are, but the critical evaluation of them as a prelude to passing beyond their given form'. Developing Hegel's distinction between what exists and potentiality, or what might yet come into being, the Frankfurt thinkers kept in mind the possibility of a rational future, of going beyond that which existed but doing so in a way that developed out of actually existing social systems. We will take up the question of globalization and this transformative, indeed utopian dimension of critical theory in the final chapter.

Box 1.2   Key Figures of the Frankfurt School

Max Horkheimer (1895–1973) was a German philosopher and sociologist who served as the primary director of the Institute for Social Research from 1930. While inspired by Marxism, Horkheimer's theoretical approach was interdisciplinary and critical of the economic determinism endorsed by many orthodox Marxists who attempted to reduce all social phenomena to economic factors. Horkheimer stressed that the economic system must be examined in connection with art, religion, ethics, ideology, and the psychic structure of consciousness, for the purpose of producing knowledge that could contribute to the struggle against all forms of political domination. Horkheimer argued that the aim of critical theory was to diagnose ideological contradictions between social theory and practice, such as liberalism's support for the concept of equality along with capitalism's creation of material conditions of inequality. His major works include *Studies on Authority and the Family* (1936), *Dialectic of Enlightenment* (1989, with Theodor Adorno), and *Eclipse of Reason* (1947).

Theodor Adorno (1903–69) was a German philosopher, sociologist, and musicologist and member of the Institute for Social Research from 1938. Adorno's primary focus was on the aesthetic dimensions of social order and the relationship between culture and politics. With Horkheimer, Adorno analyzed the emergence of the modern 'culture industry' and the increasing commodification of culture through the production of standardized forms of art and music designed for 'popular' mass consumption. For Adorno, the commodification of culture represented the political means through which dominant ideologies are imposed upon and reproduced throughout society, leading to conformism and the decline of individual thought and behaviour. The passive attitudes reinforced by popular culture, Adorno argued, threaten creativity and freedom and provide a fertile ground for the growth of authoritarian personalities. Adorno's most important works include *Dialectic of Enlightenment* (1989, with Max Horkheimer), *Minima Moralia* (1951), and *Negative Dialectics* (1966).

Herbert Marcuse (1898–1979) was a German philosopher and social theorist and member of the Institute for Social Research from 1933. As with other members of the Frankfurt School, Marcuse wrote extensively about the oppressive effects of advanced industrial society and its ability to co-opt dissent and political opposition. Incorporating the insights of Freud and existentialism with those of Marxism, Marcuse argued that the repressive alienation of modern bureaucratic capitalist society could be challenged through the creative release of eros, sensuality, and joy. Marcuse thus critiqued the narrow Marxist focus on the proletariat as the only legitimate source of social change, and suggested that positive social change could be realized by forging solidarity across a wide spectrum of disaffected groups and movements. For this reason Marcuse became a central figure in the New Left and student movements of the 1960s and 70s. His major writings include *Eros and Civilization* (1955), *One-Dimensional Man* (1964), and *An Essay on Liberation* (1969).

Box 1.2   Key Figures of the Frankfurt School – *continued*

Jürgen Habermas (b. 1929) is a German philosopher and social theorist who studied under Horkheimer and Adorno and served as director of the Institute for Social Research from 1964 to 1971. Habermas is the leading figure of the 'second generation' of the Frankfurt School, and in 1979 he was named 'the most powerful thinker' in Germany by *Der Spiegel* magazine. Habermas's early work focused on the ways in which the instrumental rationality of modern administrative and economic systems tends to dominate the 'lifeworld' of the everyday cultural environment. One consequence of this domination is that social interactions and the intersubjective relationships of individuals become increasingly weakened and distorted. Habermas's later work thus focuses on the nature of communicative action and the conditions required for undistorted communication (for example, by coercion, bias, and violence) between all participants in public discussions. For Habermas, the emancipatory potentials represented by democracy can be best realized through open yet critical communal dialogue that continuously takes into account all relevant viewpoints in deciding upon and evaluating potential outcomes. Habermas's main works include *Legitimation Crisis* (1973), *The Theory of Communicative Action* (1981), and *Between Facts and Norms* (1992).

Critical theory is also defined in a second, broad designation. Chris Brown (1994: 217) suggests that critical theory should be understood as a generic term that refers to an assortment of approaches – ranging from Frankfurt School theory to postmodernism, poststructuralism, and feminism – which share the view that the dominant discourses of modernity emerging from Enlightenment social and political thought are in a state of crisis. This crisis is the result of powerful critiques of modernity's adherence to the positivistic model of scientific practice, which neglected the rich diversity of experience and the importance of norms and values in favour of a narrowly instrumental view of rationality and knowledge. Here, as with the Frankfurt School, critical theory is directed against traditional theory's attempt to imitate the natural sciences and treat social phenomena as immutable 'facts' detached from experience. Defined in this broad sense, critical theory questions the assumptions of modern positivism, pursues alternative modes of thinking, and opens up transformative possibilities for social and political theory and practice. The implications of critical theory are significant insofar as theory is not regarded merely as the attempt to verify reality 'as it is', but to reevaluate current conditions and forge new forms of social life consistent with the goal of emancipation. As one commentator (Hoffman, 1987: 233) has put it, critical theory:

> entails the view that humanity has potentialities other than those manifested in current society. Critical theory, therefore, seeks not simply to reproduce society via description, but to understand society and change it. It is both descriptive and constructive in its theoretical intent; it is both an intellectual and a social act. It is not merely an expression of the concrete realities of the historical situation, but also a force for change within those conditions.

Given the above, critical theory by its very nature constitutes a pluralistic field populated by an eclectic mix of progressive theoretical and political perspectives. However, it can be said that what unites the different strands of critical theory is a shared commitment to human emancipation and a common concern to analyze the causes of, and prescribe solutions to, domination, exploitation, and injustice. As Marcuse suggested, 'any critical theory of society' is committed to two basic normative claims, namely, 'the judgment that human life is worth living, or rather can be and ought to be made worth living' and 'the judgment that, in a given society, specific possibilities exist for the amelioration of human life and the specific ways and means of realizing these possibilities' (Marcuse, 1964: x–xi).

Critical theory is especially concerned with addressing the forms of systematic exclusion associated with the social, economic and political status quo, insofar as the established system often replicates entrenched power relations which have detrimental effects on systematically excluded groups. Such exclusion becomes even more deleterious as power relations assume an increasingly global scope. As Scholte (1996: 53) argues, globalization has too often 'perpetuated poverty, widened material inequalities, increased ecological degradation, sustained militarism, fragmented communities, marginalized subordinated groups, fed intolerance and deepened crises of democracy'. Consequently critical theory seeks to provide for more inclusive and open forms of social, economic, political, and cultural participation, from the local to the global level.

Yet while Scholte points out the negative aspects of globalization, critical theorists are concerned to develop the positive aspects found within the same conditions of the global order. In essence, critical theory aims to exploit the 'immanent contradictions' within globalization in order to foster greater human emancipation. So, for example, while the technological transformations associated with globalization may provide the state with more powerful tools for intrusive surveillance of its citizens, it may also provide citizens with alternative means for communicating, organizing, and mobilizing. The key, then, is to identify what opportunities exist within globalization's immanent contradictions for empowering a wide variety of societal actors. Arguably, the need for empowerment has become ever more pressing as more social and political issues – ranging from human rights, to environmental degradation, to economic inequality – assume a transnational dimension and evoke an emerging global consciousness.

Critical theory thus employs a *critical* function in terms of both its evaluation of the status quo approach to praxis and its assessment of the limitations of much social and political theory. Understanding the purpose of critical theory helps to expose its methodological commitment to reflexivity, that is, a self-reflective awareness of theory's own role in constructing the reality that it examines. Whereas dogmatic or uncritical approaches to theory regard social reality as a pure 'fact', an objective given that can be apprehended in a neutral or value-free sense, critical theory considers the social order and our knowledge of it as being historically constituted and contingently situated. This has two implications: first, our understanding of the social and political world cannot be disconnected from the historically contextualized beliefs and assumptions that inform our interpretations of that reality; and, second, our interpretations and theories do not simply describe reality but also shape and produce it. For this reason theory is not a neutral instrument for passively disclosing reality, but the lens through which agents actively analyse their world and propose alternative ways to shape and reshape it. For Andrew Linklater, a critical theorist working in the field of international relations, the reflexivity of critical theory thereby challenges what he refers to as the 'immutability thesis', which is the claim that social orders are in some sense natural and therefore invariable or unalterable. Hence, as Linklater (1998: 20) describes, 'Efforts to subvert immutability claims, to debunk conventional assumptions about the natural qualities of social structures or human behaviour and to identify countervailing and progressive tendencies within existing societies are the principal hallmarks of critical social theory'.

As mentioned above, critical theory also has burgeoned beyond its Frankfurt School affiliations, leading to diverse and vibrant modes of analysis in which the phrase 'critical theory' tends to be used in a very broad sense, and it includes thinkers whose interests, approaches, and conclusions differ widely. Yet what brings together various critical theorists despite differences in their areas of focus is their attempt to move beyond unreflective and supposedly 'value-neutral' conceptions of political life and social actors, and to develop immanent potentials for emancipation. There is an important shared assumption amongst critical theorists today that we can take up and improve this world, that despite the existence of what Castoriadis (1997a, 1997b) has called the 'fantasm of full, rational mastery' in modernity, there is another rational utopian path to be trod towards positive social change under the conditions of globalization. Critical theory therefore contributes to the study of globalization in that it offers an illuminating normative framework for examining the potentials for both emancipation and oppression immanent in the new forms of interconnectedness characteristic of the contemporary global condition. Because critical theory is committed to the reconstruction of society for the purpose of emancipating it from unnecessary constraints on human freedom, it retains a utopian vitality towards opening up unrealized possibilities for the future. Yet this utopian dimension is firmly grounded within an understanding of the contemporary social reality and its immanent contradictions. Even though critical theory is immersed in the complexity and problems of the world in which we live, it refuses to relinquish the power of moral and political imagination needed to advance the transformative social and political possibilities of our global age.

Defining globalization

Having described the broad critical theoretical framework that orients our approach, a first issue to address is the very definition of our object of study: globalization. There are numerous attempts at this, and often one particular dimension of globalization is taken as key – for instance, a politically-centred definition may underscore the decline of the nation-state and the territorially-bounded societies that formed the grounding unit of analysis of modern political science, sociology, and international relations; while economically-centred definitions may underscore capitalism and the expansion of the free-market system as the key mover of globalizing processes.

For some, globalization is best understood as a legitimating cover or ideology, a set of ideas that distorts reality so as to serve particular interests (Barrett, 1991). Thus Schirato and Webb (2003: 199) view 'globalization' as a 'discursive regime, a kind of machine that eats up anyone and anything in its path'. They suggest that 'globalization functions as a set of texts, ideas, goals, values, narratives, dispositions and prohibitions, a veritable template for ordering and evaluating activities, which is "filled in" or inflected with the interests of whoever can access it' (Schirato and Webb, 2003: 200). For others, globalization is a much more 'material' reality in the contemporary world. Sometimes, as mentioned, this reality is viewed as dominated by one particular dimension as, for instance, in the following definition from *The Social Sciences Encyclopaedia* (Kuper and Kuper, 1996: 234) which privileges economics: 'The development of the world economy has a long history, dating from at least the sixteenth century, and is associated with the economic and imperial expansionism of the great powers. By globalization we refer to a more advanced stage of this process of development'. Langhorne (2001: 2), meanwhile, accents the proliferation of technology: 'Globalization is the latest stage in a long accumulation of technological advance which has given human beings the ability to conduct their affairs across the world without reference to nationality, government authority, time of day or physical environment'.

For others, a more general definition of globalization is in order. The *Dictionary of Social Sciences* (Calhoun, 2002: 192) offers the following conceptualization: globalization is 'A catch-all term for the expansion of diverse forms of economic, political, and cultural activity beyond national borders'. In Bauman's (1999a) formulation, globalization is about 'time-space compression'. And for Roland Robertson, it is 'the crystallization of the entire world as a single place' (in Arnason, 1990: 220). John Lechte (2003), meanwhile, gestures to the connectedness implied by Marshall McLuhan's 1962 phrase 'the global village', according to which globalization is to be viewed as an emerging global consciousness. This connectedness connotes a number of things: communication networks and new technology; the speed at which it is now possible to move around the world; the emergence and contemporary prominence of the multinational corporation; what Lechte calls 'decontextualization', the idea that place is not as relevant as it once was; an awareness of the finitude of global resources; and the threat of a standardization of cultural life.

It seems to us that a relatively broad and open conceptualization of globalization is most useful. A good example of such a definition is Michael Mann's (2001) understanding of globalization as the extension of social relations over the globe. This is in line with Held and McGrew's (2002: 1) definition of globalization as growing world interconnectedness, or as they put it in expanded form: 'globalization denotes the expanding scale, growing magnitude, speeding up and deepening impact of interregional flows and patterns of social interaction. It refers to a shift or transformation in the scale of human social organization that links distant communities and expands the reach of power relations across the world's major regions and continents'. In this conceptualization, globalization can be understood through the following four concepts: stretched social relations, so that events and processes occurring in one part of the world have significant impact on other parts of the world; intensification of flows, with the increased 'density' of social, cultural, economic, and political interaction across the globe; increasing interpenetration, so that as social relations stretch, there is an increasing interpenetration of economic and social practices, bringing distant cultures face to face; and global infrastructures, which are the underlying formal and informal institutional arrangements required for globalized networks to operate (Cochrane and Pain, 2000).

Perspectives on globalization

Already, these definitions signal central issues in the field of debate around contemporary globalization, and these will be taken up in an introductory way at the end of this chapter. However it is important, first, to provide further background to the discussion that is to follow by tracing the broad positions frequently taken on globalization. We will follow Cochrane and Pain's (2000: 22–4) useful characterization of the debate as broadly divided into three approaches.

First, there are the *globalists*. The globalists argue that globalization is a vital and inescapable contemporary social process. National economies, politics, and culture become increasingly part of networks of global flows, and there is little prospect for escaping these. Globalists can be either optimistic or pessimistic in their reading of globalization. For the optimists, globalization will bring raised living standards, greater democracy, and increasing levels of mutual understanding. For the pessimists, on the other hand, globalization is seen as threatening and destructive, as serving only narrow political and economic interests, and as tending to create homogeneity, dislocation, violence, and inequality (Cochrane and Pain, 2000).

Second, there are the *traditionalists*. The traditionalists are profoundly sceptical about globalization, seeing it largely as a myth or 'globaloney'. Some may contend that globalization is not at all new. For example, Marxist traditionalists would point to Marx's famous comments in the 1848 *Communist Manifesto* as evidence that globalization is a far from recent thing:

> The bourgeoisie cannot exist without constantly revolutionising the instruments of production, and thereby the relations of production, and with them the whole relations of society.... Constant revolutionising of production, uninterrupted disturbance of all social conditions, everlasting uncertainty and agitation distinguish the bourgeois epoch from earlier ones.... The need of a constantly expanding market for its produce chases the bourgeoisie over the whole surface of the globe.... All old-established national industries have been destroyed or are being destroyed.... In place of the old wants, satisfied by the productions of the country, we find new wants.... In place of the old local and national seclusion and self-sufficiency, we have intercourse in every direction, universal interdependence of nations.... The bourgeoisie ... compels all nations, on pain of extinction, to adopt the bourgeois mode of production ... to become bourgeois themselves. In one word, it creates a world after its own image. (Marx, 1987: 224–5)

Other traditionalists may view globalization as not really happening at all – for instance, some claim that, in economic terms, what we are witnessing is increased regionalization or interconnectedness between geographically contiguous states rather than globalization. Often, they insist that nation-states remain strong and central. Frequently, traditionalists contend that national economies, too, continue to be of central importance. And they tend to deny that culture is, or could be, global in any pertinent sense.

Finally, there are the *transformationalists* who seek to steer a middle way between the globalists and the traditionalists. For transformationalists it is not the case, on the one hand, that we have entered a completely new, unrecognizable era of transformation in the direction of a global economics, culture, and politics. Neither, though, is it the case that nothing has changed. Instead, contemporary global transformations issue in a 'complex set of interconnecting relationships' (Cochrane and Pain, 2000: 23). We cannot, then, predict ahead of investigation what precisely we will find. Cultural, economic, and political dimensions do not move at the same pace, and within these broad dimensions, unevenness and complexity reign. A summary of the globalist, traditionalist and transformationalist positions is presented in Box 1.3.

Box 1.3   The Globalist, Traditionalist and Transformationalist Positions

Globalist
- There is a fully developed global economy that has supplanted previous forms of the international economy.
- This global economy is driven by uncontrollable market forces which have led to unprecedented cross-national networks of interdependency and integration.
- National borders have dissolved so that the category of a national economy is now redundant.
- All economic agents have to conform to the criteria of being internationally competitive.
- This position is advocated by economic neoliberals but condemned by neoMarxists.

Traditionalist
- The international economy has not progressed to the stage of a global economy to the extent claimed by the globalists.
- Separate national economies remain a salient category.
- It is still possible to organize co-operation between national authorities to challenge market forces and manage domestic economies and govern the international economy.
- The preservation of entitlements to welfare benefits, for instance, can still be secured at the national level.

Transformationalist
- New forms of intense interdependence and integration are sweeping the international economic system.
- These place added constraints on the conduct of national economic policy-making.
- They also make the formation of international public policy to govern and manage the system very difficult.
- This position sees the present era as another step in a long evolutionary process in which closed local and national economies disintegrate into more mixed, interdependent and integrated 'cosmopolitan' societies.

Source: Held (2000: 90–1)

Globalization in history

It seems to us that the transformationalist case is the strongest: contemporary world interconnectedness is best viewed as something different from the globalization of previous periods, but we need to remain sober in our analysis of this specificity. It is clear that globalization is a hugely complex process, and theorizations that focus on the primacy of one dimension, or that attempt sweeping characterizations of all that is happening in, say, cultural or economic terms, are likely to be one-sided and unable to account in a nuanced way for the disjunctions that one is inevitably confronted with.

A good start, though, might be to take seriously the traditionalist case about globalization being 'old hat'. While globalization is often regarded as a feature of the last 30 years, or, more narrowly still, as something that arrived with the fall of communism (see, for instance, T. Friedman, 1999), traditionalists would counter that this can hardly be taken for granted, since it is obvious that world interconnectedness has much earlier origins than the last few decades. In this section, we will explore globalization in history, focussing for the most part on the period of European expansion from the sixteenth century onwards.

Held *et al.* (1999) provide a useful division of globalization into a number of historical phases. The first phase, pre-modern globalization, incorporates the period from the Neolithic Revolution, between 9,000 and 11,000 years ago, until 1500. The next phase is early-modern globalization, stretching from around 1500 to 1850. Next comes modern globalization, 1850 to 1945, which is followed by the contemporary period of globalization, from the end of the Second World War until the present.

Held *et al.* (1999: 33) contend that even the most advanced civilizations of the pre-modern period were 'discrete worlds' propelled by 'largely internal forces and pressures'. The territorial boundaries of these empires were unstable due to factors such as rebellions and alliances, and they were not so much governed as ruled: that is, regularized power and control, in administrative and military terms, was not possible. Later, the fragmented power arrangements provided by the 'interlocking ties and obligations' of Medieval Europe declined in the face of factors such as peasant rebellions, the struggles between monarchs, technological changes, religious conflict, and the extension of trade and market relations (Held *et al.*, 1999). After this time, from the fifteenth to the eighteenth centuries, began the establishment of absolute and constitutional states in Europe and the movement towards the modern state form, based on sovereignty and territoriality, with a rise in state administration, the establishment of the diplomatic system, and regular, standing armies (Held *et al.*, 1999). A central factor in this political reconfiguration was the capacity of these states for overseas operations through military and naval forces.

In the economic realm, intercontinental trade goes back to Antiquity, but such trade was constrained by knowledge, geography, and the limitations of transport technologies (Held *et al.*, 1999). The domestication of animals, and improvements in shipping, roads, and navigational techniques made trade across distances easier, and intercontinental trade, though limited in range and volume, expanded – for instance, the silk trade linking China and the Mediterranean, shipping routes between the Arabian peninsula and India, and the caravan routes of the Near East and North Africa (Held *et al.*, 1999; Osterhammel and Petersson, 2003). A world trading system, though, only emerged around the sixteenth century, with Europe's expansion outwards, and trade becoming an important means for states to gain leverage over other states (Held *et al.*, 1999).

In cultural terms, the main pre-modern stimuli to the movement of people were religion (globalizing religions such as Buddhism, Christianity, and Islam) and economics: for instance, two million migrants from China from the third century BC to the fifth century AD; the movement of armies and settlers from Greek and Roman Antiquity; the Jewish diaspora; the expansion of Islam; the conquests of the Mongol empires of the twelfth and fourteenth centuries; the voyages of Polynesian Islanders; and the expansion of Aztec, Inca, and Maya social orders in the Americas (Held *et al.*, 1999).

This brief outline demonstrates that world interconnectedness is not something that appeared suddenly in the last few decades. It is, though, in the period of the rise of the European powers that we see a globalizing process that many view as rivalling that of our own period. At this point it will be useful to follow the narrative developed by world-systems theorists such as Immanuel Wallerstein and Giovanni Arrighi. World-systems theory offers an analysis, built on Marxism, that is global in focus (taking the world-system rather than the national state as its unit of analysis) and that views globalization as tied to the development of capitalism. From the sixteenth century, Wallerstein (2005: 2) notes, 'The imperative of the endless accumulation of capital had generated a need for constant technological change, a constant expansion of frontiers – geographical, psychological, intellectual, scientific'. For world-systems thinkers, after the beginnings of the world-economy initiated by the Portuguese and Spanish voyages of discovery and conquest, the world-system has expanded through a number of fundamental reorganizations, which pivoted around the hegemony of the Dutch (the United Provinces), then the British, then America (Wallerstein, 2005; Arrighi and Silver, 1999). For a time, these hegemonic powers 'were able to establish the rules of the game in the interstate system, to dominate the world-economy (in production, commerce, and finance), to get their way politically with a minimal use of military force (which however they had in goodly strength), and to formulate the cultural language with which one discussed the world' (Wallerstein, 2005: 58). At certain points, though, the system undergoes a hegemonic crisis as competition arises (between states and enterprises), social conflict grows, and new powers emerge (Arrighi and Silver, 1999).

European expansion began with the maritime revolution around 1500 and the Spanish and Portuguese voyages to Africa, the Americas, and Asia, voyages that brought interchanges of goods (pepper, ivory, sugar, silver, gold), slaves (from the west coast of Africa and the Congo), diseases (smallpox, measles, influenza), and ideas (Held *et al.*, 1999; Osterhammel and Petersson, 2003). These contacts were often intensely destructive: the three to four million Amerindians living in Hispaniola in 1492, for instance, had virtually disappeared by 1570 (Abernethy, 2000).

The Dutch, after overcoming the overextended Spanish by way of their superior sea-power, played a lead role in the system founded by the 1648 Treaty of Westphalia, seen widely as central in the making of the modern state and the inter-state system of sovereignty and territoriality (Arrighi *et al.*, 1999). Emerging as an important slave-trading nation, controlling the Indian Ocean spice trade, and accumulating large profits from trade in the Baltic region, Amsterdam became the centre of commerce and finance in Europe; and this wealth in turn allowed greater military development and a growth in state power (Arrighi *et al.*, 1999; Arrighi, 2005b).

However, Britain were increasingly to push the Dutch aside, getting the upper hand by 1713, acquiring Hudson Bay, and wresting control of the slave trade (the trans-Atlantic triangle between Europe, Africa, and the Americas) and of Portugal's empire. Soon, the Dutch had become a second-tier naval force, and with a series of financial crises and with rising British power, the Dutch were on the decline in commercial terms too, withdrawing by 1740 to become 'the bankers of Europe' (Arrighi *et al.*, 1999; Arrighi, 2005b). From 1600–1700, Britain's foreign trade had grown by 50 per cent, but it mounted enormously through the eighteenth century by way of trade with the Americas and the plunder of India, after its victory at Plassey in 1757 (Chirot, 1986; Arrighi *et al.*, 1999). Through such trade and plunder, Britain was able to buy back the national debt from the Dutch by the 1790s, and London became the central player in international finance (Arrighi *et al.*, 1999; Held *et al.*, 1999).

Important to both Dutch and British success was the joint-stock chartered company of the seventeenth century (revived in the late nineteenth century for expansion into Africa) – for instance, the East India companies of the imperial powers, or the Hudson Bay Company operating between Britain and North America (Held *et al.*, 1999; Thompson, 1999). These organizations, a mix of government and business, are now often viewed as prototype multinational corporations (MNCs), even though they engaged in more trade (primarily in luxury goods) than production (Arrighi *et al.*, 1999; Held *et al.*, 1999). Governments gave these companies exclusive trading privileges in certain areas, and they possessed state-making functions – building armies, raising taxes, making war, and annexing territory (Held *et al.*, 1999). Thus, the British East India Company was to become the dominant governing organization in India with the disintegration of the Mughal Empire and was, by the 1760s, a powerful 'company state' (Arrighi *et al.*, 1999). By the mid-1700s, though, these stock companies were facing increasing competition with the emergence of smaller, more flexible enterprises, with the burden of costs associated with enormous bureaucracies, and with growing resentment at their trade privileges (Arrighi *et al.*, 1999). The British state eventually stepped in to take colonial control, and monopolies were abolished (1813 for India, 1833 for China).

India, with its resources and large population, provided Britain with enormous wealth – the 'principle pillar' of Britain's global power, according to Arrighi (2005b). For instance, Britain was able to extract from India 150 million pounds in gold alone between 1750 and 1800 (R. T. Robertson, 2003). Initially a major producer of textiles, and thus a competitor for Lanchashire's growing cotton industry in Britain, India was deindustrialized to become a provider of cheap food and raw materials (R. T. Robertson, 2003; Arrighi *et al.*, 1999). Thus, while the Indian subcontinent took only 11 million yards of British cotton in 1820, by 1840 it was taking 145 million yards (Hobsbawm, 1962). India also provided wealth in the form of taxes extracted by the Indian government, and power in the form of an army available to the British state (Thompson, 1999; Arrighi, 2005b).

The tea trade with China was also profitable to Britain, but it was the Opium Wars of 1839–42 and 1856–58 that forcibly opened China to purchase Indian-produced opium (which by 1870 still accounted for 43 per cent of all Chinese imports), providing Britain with silver for the purchase of Chinese teas, porcelain, and silks (R. T. Robertson, 2003; Arrighi *et al.*, 1999). These Opium Wars made clear the 'firepower gap' that had opened up between Europe and the rest of the world: in one day, the British steamship Nemesis destroyed 'nine war junks, five forts, two military stations and one shore battery' (Held *et al.*, 1999: 94). The period stretching from the fifteenth to the late seventeenth century was one of nearly constant war across Europe, and also of an accompanying series of innovations in military technology and organization (Held *et al.*, 1999). This meant that at the end of this period, by the Peace of Vienna of 1815 (which brought 100 years of relative peace in Europe), Europe was far ahead of the rest of the world in military terms. It was at this point that a shift occurs from European wars to colonial wars in the non-European world (Arrighi *et al.*, 1999).

Following its victory over the Dutch, Britain was able to draw much of the world into its trading sphere: for 20 years after the mid-1840s one-third of world exports went to Britain, which, in turn, meant the means to purchase British goods; overall, Britain was responsible for 25 per cent of world trade; and from the 1840s to the 1870s the value of exchanges between Britain, the Ottoman Empire, Latin America, India, and Australasia increased six-fold (Chirot, 1986; Hobsbawm, 1995a: 50). Unlike the Dutch, Britain was an industrial centre, 'the workshop of the world' (cotton, then railroads and iron were most important), with British industrial production increasing by 300 per cent between 1820 and 1860, and per capita GDP rising 1.4 per cent annually between 1830 and 1870 (Arrighi *et al.*, 1999; R. T. Robertson, 2003). This economic power translated into imperial power, with the British Empire covering almost a quarter of the world's land surface by 1912 (Abernethy, 2000).

It is important to note the role of new transport and communication technologies in this period. Between 1850 and 1870, 50,000 miles of new railway line was laid in Europe, against just 15,000 miles in all the years previous; and while just three countries in 1845 possessed over 1,000 km of railway line, by 1875 the number was 15 (Arrighi *et al.*, 1999; Hobsbawm, 1995a). The latter part of the nineteenth century also saw the development of fast steamers, Morse Code, telegraph (1835) and cable links (in the 1850s), telephone (1877), and radio. Such technology reduced the price of transport (freight charges fell by about 70 per cent between 1840 and 1910), meaning that, for the first time, mass trade in basic commodities rather than simply luxury goods became possible (Held *et al.*, 1999). Thus, in the case of shipping, while only 20 million tons of seaborne merchandise was exchanged between the major nations in 1840, 88 million tons was exchanged by the 1870s, with British steamship tonnage growing by 1,600 per cent between 1850–80 (Hobsbawm, 1995a). During the same period, from 1849–69, the number of telegraph lines and poles grew from 2,000 miles to 111,000 miles; and by 1880 a telegram could be sent from London to most key points of the British empire (Hobsbawm, 1995a; Osterhammel and Petersson, 2003). Rail, steamship, and telegraph were also important in military terms, and the new technology of warfare such as the Gattling gun (1861), modern explosives, and gunboats helped extend European power and thereby the territory under their control (Held *et al.*, 1999).

British historian Eric Hobsbawm (1995b) describes the period 1875–1914 as 'the age of Empire'. While international trade had doubled between 1720–80, then tripled between 1780–1840, trade volumes grew at 5 per cent per annum from 1850–70, and, by 1880, exports constituted 10 per cent of GDP for European countries (Hobsbawm, 1995a; Held *et al.*, 1999). In this period, big power expansionist rivalries increased, challenges to this expansion in the peripheral and semi-peripheral areas of the world rose, and the working class expanded in size, organizational strength, and assertiveness – these factors together destabilizing the geopolitical situation (Chirot, 1986). To remain a great power, it was felt, one had to expand, and this period saw a desperate scramble for control of overseas territory (Chirot, 1986). Thus, while in 1880 25 million square kilometres of the earth's surface was under the control of the big colonial powers, by 1913 this control had extended to 53 million square kilometres (Osterhammel and Petersson, 2003). At the same time, with international tensions on the rise, spending on arms from 1875–1914 rose by 56, 45, and 32 per cent per decade for the US, Germany, and Britain, respectively (Chirot, 1986). This rivalry led up to the catastrophe of World War I, which ushered in a new age of global conflict and massacre that left 15 million people dead (Hobsbawm, 1995b).

It should also be noted that this 'age of Empire' generated a growth in internationalism not only in terms of trade and the acquisition of colonies, but in the proliferation of international organizations and efforts at international co-ordination: for instance, the Universal Postal Union was founded in 1874, the International Railway Congress Association in 1884, the International Bureau of Weights and Measures in 1875, the International Bureau of Commercial Statistics in 1913, the International Labour Office in 1901, and the International Bureau against the Slave Trade in 1890 (Held *et al.*, 1999); the sterling-based Gold Standard was established in the 1870s to secure a stable system of international payments by fixing the price of the world's main currencies in terms of gold (Held *et al.*, 1999); Esperanto appeared in the 1880s; the socialist movement, developing into a mass movement from the 1890s (Hobsbawm, 1995b), became ever more internationalized; the woman's suffrage movement spread; in 1884, 25 states agreed to establish global time based on the Greenwich meridian; and in 1893 the World's Parliament of Religions took place in Chicago (Osterhammel and Petersson, 2003).

The period of British hegemony came to an end in a series of fundamental shocks. The first occurred during the period of the Great Depression of 1873–96. This shock was followed by a second with World War I, and then a third in the phase between the Great Depression of the 1930s and the Second World War. The costs of empire were high and rivals, political and industrial, had emerged, with 'manufacturing fever', a new industrial shift (to steel, chemical, and electrical industries), and pressures to export and to secure raw materials (Arrighi *et al.*, 1999).

The Great Depression of the late nineteenth century was followed by the rise of Germany and America as industrial powers. For instance, Germany's iron and steel production had increased five-fold from 1850–74, and by 1913 Germany's coal production rivalled Britain's (Joll, 1978); and US private enterprise in the industrialization of war dominated the world by 1890 (Arrighi *et al.*, 1999). While sterling was still the dominant currency until the mid-1940s, with half of world trade denominated in sterling, the two World Wars brought centralization of world liquidity into US hands. Already in 1913 America's industrial output outstripped Britain and Germany's, and its per capita GDP was 20 per cent higher than Britain's and 80 per cent higher than Germany's (R. T. Robertson, 2003). And, by the end of the First World War, America had been able to buy back its debt to Britain with arms, machinery, food, and raw materials; from 1924–29 the US loaned twice as much abroad as Britain; and by 1930 the US accounted for 42 per cent of global industrial output, with Britain at just 9 per cent (Arrighi *et al.*, 1999; Chirot, 1986; R. T. Robertson, 2003).

In this hegemonic reorganization, the British system of family business enterprises was transformed in the direction of the corporate or monopoly capitalism of the US and Germany (Arrighi *et al.*, 1999). With increased competition, companies began to merge in the interests of investment and survival (Robertson, 2003): 'combination advanced at the expense of market competition, business corporations at the expense of private firms, big business and large enterprise at the expense of smaller; and this concentration implied a tendency towards oligopoly' (Hobsbawm, 1995b: 44). The American version of these new business organizations was to become in the twentieth century the model of business worldwide.

While Britain continued to hold tight to the idea of free trade, the age of free trade lasted only from 1846–80 as increasingly protective tariffs were erected (Osterhammel and Petersson, 2003). This tendency away from economic liberalism was greatly accentuated after the shocks of World War I and then the Great slump of 1929–33, with world capitalism retreating 'into national and imperial preserves': the Gold Standard finally collapsed in 1931; the League of Nations became ineffective by the early 1930s; trading networks were disrupted and often discontinued; trade barriers were raised; money became largely territorialized; and trade fell so that in 1935 it was only one third of what it had been in 1929 (Held *et al.*, 1999; Scholte, 2000; R. T. Robertson, 2003). In the 1930s, the first Soviet Five Year Plan, the American New Deal, and fascism/Nazism in Italy, Spain and Germany signalled the movement away from internationalization towards national self-sufficiency (Arrighi *et al.*, 1999).

Prior to the middle of the nineteenth century, there had been important movements of people – most notably, the transfer of as many as 9–12 million Africans across the Atlantic as slaves between the mid-fifteenth and mid-nineteenth centuries. But imperial expansion, war, and economic crisis made the period from the middle of the nineteenth to the middle of the twentieth centuries one of extensive globalization. Between 1850 and 1914, 60–70 million people migrated, many making their way to the Americas; and 11 million Indians, Chinese, and Japanese left their homelands to become, in most cases, contract labourers (the so-called 'coolie' system) (Osterhammel and Petersson, 2003). Later, millions of people migrated in the face of such disparate events as the Russian Revolution, Turkish persecution of Armenians, the Nazi arrival to power, the establishment of the Soviet zone post-Second World War, the creation of Israel, the partition of India, and the Korean War (Held *et al.*, 1999; Hobsbawm, 1995b).

The massively destructive Second World War – which left 55 million people dead, and 40 million people uprooted – gave way to a reorganized world order (Arrighi *et al.*, 1999; Hobsbawm, 1995b). A new monetary order was initiated with the 1944 Bretton Woods Agreement on fixed exchange rates (fixed to the US dollar, indicating America's place as the leading economic power), and new organizations (the International Monetary Fund and the International Bank for Reconstruction and Development, also known as the World Bank) were set up, with the aim of stimulating world effective demand (Wallerstein, 2003). The Marshall Plan of 1948 saw the US giving massive aid and credits to Europe, again with the goal of allowing the purchase of US goods (Chirot, 1986). Meanwhile, to avoid the protectionism of the 1930s, an international trade organization, the General Agreement on Tariffs and Trade (GATT), was established in 1947 to open world trade on the principles of non-discrimination, reciprocity, transparency, and fairness. And, indeed, the post-war period was one of rapid expansion of world production and trade, with trade growing at 5.8 per cent a year from 1950–73 (Held *et al.*, 1999). At the same time, a new military-political order emerged with the formation of the United Nations in 1945, and the stable Yalta division of the world into blocs around the two superpowers – the USSR with one third of the world, America (the superior superpower) with the rest (Wallerstein, 2003).

However, according to world-systems thinkers, the hegemonic decline of the US was soon looming. America achieved only a 'draw' in the Korean War, and was defeated in Vietnam, a defeat that came at enormous cost (using up US gold reserves) (Wallerstein, 2003). Stagflation (the combination of high inflation, low economic growth, and high unemployment) set in across the world during the 1970s. And the productivity gap between the US, Japan, and Western Europe was closed: US productivity increased only 4.1 per cent between 1950–69, against 6.7 per cent for Western Europe and 13.8 per cent for Japan; the US share of world trade declined from 21 to 12 per cent between 1950 and 1978, and it became dependent on the flow of capital from the rest of the world (R. T. Robertson, 2003; Wallerstein, 2003). The Bretton Woods system collapsed in 1971 with a massive flight of US capital offshore and with the fiscal crisis of the US government (R. T. Robertson, 2003). MNCs developed new systems of flexible and decentralized production and exchange, bringing a shift in the centre of gravity of manufacturing, and escaping the control of states (Wallerstein, 2003). Meanwhile, East Asia expanded economically. Though America was able to drive the USSR into bankruptcy through an arms race that it won with its greater financial resources – bringing a 'unipolar moment' – the collapse of communism, argues Wallerstein (2003), actually meant a further decline for the US, because of the demise of a foe that provided significant legitimacy to American power. And while America continues to be vastly superior militarily to any other nation, the inconclusive first Gulf War of 1991 indicated that it could no longer finance by itself such military operations as Kuwait, Japan, and Saudi Arabia funded much of the cost (Wallerstein, 2003).

Turning back now to consider the social dimension of the world-system, the French and American Revolutions often are viewed as central in promoting global ideals of democracy and liberty. For Wallerstein (2005), the French Revolution, in particular, inspired two crucial ideas in terms of global social contestation: (1) that political change was normal and constant, and (2) that sovereignty resided in the people. Thus, in the periphery of the world-system, in St Dominique a slave rebellion fended off European attempts at restoration and the independent republic of Haiti was proclaimed in 1804, resonating across the Atlantic world and spelling the end for slavery (Silver and Slater, 1999; Osterhammel and Petersson, 2003).

In the 1830s in Britain, meanwhile, as workers' living conditions worsened, there was a large swell of political mobilization around the issue of the extension of the franchise, with the movement for the People's Charter peaking in 1839–42 and ruling groups responding with both reaction and reform (Silver and Slater, 1999; Hobsbawm, 1962). Wallerstein (2005), though, suggests that 1848 was the crucial year that witnessed the first social revolution of the modern era. As economic crisis deepened, a wave of rebellions in Western and Central Europe spread, with the popular objective of establishing a 'democratic and social republic' (Hobsbawm, 1995a). Nearly all rebellions were defeated within 19 months and an 'age of capital' was ushered in, where social costs were transferred to the colonies, some workers experienced a 'trickle down of wealth', and trade and production grew (Hobsbawm, 1995a; Silver and Slater, 1999).

This age of capital soon came to an end, however, with the depression beginning in 1873. This meant a worsening of working conditions and increasing resistance, with growth in the size of the working class (in Germany, for instance, the 50 years from 1850 to 1900 saw the number of workers in mining and manufacturing grow from 600,000 to 5.7 million), trade unions (which became less sectional), and working class and socialist parties (with mounting electoral strength – for instance, by the start of World War I, one in three German voters were voting socialist) (Silver and Slater, 1999; Joll, 1978). Repression alone was no longer sufficient to contain the impulses of working class movements: in 1890 the ban on the German SPD, the biggest social democratic party in Europe, was lifted; and in Britain reforms in the 1860s and 1880s nearly quadrupled the electorate (Silver and Slate, 1999; Hobsbawm, 1995b). At this time, too, in some countries the beginnings of the welfare state appeared, as a response to working class demands and as an effort towards reducing working class militancy.

The age of empire, which for Hobsbawm follows the age of capital, was a period of the spread of secular ideologies, most importantly those of nationalism and socialism (Wallerstein, 2005). These secular and universalizing modes of thought deepened in the West and spread beyond North America and Europe, into Asia, the Middle East, the Baltic, and Latin America. Already, rebellions in the periphery contested European power – for instance, in India in 1857–58 and Algeria in 1871 – but the First World War and, especially, the Great Depression of 1929–33 shook colonialism: from 1919 to 1922 waves of protest against European powers erupted in India, Egypt, Iraq, Sierra Leone, Vietnam, and the Congo. In addition, the collapse of prices for Third World primary products between 1929–33 made colonialism and dependency less sustainable (Hobsbawm, 1995b; Abernethy, 2000). After the Second World War, a wave of decolonizing movements brought independent statehood for non-Western peoples, from Asia, to Africa, to Latin and Central America, to the Middle East: between 1940 and 1980, 81 colonies gained independence from their European rulers (Abernethy, 2000; Chirot, 1986). In Europe, the influence of socialist ideals became clear in the aftermath of the destruction of World War I, as a wave of rebellions ignited in Italy, Germany, Russia, Hungary, and elsewhere. While all were defeated, save for the Russian Revolution, socialism became a truly threatening spectre in Europe.

In the 1970s the world-system entered a new 'period of transition' (Wallerstein, 2003). One central marker of this new period is what Wallerstein calls the 'world revolution of 1968' which contested both US hegemony and the communist model of the USSR. This 'revolution' – manifested, for instance, in student revolts across Europe and the US – expressed a generalized scepticism towards the state and towards the socialist and nationalist anti-systemic movements that had dominated since the last half of the nineteenth century. Following this period, notes Wallerstein (2003), an important set of world-systemic changes occurred: world production and trade expanded; a global reorganization of production took place; the process of the death of the peasantry gained momentum; and America lost in Vietnam, was shaken by the Iranian Revolution of 1979, was subsequently forced out of Lebanon, and became the world's biggest debtor nation (with public debt presently sitting at $7.4 trillion) (Wallerstein, 2003).

Additional world-systemic changes have led us to our current global era: the notion of 'development' in the Third World gave way to structural adjustment and an increasing global polarization of wealth; the world trend towards democratization in education, health, and guaranteed income began to threaten accumulation, as have rising costs of production, diminishment of inputs (natural resources and dumping space), and exhaustion of areas to which factories might relocate in order to cut costs (Wallerstein, 2003, 2005); new information and communication technologies such as satellite, fibre-optics, and the Internet appeared; world air traffic became denser (from 25 million passengers in 1950 to nearly four billion in 1996) (Scholte, 2000); the globalization of money occurred, in the 1980s and 1990s, after the demise of Bretton Woods; East Asian economic power – for instance, Hong Kong, Taiwan, China – emerged and the European Union grew; and, last, 'really existing socialism' collapsed from 1989–91 (Wallerstein, 2003). These monumental changes form the vital backdrop to thinking about the specificity of our globalizing period.

Theories of social change

We will take up and develop certain dimensions of this discussion in the following chapters. A major point to be noted here is that globalization is not just a feature of the last 30 or so years. Such interconnectedness can be found much earlier, and contemporary globalization is to be understood, to varying degrees, in light of these processes and relationships established in earlier periods. The world-systems analysis has the virtue of guarding us somewhat against the tendency to chronocentrism – that is, the tendency to regard the present as a completely unique moment of transformation, dynamism, and novelty.

A central part of the vocation of the social sciences is reflecting on social change, tied to ideas of societal evolution, the delineation of trends of transformation, and the exploration of different social forms and logics of development. It is often pointed out that such a vocation predisposes social scientists to overestimate the newness and extent of the change they focus upon. This is an important warning not only in relation to considerations of the historical specificity of globalization in our period, but also as a preface to this section in which we are concerned with theories of social change in the last two or three decades. These theories are outlined here because they have significant connections to, and affinities with, analyses of contemporary globalization, and they provide important tools of understanding for the critical theoretical assessments of globalization that we will focus on in the chapters that follow. While we think each of these theories has important merits, and we see them as provocative and helpful tools in theorizing our globalizing moment, it is important to keep in mind the ease with which these theories might be overreaching in describing the novelty of the current social order.

Postindustrialism, information societies, and postfordism

Marx, Weber, and Durkheim, the three founding fathers of social theory (see Box 1.4), were all concerned to understand the transformation of European social orders from traditional, feudal, agriculture-based, and religious configurations towards modern, industrial, and secular social formations. From the 1960s, some commentators contended that another shift was taking place, a shift that entailed a move from the centrality of factories, heavy machinery, and blue-collar labour to the primacy of information, new technologies, knowledge, and service work. We will look, here, at theories of postindustrialism and at theories of an emerging information or knowledge society.

Box 1.4   Marx, Weber, Durkheim and Social Change

Karl Marx (1818–83) was a German philosopher, political economist, and social theorist, and the founder of modern communism. Marx studied philosophy at the University of Berlin, where he also became involved in radical politics. Because of his involvement in revolutionary politics, Marx eventually was compelled to leave Germany, first for France and then for Great Britain, where he was supported in large part by his friend and collaborator, Friedrich Engels. Marx's theories were developed in response to classical political economy and the emergence of bourgeois liberalism and capitalism. For Marx, economic systems or modes of production determined the structure of social orders and consequently the course of social change. According to the Marxist theory of historical materialism, changes in the 'superstructure' of society – state and legal institutions, religion and morality – result from changes in the 'base' or economic mode of production. Marx argued that because the capitalist mode of production, with its emphasis on competition, consumerism and profit, leads to domination, class conflict and alienation, only a radical transformation to a communist mode of production will enable genuine emancipation. 'Scientific' or 'orthodox' versions of Marxism adopted a positivist view of historical materialism as revealing empirical 'laws' that can enable the prediction of supposedly inevitable future events. Marx's most influential works include *The German Ideology* (1846), *The Communist Manifesto* (1848), and the three-volume *Capital* (1867, 1885, 1894).

Max Weber (1864–1920) was a German political economist and sociologist. Weber's most important contributions were to the study of the modern state and bureaucracy, and the connections between economics, politics, and religion. For Weber, the modern state has a monopoly of the means of 'legitimate violence', and modern forms of authority are characterized by

---

Box 1.4   Marx, Weber, Durkheim and Social Change – *continued*

rational administrative procedures and impersonal legal rules rather than the personal characteristics of a charismatic leader. In contrast to the Marxist emphasis on economic systems as the ultimate determining factor of social change, Weber argued that historical change must be understood in light of the interaction between many factors, including cultural, economic, political, and religious values. For instance, Weber viewed modernity as defined by the kind of instrumental or 'means-end' rationality associated with Protestantism and, ultimately, with the bureaucratic nation-state. Consequently, Weber contended that the subjective meaning of social action could not be reduced to 'evolutionary laws' about economic systems which supposedly determine the course of history. Weber's major works include *The Protestant Ethic and the Spirit of Capitalism* (1902), *The Sociology of Religion* (1920) and *Economy and Society* (1922).

Émile Durkheim (1858–1917) was a French sociologist and philosopher who helped to found sociology as a distinct discipline within the social sciences. For Durkheim, sociological explanation must be functional in orientation, by considering 'social facts' in relation to the whole structure of social life and the values embedded within it. According to Durkheim, societies evolve from simple, non-specialized forms towards highly complex, specialized forms. In more complex modern societies, work becomes specialized – the division of labour – providing a new basis for social solidarity. Social change, Durkheim argued, can result in the condition of 'anomie', which refers to the breakdown of social codes and norms within communities leading individuals to experience greater dissatisfaction, conflict, and unhappiness. For Durkheim, the social disintegration characteristic of anomie should be countered by the emergence of new forms of cultural integration based on commonly shared values, beliefs, and institutions. His most important works include *The Division of Labour in Society* (1893), *Suicide* (1897), and *The Elementary Forms of Religious Life* (1912).

The argument for an emerging postindustrial age is most famously put forth in sociologist Daniel Bell's 1973 work, *The Coming of the Post-Industrial Society*. Bell maintains that in advanced social orders a 'vast historical change' is taking place, in terms of social relations, culture, and power. For Bell (1999), a society is best understood as composed of a social structure, a polity, and a culture. Social structure encompasses the economy, technology, and the education system, and it is at the social structural level that Bell's comments on the emerging postindustrialism are focussed. For Bell (Bell, 1999: xc), the industrial society 'is primarily *fabricating*, using energy and machine technology, for the manufacture of goods', while a postindustrial sector 'is one of *processing* in which telecommunications and computers are strategic for the exchange of information and knowledge'. Furthermore, 'industrial society is based on machine technology, post-industrial society is shaped by an intellectual technology.... Capital and labour are the major structural features of industrial society, information and knowledge are those of the post-industrial society' (xci).

Five dimensions or components of the postindustrial society are particularly singled out by Bell (1999): a movement from a goods producing economy to a service economy; a change in occupational distribution, which sees the emerging dominance of a professional and technical class; a new 'axial principle', from private property to the pivotal importance of theoretical knowledge as source of information and policy formulation; a future orientation centred on the control of technology and technological assessment; and changes in decision-making with the creation of a new intellectual technology. In addition, he mentions a movement from the importance of inheritance to education for social mobility, from financial to human capital, from transportation to communication in infrastructural terms, changes in the character of work so that work increasingly is a 'game between persons' (xcv), and a change in the role of women.

In a more recent analysis, Liagouras (2005: 32) sees postindustrialism as an age in which 'knowledge, communication, and aesthetics are the most important inputs and outputs of economic activity'. This postindustrialism combines a transition from energy-intensive to information-intensive technical systems, towards a new weightless economy; a move from the accumulation of goods to the 'proliferation and amelioration of symbolic and relational systems' (21); the growing predominance of soft- over hard-ware; a new economic integration with time-space compression; and a shift in business organization, from 'material-processing' to 'knowledge-creating' (23).

In terms of changes in power and conflict, for Bell, this transformation means a decline in traditional class conflicts between labour and capital. But he also suggests that this transition will bring a rising disjunction between social structure and culture, especially with the rise of standards of living, individualism, and expressive lifestyles, against the restraint and character structure linked to the economic realm (such as efficiency, respectability, delayed gratification, and so forth). In contrast, French social scientist Alain Touraine, while concurring with much of Bell's analysis, contends that the arrival of postindustrialism would not so much end social conflict as lead to its reconfiguration, most notably, centred on the divide between the new technocracy and those subjected to their attempts at technocratic control (Mackay, 2001).

The idea of a postindustrial society is closely connected to the idea of the contemporary social order as an information or knowledge society: Bell, for instance, explicitly remarks that the postindustrial age is an information society. Although the notion of a knowledge or information order is frequently tied to developments in information and communication technologies, as well as with new systems of management and new production technologies, as Frank Webster (2002) points out, variations of this thesis associate the idea of an information society with technology, media, education, occupational structure, and the shrinking of time through the conquest of space. The reality of this information or knowledge order is said to be clear in a number of realms of modern life: in the home, at work, in the military, and in the sphere of the state and surveillance (Mackay, 2001). The arrival of this new order, with the primacy it accords knowledge, is often viewed optimistically as expanding the powers of individual and collective actors against larger institutions, which are no longer able to impose their will or claim a monopoly on truth (Stehr, 2003).

While these closely connected arguments about social change evidently point to important trends in social orders over recent decades, there are a number of pertinent critical points to be made. A first is the frequent determinism of these theories, where one dimension – such as technology – acts as the primary and independent facet in social change (Webster, 2002). In addition, it is often said that these ideas are historically short-sighted (Kumar, 1995). That is, the particular changes detailed have been emerging for a long time and critics might ask, for example, what society is not a knowledge society? (Kumar, 1995; Stehr, 2003). In terms of the alleged transitions in employment and in the key facets of the economy, Callinicos and Harman (1987), for instance, claim that even in Marx's time, the majority of the working class were service workers; others have pointed to the similarity of blue collar and much white collar work in terms of the knowledge component, working conditions, and autonomy; and some have maintained that continuity – for instance, in terms of technical innovation or rationalization – rather than discontinuity is to be underscored (Kumar, 1995).

Finally, a debate that is related to both the postindustrialism and information society theses (for instance, in the importance lent to new information technology) is the idea of a transition from Fordism to post- or neo-Fordism. Lash and Urry (1987) develop a similar thesis in the notion of a transition from 'organized' to 'disorganized capitalism'. What is important here is the notion of a movement towards flexible specialization of machinery and workers (Kumar, 1995).

The Italian Marxist Antonio Gramsci used the term 'Fordism' to capture the new industrial mode seen in the manufacture of Ford's Model-T car in Detroit in the early twentieth century (Cohen and Kennedy, 2000). This mode of production consisted of a moving assembly line, repetitive work, and so-called 'Taylorist' methods of measurement of work tasks (a functionalist approach to the 'scientific' management of work so as to improve worker efficiency, developed by Frederick Winslow Taylor in the late nineteenth century) (Allen, 2001). Fordism is commonly characterized by a number of features: the fragmentation of labour skills and the moving assembly line; economies of scale, with the predominance of mass production of standardized goods for a protected national market; the centrality of semi-skilled 'mass workers' in large factories; a hierarchical, centralized, and bureaucratic mode of work organization; Keynesian state management of the national economy; and a link between mass production and mass consumption (Cohen and Kennedy, 2000). Since the 1970s, the transition from Fordism to postfordism is supposedly characterized by an increasing emphasis on flexible specialization, the dispersal and decentralization of production, an increase in subcontracting and 'outsourcing', the decline of mass unions and centralized wage bargaining, and an increase in flexi-time, part-time, and temporary workers (Kumar 1995: 52).

Again, important criticisms can be raised against this notion of epochal transition. For instance, some critics point to the important continuities between Fordism and the postfordist system that was apparently replacing it, insisting that Fordism was precisely about flexibility and 'constant technological dynamism and maximum adaptability of production methods' (Kumar, 1995: 60). In a similar vein, American sociologist George Ritzer offers a partial counter to such arguments in his notion of McDonaldization. For Ritzer (2001), there has been a generalization of the principles of the McDonald's fast food empire to more and more sectors of society – education, work, health, leisure, politics, family – and across the globe. Four dimensions of this McDonaldization are particularly important: efficiency, calculability, predictability, and control. In short, the McDonaldization thesis is, in a sense, precisely about the global expansion of the sort of standarization and rationalization that is central to Fordism, against arguments about growing flexibility and decentralization (see Beilharz *et al.*, 2004).

The postmodern condition

In our view, the idea of an emergent postmodern condition is the most important of the theories that we are dealing with here. Postmodernism is related to globalization, as well as to some of the other theories already examined; for instance, the emphases on 'diversity, differentiation and fragmentation' (Hall and Jacques in Kumar, 1995: 51) found in postfordism are central to emphases in work on postmodernism.

As Perry Anderson (1999) has shown, the term 'postmodern' has appeared and reappeared numerous times from the nineteenth century onwards. Yet it was only in the 1970s in the realm of the arts (and architecture, first and foremost) that the term really took hold, expressing a changing cultural sensibility and announcing a break from the principles of modernism that had dominated for around a century (Sim, 2002; Bertens, 1993; Lucie-Smith, 1990). According to such arguments, modern art is characterized by seriousness of purpose, austerity, absence of ornamentation, the idea of progress, and an elitist distinction between the high and low or 'popular' in aesthetic terms (Sim, 2002; Bertens, 1993; Harvey, 1989). The postmodern questions such emphases, and is characterized, in contrast, by a turn to stylistic eclecticism, a concern for popular taste, and a move from the serious to the playful (Sim, 2002; Harvey, 1989; Jameson, 1991). With the exhaustion and suspicion towards the assumptions of the modernist avant-garde (such as progress), irony becomes the pivotal characteristic of the postmodern.

For Fredric Jameson (1984), central features of the new postmodern art include a move from depth to surfaces, and a waning of historicity and affect. A good example of the shift to the postmodern, for him, is provided by a comparison of Van Gogh's work 'Peasant Shoes' with Andy Warhol's 'Diamond Dust Shoes'. The former work has layers, signalling a whole way of life and struggles, which cannot be found in the blank, glossy surface of the latter work. And Andy Warhol's 'studied superficiality' captures perfectly, for Jameson, the postmodern personality: as Warhol declared, 'If you want to know all about Andy Warhol just look at the surface of my paintings and films and me, there I am. There's nothing behind it' (quoted in Rojeck, 1993: 117). The problem for critics, especially Marxist critics, was that postmodernism reduced itself to ironic detachment, frivolous, shallow, and purposeless enjoyment, disregard for progressive ideals, rejection of evaluation for populism, and play and delirium rather than purpose, rationality, and emancipation. Much the same can be said for reactions to postmodern theory and philosophy, to which we will now turn.

The seminal statement of postmodern theory is Jean-François Lyotard's 1979 work, *The Postmodern Condition*, ostensibly a report on the contemporary condition of knowledge. For Lyotard, the postmodern 'designates the state of our culture following the transformations which, since the end of the nineteenth century, have altered the game rules for science, literature and the arts' (Lyotard 1984: xxiii). This condition is bound up with alterations in production techniques and technologies that coincide with capitalism, as well as with our entry into a period of generalized scepticism towards what Lyotard refers to as 'metanarratives'. These metanarratives are far-reaching stories about the world and about social transformation, which exist in such forms as Marxism's conclusion that the development of class struggle will usher in a classless utopia and thus an effective end to human history (Smart, 1992). In the face of the disasters of the twentieth century, these metanarratives had lost their legitimacy, argued Lyotard – we are no longer able to believe in them. What we are left with instead are little narratives, stories about the world that are limited and situated, stories that do not pretend to universality or finality and that cannot, for moral and epistemological reasons, be confidently evaluated and ranked one above the other.

Importantly, postmodern thinkers want to escape the supposedly totalizing impulses of modernity by accenting difference, otherness, and contingency, against sameness, cohesion, and order (Sim, 2002). Grand theories of everything and huge utopian schemes of social change are usually considered by postmodernists as obscuring or marginalizing particularities in the name of order and finality – weaving happy stories of complete harmony, which become nightmares when people try to establish them in the messy, complex world.

Postmodern thinkers are generally sceptical too about the modern tendency to posit meaning and identity as stable. Both meaning and identity, they counter, are without sure foundations: they are in flux, in a process of constant change that cannot finally be arrested, and there is nothing *essential* to them (meaning and identity, that is, are constructed and relational). Similarly, postmodernists often follow Friedrich Nietzsche in his insistence that value judgements are essentially conventional: that is, we can not provide any objective and solid grounds for our politics, morals, or social observations, but are instead reliant on rhetoric, on the same sorts of persuasive devices found in fiction (Sim, 2002). For critics, the problem with this is that the boundaries between fiction and reality and fiction and history seem to thereby undergo a crucial weakening, threatening to throw us into a mindless relativism where anything goes, where anything is as true or false as anything else, and where morality and politics simply end up collapsed into aesthetics, into a matter of personal taste or whim (see Callinicos, 1989; Eagleton, 1991; Anderson, 1983).

Box 1.5   Nietzsche's Critique of Modernity

Friedrich Nietzsche (1844–1900) was a German philosopher whose work mounted a sustained critique of the values, beliefs, and ideals of modern Western societies. In regard to science and philosophy, Nietzsche argued that truths are the artificial constructs of creative acts of interpretation and not natural facts that exist independently of such interpretation. For Nietzsche, knowledge is always constructed from some particular point of view and thus cannot be objective or impartial. Instead, our interpretations are expressions of what Nietzsche called the 'will to power' – the physical and psychic drives through which all forms of life seek to enhance their power or ability to achieve goals – and thus give expression to either life-affirming or life-denying values. Consequently, in regard to morality and politics, Nietzsche argued that Judeo-Christian morality was life-denying in that it promoted the values of humility, self-denial, meekness, and submission to authority. By extension, modern egalitarianism and democracy exhibited the same 'levelling' tendencies as Christian 'slave morality', by promoting notions such as the equal worth and equal rights of the 'common man' and conformity to majority opinion. In Nietzsche's estimation, individual self-creation and the affirmation of difference and one's own values were the means by which 'free spirits' could transcend the dominant norms of modernity. Nietzsche's most important works, which have had a profound influence on many postmodern thinkers, include *Beyond Good and Evil* (1886), *Genealogy of Morals* (1887), and *Thus Spoke Zarathustra* (1883–85).

However, postmodernists, in the main, are not rejecting morality and politics as such, and theirs is frequently a strong political and moral critique and social alternative. A large factor in their work is the critique of modernist confidence in notions such as progress, science, the reasoning individual, universalism, and secularism. This confidence is ill-founded, it is argued, because for all our achievements in knowing and controlling things, we have failed to prevent the multiple disasters of the modern period. In fact, this anxious will to know and control – what Cornelius Castoriadis has called the fantasy of 'full rational mastery' and what Michel Foucault referred to as the 'will to knowledge' – might even be responsible for such disasters. For Zygmunt Bauman (1999b), for instance, we moderns have found it almost impossible to live with ambivalence, with the marginal, questionable, not fully resolved, with that which does not fit into schemes of what is 'normal'. This has led to all sorts of distortions, including the Holocaust and Stalinism. Bauman suggests that the postmodern is best read as simply 'modernity without illusions', about learning to live with ambivalence, and without guarantees. In this way it is potentially a reinvigoration of both politics and morality, insofar as these now might be free from the illusions of final completion, absolutist foundations for knowledge and politics, and evolutionary ideals of social destiny.

Critics of postmodernism, on the other hand, have viewed it as all-too-quickly giving up on the aims of Enlightenment, on the progressive features of modernity which need to be completed rather than jettisoned (see Habermas, 1987). For instance, these critics often make the point that it is only with these modern and Enlightenment resources – intellectual, material, moral – that we can understand, criticize, and guard against the barbarisms that postmodernists point to. From this perspective, the postmodern simply collapses into relativism, irrationalism, and nihilism, throwing the baby out with the bathwater (Sim, 2002).

Another variety of postmodern theory is developed by the French sociologist Jean Baudrillard, whose diagnosis of postmodernism is tied to the ubiquity of media and advertising, the relentless turnover of fashions, new technology and the extraordinarily fast circulation of information, and the predominance of the image in contemporary consumer societies. Baudrillard (1983) argues against theories such as Marxism and psychoanalysis that posit an underlying essence beneath appearances ('the hermeneutics of suspicion'). Baudrillard, in contrast, focuses on surfaces and seduction by these surfaces. In his 1983 work, *Simulations*, Baudrillard suggests that we are now in a 'hyperreal' period in which we have moved from an older regime in which signs dissimilate something. Today, by way of contrast, illusion is no longer possible because the real itself is no longer possible. In hyperreality, there is no longer a clearly demarcated origin or underlying reality, as the artificial and real mix to leave us in an age of simulation. Thus, in his book on the 1991 Gulf War, Baudrillard (1995) insisted that the war did not happen insofar as we cannot distinguish the *image* of the war from the war *itself*. It had been so thoroughly played out ahead of time, we had been exposed to such a mass of speculation, models, and expert opinion, that the real events were inaccessible. Here, Baudrillard was not contending that people were not killed and that destruction did not take place – in fact, he condemned as a 'heap of stupidity and cowardice' what was taking place on the ground; what he was pointing to was the interminable blurring of image and reality in the contemporary period and to the obsolescence of older forms of political intervention in the face of these changes.

Reflexive modernity: risk society and detraditionalization

Two notions of social change that are intimately related both to post-modernism and to globalization are contained in the ideas of an emerging 'risk society' and in the arguments about 'detraditionaliza-tion' as a central cultural-intellectual feature of the present period of 'reflexive modernization'. These notions are associated, first and fore-most, with the work of British sociologist Anthony Giddens and German sociologist Ulrich Beck.

According to Giddens (1990: 10), our world is a particularly 'fraught and dangerous one', in the sense that our 'second' or 'reflexive moder-nity' is, Beck (2000) argues, burdened by problems, crises, and hazards. These risks have become central ahead of the distributional questions that had dominated first modernity. Risk is about the unintended con-sequences of the first modernity of Enlightenment, scientific progress, collectivism, and technological advance and control (Debrix, 2005), and these consequences 'come to be a dominant force in history and society' (Beck, 2000: 400). For instance, decisions made about genetic engineering 'are unleashing unpredictable, uncontrollable and ulti-mately incommunicable consequences that might ultimately endanger all life on earth' (Beck, 2002: 40).

The new risks, such as environmental risks (pollution, genetic engi-neering, the impact of pesticides), do not tell us what to do, only what should not be done, and they are simultaneously local and global – they can no longer be viewed solely as national questions. Beck notes that these risks are 'deterritorialized', that is, they 'endow each country with a common global interest ... [so that] we can already talk about the basis of a global community of fate' (Beck, 2002: 42). The age of risk, then, entails a transformation of politics. Without definitive answers, in the face of contradictory information, and with a loss of faith in the state and older hierarchies, a new 'sub-politics' emerges, which shapes society from below (Beck, 1999: 39). Both Giddens and Beck are optimistic about the implications of this new age, seeing the growing reflexivity, individualization, and deterritorialization of second modernity as real opportunities for the development of a global consciousness and sense of responsibility, a new world community of shared global risks.

Some critics believe that such a thesis overreaches. As Lechte (2003: 191) succinctly puts it: 'Beck overdoes it here. Risk, yes; but risk society, no'. For Debrix (2005), meanwhile, the risk society thesis is plainly eth-nocentric, elevating specifically Western fears to an unfounded universal status, and leaving unanswered pressing questions 'such as who bears the risks, who profits from risks, what or whose risks are more valued in the global polity, and what dominant perceptions of risks are in charge of ordering and organizing globalizing processes'.

Beck, Giddens, and others also view the latest phase of modernity as a 'detraditionalized' age. Of course 'first modernity', with the Enlightenment emphases on secularism, individualism, and science, is associated with the idea of a wide-ranging emancipation from the weight of tradition. For some, though, this modernity simply succeeded in installing *another* traditionalism centred around notions of science, progress, individualism, and so forth (see Coicaud, 2002). The notion of detraditionalization developed by Beck and Giddens is linked to the reflexive modernization of the past couple of decades where beliefs and customs recede, where individualization and life as experimentation are pivotal, and where globalization brings cultural-intellectual mixing. Heelas (1996: 2) defines detraditionalization as involving a 'shift of authority: from "without" to "within". It entails the decline of the belief in pre-given or natural orders of things. Individual subjects are themselves called upon to exercise authority in the face of the disorder and contingency which is thereby generated. "Voice" is displaced from established sources, coming to rest with the self'. While Giddens and Beck are optimistic about detraditionalization as bringing greater choice, openness and reflexivity, and loosening the hold of older hierarchies, more pessimistic commentators have pointed to the sense of normlessness and homelessness entailed by the demise of tradition (Heelas, 1996). As with the risk society thesis, sceptics suggest the strong reading of detraditionalization goes too far. Such a reading perhaps caricatures 'the traditional', and it ignores the realities of simultaneous detraditionalization, tradition maintenance, and tradition reconstruction at work in the world today (Heelas, 1996).

'Development' and 'modernity'

Two more important ideas are often evoked – sometimes explicitly, sometimes implicitly – in discussions of globalization: 'modernity' and 'development'. We will first examine the notion of 'development' through the exploration of two competing paradigms. We will then discuss the notion of modernity, which is closely linked to the idea of development and a topic of renewed interest with the rising fortunes of 'postmodernity'. Modernity also is an important concept in theoretical discussion of globalization – for instance, modernization is often viewed as one of the logics or component parts of globalization.

Development

In this section, we will explore two prominent theoretical paradigms – the 'modernization' and 'dependency' approaches – which were popular as ways of accounting for global inequalities and for framing progressive responses to such inequalities, as contained in the post-Second World War idea of 'development'. These two approaches to the goal of development have subsequently gone into decline. Nevertheless, both modernization and dependency approaches continue to function within the broad discourse of globalization, and this section is therefore a crucial backdrop to discussions of global inequality in Chapter 2.

It is clear that those in the so-called 'third world', the South, or 'developing' nations suffer greatly unequal life chances compared with those in the 'first world', the North, or the developed world. The term 'third world' was coined by French economist Alfred Sauvy in 1952, and denotes the states not of the capitalist, developed first world or of the socialist second world (Hobsbawm, 1995b; Hulme and Turner, 1990). It also denotes a state of economic development often designated today as 'underdeveloped', 'less developed', or 'developing'. The term has become less fashionable with the end of the Cold War and with recognition of the variety of experiences lumped into that category (Hulme and Turner, 1990; Dirlik, 1997). In general, 'the third world' encompasses societies exhibiting low growth rates, high incidences of poverty, poor sanitation and health, comparatively high population growth rates, higher fertility rates, lower life expectancy, a higher proportion of the economy dedicated to agriculture, lower rates of urbanization, inadequate housing, extensive internal inequality, high levels of gender inequality, and adult illiteracy (Hulme and Turner, 1990; Webster, 1990). Many of these countries are often said to suffer from the colonial legacy of having 'plantation' or 'quarry' economies that rely on exporting a handful of commodities to rich countries, which makes them extremely vulnerable to price fluctuations caused, for instance, by climate change or crop diseases (Hulme and Turner, 1990; Webster, 1990). These countries often also suffer high levels of indebtedness, and much of their budgets are taken up making payments on loan interest and principal. In addition, democracy is often weak or non-existent in these countries, with military expenditure often dwarfing spending on health and education.

Let us look briefly at some selected details of the global inequality between rich and poor countries. Life expectancy for those in countries such as Japan, Sweden, Australia, France, and the United

Kingdom is above or close to 80 years of age, while it is less than 40 for persons living in Rwanda, Zambia, Lesotho, Zimbabwe, and the Central African Republic. While GDP per capita in Norway, the US, Denmark, Switzerland, and Ireland is above $30,000, it is below $1,000 for Ethiopia, Tanzania, Nigeria, Yemen, and the Democratic Republic of Congo. Norway, Australia, Sweden, the US, and Belgium register as having none of their population living on less than $2 per day, while over 40 per cent of the population of Ecuador, Indonesia, Nicaragua, Egypt, and Nigeria live on less than $2 per day. Relatedly, over 40 per cent of the population are undernourished in Angola, Tanzania, Haiti, Mozambique, and Tajikistan. The prevalence of HIV in Japan, New Zealand, Slovenia, Hong Kong, and Korea is less than 0.1 per cent of the population; in contrast, it is over 20 per cent in Swaziland, Botswana, South Africa, Namibia, and Lesotho. Cases of malaria per 100,000 of the population are negligible in the US, the UK, Japan, Netherlands, and Canada, while they reach over 20,000 in Botswana, Burundi, Zambia, Malawi, and Guinea. The adult literacy rate in Albania, Estonia, Slovenia, Ukraine, and Lithuania is over 98 per cent, compared to less than 50 per cent for Bangladesh, Chad, Ethiopia, Niger, and Senegal. In terms of technological diffusion, telephone mainlines per 1,000 people reaches over 6,000 for Norway, Sweden, Switzerland, Denmark, and the US, in comparison with less than 10 for Tanzania, Angola, Niger, Mali, and Rwanda; and Internet users per 1,000 people sits at over 500 for Singapore, Finland, the US, Canada, and Norway, compared to less than five for Burkina Faso, the Central African Republic, Rwanda, Eritrea, and Sudan (United Nations Development Programme, 2003).

We will now focus on the two broad paradigms that seek to explain and remedy global inequality. First, modernization theory follows the interests of the classical social and political thinkers in their concentration on the supposedly progressive movement from traditional to modern social orders. Emerging from this evolutionist perspective – especially from Durkheim and from Weber – modernization theory came to prominence in the 1950s and 1960s. The context of this approach is the polarization and global competition of the Cold War period, as both superpowers sought allegiances with non-European societies. Theorists of this paradigm draw on the tradition-modernity distinction. Talcott Parsons, America's leading sociologist of the period, had already drawn up a list of traits ostensibly dividing traditional from modern social orders: affectivity versus affective neutrality; collective versus self-orientation; particularism versus universalism;

ascription versus achievement; diffuseness versus specificity (Hoogvelt, 1978). In this perspective, tradition and the past provide the key sign posts, along with kinship and the collective, for those living in traditional social orders (Webster, 1990). People's place in the social order is ascribed (rather than achievement-based), allowing little mobility, and thus inclining people towards a worldview that is characterized by emotion, fate, and religion (Webster, 1990). One consequence of this, it was argued, is that they tend to lack the desire for new skills and technology, for new ways of thinking and acting (Webster, 1990). By contrast, people in modern societies are future-oriented, not as tied to tradition, kinship, and the collective, with achievement more important than ascription in determining one's place in the world, and equipped with a rational, scientific, and entrepreneurial approach to the world (Webster, 1990; Hulme and Turner, 1990).

While modernization theory is not all of a piece, emphasizing different factors in the move to modernity, there are important commonalities. For example, modernization theory views values, beliefs, and norms as important for progressive social change (Webster, 1990). Thus, David McLelland (1970) underscores the need for achievement and entrepreneurship in the modernization process. Modernization theory also tends to view the West as a map for development globally. It is thought that modern societies will develop as traditional ways are replaced with more modern practices and modes of thought, and these can be introduced from without, so that the West has a central role to play in the modernization of developing social orders (Hulme and Turner, 1990). Further, modernization thinkers identify a number of logics, tendencies, and institutions that should be encouraged so as to generate development, such as urbanization, nuclear families, growth of education and the mass media, and the emergence of a system of rational law (Webster, 1990; Hulme and Turner, 1990). The modernization approach also assumes that less developed social orders are in a state prior to their 'take off' into modernity, that the obstacles to such development or modernization are merely internal, and that development is a relatively linear process (Webster, 1990).

From the 1960s, these assumptions were heavily criticized, and modernization theory's popularity waned. A first counter-argument is that the dichotomous schema of 'tradition-modernity' is far too simplistic to account properly for a whole variety of experiences (Webster, 1990). This schema was also criticized as highly problematic in basing itself on the experiences of a small number of Western nations, and in being founded on the questionable assumption that the West was superior

(Webster, 1990). Next, modernization approaches seemed overly simplistic, when, for instance, modernization might not at all mean the decline of traditional beliefs and practices, especially since these might prove highly functional as resources in changing social orders (Webster, 1990). Most importantly, though, a number of thinkers influenced by Marxism objected that modernization theory had blindly ignored the impact of Western imperialism and colonialism on these third world orders: that is, modernization theory was deemed profoundly ahistorical (Hulme and Turner, 1990; Webster, 1990; Hoogvelt, 1978).

The second paradigm, emphasizing Western impact as an explanation for underdevelopment, is labelled dependency theory. We have already referred to Marx's assumption that capitalism would spread inexorably around the world, creating, in the process, a global capitalist order, which he believed was a progressive step insofar as it would pave the way for communism. Capitalism, that is, would generate the necessary productive forces and skills and create a human force – the working class – that would bring a higher stage of human social organization. Marx was impressed by capitalism's dynamism and progressiveness, and was often contemptuous of the traditional ways of life capitalism swept away. While Marx recognized the disruption and barbarism that can come with this expansion – the slave trade and the colonization of India are singled out – he viewed this process as inevitable and as ultimately progressive.

However, Marx does also note that, at least in part, the development of the Western capitalist nations is related to their ability to exploit the less advanced countries (Hulme and Turner, 1990). It is this idea that is very important to the thinkers who were to draw on Marx and Marxism to criticize and offer an alternative to modernization theory. For these Marxist thinkers, we need to turn to the history of Western exploitation of what is now the third world in order to understand why these countries did not and could not simply 'take off' into development, but were, quite the reverse, underdeveloped and made dependent by their contact with the West.

The leader of the Russian Revolution, Vladimir Lenin's 1917 pamphlet *Imperialism as the Highest Stage of Capitalism* is also important for thinkers of the dependency school. Imperialism, in brief, refers to the domination of less developed by more developed nations in the interests of economic gain (Marshall, 1994). For Lenin (1970: 106), the imperialistic stage of capitalist development was marked by the following: the concentration of production and capital towards monopolies;

the merging of bank and industrial capital; the export of capital; the creation of 'international monopolist combines which share the world among themselves'; and the complete division of the world between the major capitalist powers. Imperialism was, for Lenin, the result of the capitalist system attempting to overcome its crisis of profitability. Expansion outwards, suggests Lenin, solves this problem, allowing control over the global market, access to cheap labour, and a supply of cheap raw materials. This means as well the centralisation and concentration of capital by large monopolistic companies. For Lenin, capitalism inevitably generated imperialism, which inevitably generated conflict, war, and misery for the working class – recall that Lenin is writing in the period of the First World War – and this, in turn, would bring world socialist revolution. According to Lenin, though, because of the benefits accrued to the aristocracy of labour in the capitalist nations, the agent of revolution might not, first and foremost, be the Western working class, but might now be located in the less developed, exploited nations suffering from imperialistic plunder. A central innovation here, in contrast to the supreme optimism of many thinkers of socialist orthodoxy at the time, is that there are limits to the progressiveness and development of capitalism. At a certain stage, capitalism reaches decadence (it is no longer progressive), the end of its historical ascendancy and the end of its usefulness for the people of the world.

Scepticism about the inevitability of capitalist progress and development was taken up later in the Latin American context, and was vital for the development of dependency theory. The negative impact on Latin America of the Great Depression of the 1930s meant that the countries of this region began looking inwards for development strategies (Hulme and Turner, 1990). The Economic Commission for Latin America (ECLA) was established in 1948 and tried to explain and combat the persistence of underdevelopment in that continent (Hulme and Turner, 1990). Though their policies failed to achieve the development sought, as Hulme and Turner (1990: 47) note, they came to two important conclusions: (1) the world could be understood in terms of a 'core' of developed industrial nations and a 'periphery' of underdeveloped nations; and (2) that the core and periphery were closely linked, in such a way that these links made the periphery dependent on the core.

This dependency is frequently explained through a three-part account of the relations between core and periphery (see Webster, 1990: 70–81). The first phase began with merchant capitalism, the accumulation of capital through trade and plunder, starting in the sixteenth century. The second phase was colonialism in the nineteenth century, which involved greater wealth extraction from peripheral areas through tightened control over the labour force and the industrialization of production (Hoogvelt, 1978; Webster, 1990). Here, peripheral areas increasingly geared production towards the needs of European countries, so that, as Hobsbawm (1995b: 64) puts it, 'Malaya increasingly meant rubber and tin, Brazil coffee, Chile nitrates, Uruguay meat, Cuba sugar and cigars'. In the third phase of neocolonialism, the former colonies achieved independence, but a new form of socio-economic domination from outside has meant continuing dependence (Webster, 1990; Hoogvelt, 1978). Some support for this dependency thesis is given by the growing inequalities of wealth between Europe and its colonies: from 2: 1 in the eighteenth century, to 5: 1 in 1900, to 15: 1 by the 1960s (R. T. Robertson, 2003).

These ideas are most famously developed by the political economist, Andre Gunder Frank. Frank (1971) suggests that poverty in the third world, the satellites, is the result of dependency on the metropolis: in other words, development and underdevelopment are two sides of the same coin. The economic and political fabric of the now underdeveloped countries was distorted by expanding capitalism, and these countries became linked to the capitalist metropolis through narrow economic specialization. The elites in the third world act as intermediaries who benefit from this situation, while the mass of people in these satellites have the wealth or economic surplus they produce transferred back to the metropolis through 'a whole chain of metropolites and satellites, which runs from the world metropolis down to the hacienda or rural merchant who are satellites of the local commercial metropolitan centre but who in their turn have peasants as their satellites' (Frank in Long, 1977: 74). Influenced like others from the dependency paradigm by the Cuban Revolution, Frank contends that the source of underdevelopment can only be eliminated by breaking these ties of dependency.

While the dependency paradigm did much to discredit modernization theory, shifting the blame away from the third world, it too came in for a substantial amount of criticism and has since gone into decline or been modified. In particular, the concept of dependency was criticized as being of limited explanatory value (Webster, 1990): for instance, New Zealand has been heavily dependent on overseas markets for a narrow range of products (such as wool, meat, and dairy products) yet has a very high standard of living and might be considered as part of the core states. Second, even some Marxists (such as

Warren, 1973) claimed that third world nations are far from static, as dependency theory assumes, and development is occurring in a number of peripheral countries (Webster, 1990). Dependency theory thus is seen as providing too simple and unnuanced an account of global inequality. Nevertheless, as noted, while both modernization and dependency paradigms have been subjected to heavy critical interrogation, both continue to have resonance in popular, governmental, and academic discourse as ways of understanding global inequality.

Modernity

The question of modernity is obviously linked closely to ideas of development and modernization. And modernity has become a renewed focus of investigation, as we suggested earlier, with the challenges of postmodernism. As Jameson (2002) says, 'Modernity is back in business', and this is, paradoxically, a postmodern phenomenon.

Marx, Weber, and Durkheim were each wrestling with the advent of modernity and conceptualizied it, respectively, as dominated by capitalism, rationalization, and the expansion of the division of labour. In all three accounts, modernity is double-sided (Lemert, 1998; Berman, 1983), at once promising and dynamic but also disruptive and threatening – alienation and exploitation accompany capitalism (Marx), disenchantment of the world (a loss of the magic quality of life) comes with rationalization (Weber), and anomie (normlessness) with the expansion of the division of labour (Durkheim). And, as we have seen in Marx's account, modernity was linked to what is now called globalization, with capitalism spreading across the world.

In the social sciences today, modernity is often understood as a political, cultural, intellectual, and economic cluster that includes the following facets: the Industrial Revolution and the application of science and technique to production; capitalism, the generalized production of commodities for a market, and the relentless search for profit; the advent of the modern nation-state, nationalism, and the category of the citizen; the beginnings of the socialist movement and the coming into political life of the masses; Western global expansion and the emergence of the discourse of the 'West versus the Rest'; the intellectual-cultural revolution of the eighteenth century Enlightenment, with its emphasis on Reason, empiricism, science, universalism, progress, individualism, toleration, freedom, and secularism (Hamilton, 1999).

There has, then, been a movement away from conceptualizing modernity in terms of a single dominating dimension. Thus, influenced by but critical of Marx, the Hungarian political philosopher Agnes Heller insists

that modernity cannot simply be understood as solely about the unfolding of capitalism (Feher and Heller, 1987). Instead, Heller understands
modernity as made up of a number of competing and intertwining
logics – capitalism, industrialism, and democracy – which develop and
mix unevenly and unpredictably. As Beilharz (1994) suggests, we
could easily add others – for instance, nationalism, rationalization,
bureaucratization, relativization, pluralization, and globalization.

Another pluralizing move in the theorizing of modernity has seen a
shift away from the simple tradition-modernity dichotomy that is
based on a small part of the Western world as blueprint of modernity,
towards an attempt at a pluralistic and non-Eurocentric conceptualization of competing projects of modernity. The idea here is, in Andre
Gunder Frank's words, that 'If you look only under the European street
light you won't see much beyond Europe' (quoted in R. T. Robertson,
2003: 87). Rather than a single type of modernity, then, it is necessary
to speak of diverse *modernities* or projects of modernity that emphasize
a variety of distinct values, aims, ideals, practices, and institutions. For
example, Nicos Mouzelis (1999) considers modernity as introducing an
unprecedented mobilization of peoples that weakens local ties and
brings them to an economic, social, political and cultural centre. In
addition, he points to institutional differentiation, that is, the separation and autonomization of institutional spheres, as a central aspect of
modernity. This mobilization and differentiation are linked to the
scientific revolution. Further, in the cultural sphere, cultural technologies, for instance, help make mass literacy and education possible,
while in the social domain, technologies are employed for care of the
weak and destitute. This broader conceptualization aims at allowing us
to see varieties of modernity, modern institutions, and modern possibilities beyond the West, so that, for example, the idea of an Islamic
modernity that embraces certain Islamic traditions as well as Western
techno-capitalism no longer appears as a contradiction in terms.

Conclusion

We have argued in this chapter for the utility of critical theory in
approaching globalization. Such an approach is useful in that it refuses
to treat globalization as a simple 'fact' that can be straightforwardly
apprehended in a purely empirical manner. Critical theory instead
insists on the inescapability of theorizing, and thereby provides us
with challenging and enlightening ways of seeing and understanding
the world. Moreover, by refusing the possibility of an easy separation

of fact and value, and arguing that we can take up and transform the world, critical theory generates not only intellectual challenge and stimulation but also alternative political possibilities. We hope that this book will demonstrate not only the excitement of the alternative ways of seeing associated with critical theorizing, but also the necessity of confronting contemporary globalization and imagining other global futures.

Further reading

Arrighi, G. *The Long Twentieth Century: Money, Power, and the Origins of Our Times* (London: Verso, 1994).

Calhoun, C. *Critical Social Theory: Culture, History and the Challenge of Difference* (Oxford: Blackwell, 1995).

Held, D. *Introduction to Critical Theory: Horkheimer to Habermas* (Berkeley: University of California Press, 1980).

Hirst, P. and Thompson, G. *Globalization in Question* (Cambridge: Polity, 1996).

Jay, M. *The Dialectical Imagination: A History of the Frankfurt School and the Institute of Social Research, 1923–50* (London: Heinemann, 1973).

Linklater, A. *Beyond Realism and Marxism: Critical Theory and International Relations* (New York: St Martin's Press, 1990).

Mittelman, J. H. (ed.) *Globalization: Critical Reflections* (Boulder: Lynne Rienner, 1996).

Scholte, J. A. 'Beyond the Buzzword: Towards a Critical Theory of Globalization', in E. Kofman and G. Young (eds), *Globalization: Theory and Practice* (London: Pinter, 1996).

Wallerstein, I. *World-Systems Analysis: An Introduction* (Durham: Duke University Press, 2004).

Webster, A. *Introduction to the Sociology of Development*, 2nd edn (London: Macmillan, 1990).

2
Economic Globalization

Introduction

Economic globalization is without doubt the most commented upon, debated, and controversial of topics within the literature on globalization. Economic globalization appears spectacular, and its consequences seem most tangible. In fact, it often seems that economic globalization is the driving force behind the various changes bound up with culture and politics in the contemporary world, as well as being the principal concern of the alternative globalization movement. Consequently, it is often suggested that contemporary globalization is a historical moment in which the economic attains autonomy from, and exerts its weight upon, other spheres such as politics, society, and culture. In this chapter we examine how this purported economic autonomy is, above all, tied up with questions of inequalities in wealth and power – between MNCs and citizens, between countries in the North and countries in the South, between the connected and the unconnected, and between employers and employees.

Capitalism, social democracy, and neoliberalism

Whenever one talks of globalization in economic terms, there is frequent reference made to capitalism, neoliberalism, and socialism or social democracy. In particular, one vital ingredient in the emergence of the new global economy has been a set of deregulating policies pushed by neoliberals, which have come to replace the previous social democratic consensus in Western nations (Castells, 1996). It is therefore necessary to unpack these terms and examine this shift before proceeding to discuss other central considerations in the literature around economic globalization.

Capitalism is an economic system based on the generalized production and circulation of commodities – goods and services on sale on a market – and the production and circulation of these commodities is centred around the drive for profit (Buick and Crump, 1986). For Marxists, the existence of capital implies as a corollary the existence of waged labour – that is, men and women who own no means of production (factories, tools of production, products of labour) and sell their labour power, their capacity to labour, to the capitalist class (the owners of the means of production). This relationship entails exploitation of the worker by the capitalist – profits are derived from the worker's surplus labour time (the time over and above that taken to produce an amount equivalent to the costs of sustaining the worker and reproducing the next generation of workers). Profitability, the market, competition, and inequality are thus all central to capitalism.

According to Osterhammel and Petersson (2003), the period 1846–80 was an 'age of free trade'. Britain, in particular, held fast to this idea, even as it started losing popularity from the 1870s and country after country raised protective barriers to shelter national economies (Hobsbawm, 1995b). For enthusiasts of free trade, markets were self-regulating; as Adam Smith had argued a century earlier, the market worked as if guided by an 'invisible hand' to produce social welfare as a by-product of the self-interested pursuit of profit. That is, people enter the market with certain capacities, products, and needs, and there will be a resulting complementary harmony of interests and abilities that would flow from the pursuit of individual self-interest.

However, this notion of the spontaneous harmony generated by the pursuit of self-interest, and that of the self-regulating capacity of markets, increasingly fell into disrepute, partly as a result of the rising socialist challenge, partly as a result of economic dislocation. The effects of unrestrained capitalism led, in the course of the nineteenth century, to attempts – in such far-flung places as Germany and New Zealand – to introduce measures to restrict and regulate market forces. (Smart, 2003). And though confidence in the market was restored for a period, the Great Depression of 1929–33, bringing economic ruin, unemployment and political instability, allowed no return to the unrestrained capitalism of the 'age of imperialism' (Hobsbawm, 1995b; Smart, 2003).

Thus, in his 1944 work *The Great Transformation*, Karl Polanyi offered a strong critique of the market model, and he hailed the retreat from faith in free markets towards growing state intervention as a positive and irreversible move (Smart, 2003). For Polanyi, 'To allow the market mechanism to be sole director of the fate of human beings and their natural environment ... would result in the demolition of society' (in George 1999). And increasing state intervention meant 'a development under which the economic system ceases to lay down the law to society and the primacy of society over that system is secured' (in Smart, 2003: 31). Polyani's confidence in the retreat from the market seemed well grounded, as liberal economics gave way increasingly to an economic common sense that emphasized equality, state intervention, collectivism, and welfare. For about 30 years, then, Keynesianism, basing itself on the kind of assumptions offered by Polyani, constituted conventional economic wisdom for Western governments. Drawing from the ideas of economist John Maynard Keynes, numerous states stimulated the growth of production and demand by fiscal and monetary measures, for instance, in abandoning concern with inflation and introducing money into circulation so as to promote economic growth. Here, the state sought to foster a mixed economy (a combination of state and private enterprise), full employment, and national cooperation between labour and capital towards the goal of national prosperity. In this period, too, the welfare state grew in many nations, with the state agreeing to provide social protection for the unemployed, the sick, and the elderly, from the often brutal outcomes of free markets.

Box 2.1 Keynesian Economics

John Maynard Keynes (1883–1946) was a British economist who advocated interventionist government policies, such as monetary control, public debt and fiscal regulation, in order to mitigate the adverse effects of capitalism, including high unemployment, recessions and depressions, and the 'boom and bust' business cycle. Keynes' theories had a major influence on US President Franklin D. Roosevelt's 'New Deal' policies in response to the Great Depression of the 1930s. In particular, Keynes argued that the depressed economy would be 'primed' or stimulated back into growth by the federal government borrowing and spending money on public-works projects and social services. In Keynes' estimation a 'mixed' or socially regulated market economy would avoid the disadvantages of both pure capitalism and pure socialism. Keynes' economic theories subsequently gained ground in the form of the welfare state in the Western world. Keynes served as leader of the British delegation and chairman of the World Bank Commission during the negotiations that established the Bretton Woods system near the end of the Second World War. While Keynes lobbied for a socially regulated global economy this move was opposed by the US.

However, from the early 1970s, a multi-pronged crisis started to eat away at the Keynesian compromise or the 'social democratic consensus': a crisis of governability with rising social antagonism, economic down turn (with growing unemployment, economic contraction, profit losses, and bankruptcies), and a growing recognition of the rigidity of the Fordist system (Cohen and Kennedy, 2000). From the 1970s, neoliberal ideas became increasingly influential, signalled by the award of Nobel prizes in economics to Friedrich von Hayek in 1974 and Milton Friedman in 1976, two of neoliberalism's most influential thinkers (Hobsbawm, 1995b). Neoliberals called for extensive economic reorganization, and, harking back to the ideas of the age of free trade, insisted that the market, free of state intrusion, would spontaneously and neutrally order the complex web of decisions, actions, needs, and abilities of a multitude of individuals (Smart, 2003). For neoliberals, this market mechanism is infinitely more efficient and just than state attempts to order and plan the economy. For Hayek, it was a 'fatal conceit' to imagine that that state could know of and plan for the totality of individual needs, interests, and capacities. He argued that attempts at such state-led planning in the economic and social realms would undermine efficiency, innovation, and wealth generated by competition, and it would inevitably lead to coercion, the extreme tendency of such coercion leading in the direction of Soviet communism. Thus, for Friedman, it is a crucial mistake to imagine that one could achieve political freedom while undermining economic freedom (Green, 1987). While frequently giving the state a continued role in the protection of private property, defence from external enemies, and even construction of a modest safety net for those who fail in the market, neoliberals argue for a reduction of state involvement in economic life to a minimal level. Here, freedom is elevated as a societal goal above the social democratic emphasis on equality, though many neoliberals would still view equality of opportunity (as opposed to equality of outcomes) as important. For neoliberals, freedom is closely linked to capitalism, and is often said to be a 'negative' freedom, a 'state in which a man is not subject to coercion by the arbitrary will of another or others' (Hayek in Hindess, 1987: 128).

Neoliberal ideas came increasingly to constitute the new economic common sense after the 1970s, and the powerful criticisms that can be levelled at neoliberal contentions have often been marginalized as unrealistic or extremist. Thus, neoliberalism, in Susan George's (1999) estimation, has emerged as a new 'worldwide religion', and Perry Anderson (2000) names neoliberalism as the most powerful and successful ideology in world history. Especially important for the achievement of neoliberal hegemony were the electoral victories of Ronald Reagan in America (1980) and Margaret Thatcher in England (1979). From this time, in many parts of the world, attempts were made to reduce social spending, deregulate markets (including labour markets), 'rationalize' and privatize state enterprises, and promote an ethos of self-reliant, competitive individualism: for instance, between 1979 and 1994, the number of jobs in the British public sector were reduced by 29 per cent (George, 1999); between 1990 and 1999, the value of state assets sold worldwide reached $900 billion, from $30 billion in 1990 to $145 billion in 1999 (New Internationalist, 2003b); the percentage of those in Germany in insecure forms of work rose from 10 per cent in the 1960s to 30 per cent in late 1990s (Smart, 2003); corporate and top income bracket tax rates fell; and social spending was attacked, with mixed results, ranging from moves towards more residual welfare systems in Britain and New Zealand, to more modest cuts in countries such as Austria, Germany, Canada, and Australia (Huber and Stephens, 2001).

The socialist movement, growing from about the time of Marx and Engel's 1848 *Communist Manifesto*, had posed capitalism a series of intellectual, moral, economic, and political challenges. These challenges, at first glance, seem now to have largely passed away. As Ulrich Beck says, 'No one today questions capitalism' (in Smart, 1993: 27). In the face of such neoliberal hegemony, we believe that it is vital to return to the socialist critique of this 'bankers' fatalism' (Bourdieu, 1998), because, in our view, such fatalism and the widespread submission to the market mechanism are threats to the still resonant values of democracy, freedom, and equality. Critique is also called for because it appears that neoliberalism is facing something of a crisis, manifested in both the turn to 'tribal politics' and the emergence of the alternative globalization movement (Rapley, 2004).

For socialists, capitalism's overriding logics of the pursuit of self-interest, competition, and profitability are chaotic, socially divisive, and inefficient. At base, for socialists, the main goals of an economic system should be about the satisfaction of needs and the achievement of co-operation, rather than about profitability (which, they maintain, is attained by exploitation of the majority of people) and competition. If economics are not organized according to need and solidarity, monetary value would come to outweigh and colonize all other values. And because of capitalism's insatiable drive to profit and expansion, crisis and conflict are unavoidable.

Within socialism's radical communist wing, the argument held that capitalism could never be humanized and therefore must be abolished. Within socialism's moderate wing, social democracy, we find a social or 'soft' capitalism, with extensive state involvement, collectivism, and 'cradle to grave' welfare provision. While social democracy has, world-wide, tended to become much more accommodating to neoliberal arguments (as we will detail in Chapter 5), and while the communist movement and the ideas of Marx have become less popular, it is our view that the socialist critique of capitalism still stands as intellectually and morally compelling. We believe that the exploration of some of the dimensions of economic globalization that follows demonstrates the continued relevance of this critique. Moreover, the existence of a diverse and vigorous alternative globalization movement indicates that there is still an agent or carrier of this critique.

Against the neoliberal argument about the neutrality of the market and the insistence that the poor cannot be regarded as coerced (because coercion only results from intentional acts), Marx's reminders that people do not meet in the market on equal terms, that private property is always a distribution of freedoms and unfreedoms, and that markets and distributions of private property are not natural but have a history that often entails violence and exclusion, are all important. On this last point, Castoriadis (2005) insists that the market has seldom if ever been perfect or even truly competitive, characterized as it is by the endless interventions of the state, coalitions of capitalists, the manipulation of consumers, and violence against labouring people. We would suggest, in particular, that it is necessary to contest the way in which, ever increasingly, 'the social world is written in economic language' (Bourdieu, 1998). The autonomy and primacy given to the economic, to productivity and profitability, clearly represent threats to other values and needs, and many people would accept that some restraints need to be placed on the search for growth and profits: for instance, as Smart (2003) suggests, most people would object to a market in human organs; therefore, there must be limits on the market's operations, to its tendency to function, as Weber noted, 'without regard for persons' (in Smart, 2003: 84).

Further, the negative freedom praised by neoliberals is arguably not enough. Marxists often contrast such an emphasis with a 'positive' conception of freedom that specifies how we should live and what we should be as human beings (social, productive, creative beings, according to Marx). So, with respect to the emphasis on choice within neo-liberalism, we need always to consider the critical issues of '*what* can be chosen and what *is* chosen' (Marcuse in Smart, 2003: 44). That is, needs and desires are not natural and obvious but socially produced, often imposed or improperly thought through, and consumption, then, is to an extent 'controlled': as Castoriadis (2005) puts it, people want the goods they want because they are raised to want them. It is necessary, at the very least, to have domains outside of the market that allow for the development of the autonomy and discrimination required for informed choice, and without such domains and regulation, we face clear threats to civic life and to democracy itself (Smart, 2003).

Neoliberalism and the IMF, World Bank, and WTO

For critics of economic globalization, some of the most damaging outcomes of globalization can be attached to the neoliberal orientation of institutions such as the International Monetary Fund (IMF), the World Bank, and the World Trade Organization (WTO). These institutions are commonly viewed as working according to the so-called 'Washington Consensus', a neoliberal agenda that originated with policies directed towards economic reform in Latin America from the late 1980s, and which Steger (2003: 53) defines as follows:

1. A guarantee of fiscal discipline, and a curb to budget deficits;
2. A reduction of public expenditure, particularly in the military and public administration;
3. Tax reform, aiming at the creation of a system with a broad base and with effective enforcement;
4. Financial liberalization, with interest rates determined by the market;
5. Competitive exchange rates, to assist export-led growth;
6. Trade liberalization, coupled with the abolition of import licensing and a reduction of tariffs;
7. Promotion of foreign direct investment;
8. Privatization of state enterprises, leading to efficient management and improved performance;
9. Deregulation of the economy;
10. Protection of property rights.

The Bretton Woods Conference of 1944 aimed at establishing a new global economic order at the end of the war, moving away from some of the destabilizing economic problems that had characterized the interwar years (Steger, 2002). Under the agreement, the American dollar was to function as an effective world currency, so that, in theory, the dollar could be redeemed in gold at $35 per ounce, thus setting in place a system of fixed exchange rates between currencies, which would protect the global economy from the competitive devaluations of the interwar period (Cohn, 2003). However, with the expansion of the global system of production and finance, the oil crisis of the early 1970s, and the declining place of America within the system, the relationship between the dollar and gold became unstable (Cohn, 2003). When, in 1971, the US experienced its first balance of trade deficit since 1893, President Nixon announced that America was removing convertibility between the dollar and gold (Cohn, 2003). After this time, currency values were determined by the market, and capital flows expanded steadily.

Importantly, the Bretton Woods Conference saw the establishment of a UN agency, the International Monetary Fund (IMF) to secure financial stability in the world economy. The IMF was formed to guard monetary stability and to make short-term loans to members who

---

Box 2.2   Structural Adjustment Programmes

Structural Adjustment Programmes (SAPs) originated in the late 1970s under the influence of neoliberal economic policies favouring the deregulation of capital and labour markets, as a means to foster free-market liberalization across borders. SAPs were introduced as conditions on loans by the International Monetary Fund (IMF) ostensibly to help attract investment into developing countries. These 'conditionalities' required developing countries to modify their economic policies in order to support privatization and deregulation and reduce barriers to trade. Such programmes included cutting public spending, placing limitations on wages, removing price controls and state subsidies, and devaluing currencies against the US dollar. For critics, SAPs have had hugely detrimental effects on the populations of developing countries, as reductions in state spending, reductions in wages, and the privatization of land and public enterprises have contributed to further impoverishment, the displacement of local production, and the expropriation of national resources. Due to public criticism of SAPs they were replaced by the IMF and World Bank in the late 1990s by 'Poverty Reduction Strategy Papers', although many regard this change as merely terminological since neoliberal conditionalities are still imposed on loans provided by these institutions. For example, in Colombia, the IMF Stand-by Arrangement signed by the government in 2002, made new loans conditional on labour reforms that 'should reduce labour costs by extending daytime working hours and reducing overtime charges and severance payments'.

Source: (IMF 2002).

found themselves facing balance-of-payment difficulties (*Guardian*, 2001a; Cohn, 2003). However, critics charge that over the years, particularly since the debt crisis of the 1980s, the IMF's role was redefined towards the surveillance of the economic performance of countries, offering loans conditional on the adoption of a number of free market measures or so-called 'structural adjustment programmes' (Burton and Nesiba, 2004; Cohn, 2003; *Guardian*, 2001a).

The oil shocks of the 1970s, the expansion of money flowing into less developed nations, global recession and structural dependence, hit many less developed nations hard and led to requests for debt restructuring (Cohn, 2003), with debt burdens of low income countries rising from $21 billion in 1970 to $110 billion in 1980 (Burton and Nesiba, 2004). In this situation, the IMF stepped in and demanded structural adjustment conditions on countries seeking rescheduling of debt. Such conditions included policies such as the removal of trade barriers, the removal of restrictions on the in- and out-flow of capital, the sale of national assets to foreign investors, and cuts to social spending (*Guardian*, 2001a; Albert, 2000). As Stiglitz (2004) notes, the IMF acted as a hospital that made its patients sicker, focussing on protecting foreign lenders rather than on the fate of these countries in crisis, and contributing to a 'lost decade' for nations in Africa and Latin America (Cleaver, 2002; Burton and Nesiba, 2004; Cohn, 2003). The IMF has, in line with this, frequently been viewed as an institution favouring the developed countries of the world at the expense of the poor, with the G8 countries controlling nearly half of votes in the Fund and the US over 17 per cent (New Internationalist, 2004a).

The World Bank is also a UN affiliate, originating at the Bretton Woods Conference and commencing operations in June 1946. Its original brief was to aid in the reconstruction of Europe, as well as act to lend money to poorer countries (*Guardian*, 2001b; Cohn, 2003). Thus, as George (1999) says, initially both the World Bank and the IMF were widely viewed as relatively progressive institutions, even if part of their function was linked to the Western Cold War aim of containing communism (Steger, 2002). It is often said that with the debt crisis of the 1980s there emerged a convergence between the IMF and the World Bank (Cohn, 2003), with the Bank granting loans for purposes it deemed would result in sustainable and equitable growth in developing countries. This growth was seen as most likely in economies that are open to international trade, manage to attract foreign investment, and adhere to free market policies (*Guardian*, 2001b). However, critics maintain that such loans leave developing countries even poorer because of the hefty interest payments required, and the Bank is criticized for attaching too many strings to loans, requiring structural adjustments that protect private investors at the expense of national economic independence, employment, wages, and human development in general. In addition, as in the case of the IMF, voting power is not evenly spread across member states, with the G8 countries controlling nearly half of the votes in Bank decisions (New Internationalist, 2004a).

In January 1995, a new World Trade Organization (WTO) replaced the General Agreement on Tariffs and Trade (GATT). The GATT was a pact, operating since 1947, that governed tariffs and quotas on the trade in goods (Wallach and Woodall, 2004). The aim of the informal and flexible GATT was to lower tariff rates through multilateral negotiations so as to protect against the protectionism of the interwar years, negotiations based on principles of trade liberalization, non-discrimination, and reciprocity (Cohn, 2003). The WTO, in contrast, is formal and legally constituted (Cohn, 2003), a more powerful organization that administers trade agreements, acts as a forum for trade negotiations, handles trade disputes, monitors national trade policies, and seeks to remove barriers to free trade (Wallach and Woodall, 2004). Its disputes settlement process is binding, it is able to implement retaliatory measures on offending countries, and its brief extends beyond just goods to services and intellectual property rights (Cohn, 2003).

The WTO is much criticized, and has been the focus for alternative globalization activists, on a number of counts. According to Michael Albert (2000), for instance, 'The WTO is about protecting corporate ownership and monopoly... and breaking down any protections of labour, the environment, health and safety, that might limit corporate profit making'. For Wallach and Woodall (2004: 2, 13), the WTO is a mechanism for 'spreading and locking in corporate-led globalization'; in other words, 'global commerce takes precedence over everything – democracy, public health, equity, access to essential services, the environment, food safety and more'. One of the main arguments from alternative globalization critics, then, is that the blind commitment to free trade over all other values (such as democracy, human rights, local economic development, and the prevention of health risks) will see countries forced to accept imports from places with lower health and safety or environmental protection standards (Albert, 2000). It is, for instance, counter to free trading rules to discriminate against a product because of the way it was produced, and this could mean that states may not be able to keep out commodities produced, say, with child labour or in an environmentally destructive way. Critics also charge that, because of the wide-ranging impact of WTO decisions, discussions should involve wider civil society, not merely state-appointed delegates (Wallach and Woodall, 2004). In addition, critics maintain, despite the consensus mechanism of decision-making, secrecy and lack of transparency within the organization is rife, and power politics and bullying within the organization, whereby more vulnerable countries are coerced into agreement with the wishes of more powerful nations, is commonplace (Wade, 2004). Developing countries are frequently seen as the real losers, forced away more easily from measures that might protect and develop their domestic economies, while protectionism remains heavy in certain sectors in the economies of more developed nations (Wallach and Woodall, 2004).

Global finance

In 1997 a major financial crisis spread through Southeast Asia, across countries such as Thailand, Malaysia, and Indonesia, countries generally viewed in a positive light because of their openness and solid rates of economic growth. Investors panicked and withdrew well over $100 billion, leading to rapid falls in currency values (the South Korean *won* fell from 800 to the dollar on the 10th of January to 2000 to the dollar just two days later); depletion of foreign exchange reserves (the Bank of Thailand lost nearly all of the $38.7 billion in foreign exchange reserves it had held in 1996); declining economic output and wages (between 1997 and 1998, GNP per capita fell by 8.5 per cent for Thailand, 7.4 per cent for South Korea, 9.6 per cent for Malaysia, and 18 per cent for Indonesia); and massive unemployment (by 1999, an estimated 27 million workers had lost their jobs) (Cleaver, 2002; Bello *et al.*, 2000; Steger, 2002; Volcker, 2000; Short, 2001; Grimwade, 2000; Andersen *et al.*, 2000). The crisis was viewed by many as a signal of the growing centrality and volatility of financial globalization.

For Castells (1996), the globalization of financial markets is the very backbone of the new global economy. According to Cetina and Preda (2005: 2), 'finance has perhaps risen in importance in the last quarter century more rapidly than any other sector of the economy', with enormous consequences in terms of 'production, consumption, and social welfare'. This new centrality of finance is connected to the liberalization of financial flows after the demise of the Bretton Woods system, deregulation of the financial sector, a new communications infrastructure that allows round the clock and instantaneous transactions of enormous amounts of money, and the emergence of new financial instruments such as derivatives (Castells, 1996; Khor, 2001).

Let us examine some of the elements of this explosion of global finance. In 1973, just $15 billion was exchanged daily in currency markets; this rose to $900 billion per day by 1992, and again to $1.5 trillion per day in 2004 (Burton and Nesiba, 2004; Khor, 2001). By 1999, foreign exchange transactions were over 70 times the volume of world trade, up from 10 times world trade in 1983 (Cetina and Preda, 2005). The international trade in derivatives, such as futures, where buyers and sellers agree to buy or sell a certain commodity at a future date for a fixed price has, in similar fashion, risen in value from $30 trillion in 1994, to $80 trillion in 2000, to $192 trillion in 2002 (Cetina and Preda, 2005; Sassen, 2005). Trade in international debt securities doubled between 1993 and 1999 to 17.4 per cent of world GDP (Hout, 2004). And, increasingly, transactions in bonds and equities are global: 'the value of cross-border transactions in bonds and equities as a percentage of GDP in the leading economies was 4 per cent in 1975 in the US, 35 per cent in 1985 ... and had risen to 230 per cent in 1998' (Cetina and Preda, 2005: 5).

For enthusiasts, the growth of financial globalization provides new opportunities for wealth creation and democratizes investment opportunities. According to Thomas Friedman (1999), for instance, now everyone can be a player, and the power of global finance, what he calls 'the electronic herd', while potentially devastating in its impact, is a positive development that disciplines wayward economies (such as the 'crony capitalism' of East Asia), by pushing towards less corrupt, more transparent, and healthier economic practices.

For critics, on the other hand, the speed and uncontrollability of global financial flows is an urgent problem. An enormous amount of money can move in and out of markets at a very fast pace. This may be profitable for some investors, but it is potentially harmful for many countries – for instance, in reducing a nation's sovereignty in economic and social policy. In particular, smaller countries are very susceptible to the sudden withdrawal of capital inflow, and thus are more vulnerable to economic insecurity as the Southeast Asian crisis showed. For George Soros (2002), financial markets are quite different from other markets in that they do not tend to equilibrium, are not based on knowledge but, instead, on speculation, and tend to spiral out of control. The 'market fundamentalist', neoliberal optimism about global finance refuses to take these realities into account (Soros, 2002). Furthermore, very little of the massive volume of capital circulating today has any real productive function: Scholte (2000) estimates that less than 5 per cent of foreign exchange dealings relate to transactions in real goods. That is, much of such investment is speculative and short-term (such as the bulk of funds coming into East Asia), and therefore it has very little real benefit to countries and their peoples. In Chapter 5 we will explore proposals for containing the power and volatility of financial markets.

New technology

As Mackay (2002) notes, one vital feature of modernity is its increasingly mediated nature. This rising mediation is seen by Giddens (1990, 2005) as important in the stretching of social relations ('time-space distanciation'), making social life less centrally about immediate locality – a key factor in globalization. New information and communication technologies are frequently viewed as crucially linked to contemporary globalization – for instance, in the notion of an 'end of geography' brought by 'fast capitalism's' instantaneity and erosion of boundaries (Agger, 2004), which transforms identity, as well as social and economic life. In economic terms, just as the spread of rail, fast steamers, and telegraph in the 'age of imperialism' facilitated a great expansion of world interconnectedness, so too satellite, digitization, video conferencing, mobile communications, electronic data exchange, and networking appear to facilitate a growing density of transnational economic interaction.

For some, new technology is the defining feature of the current economic system, a new information or postindustrial era. For Castells (1996), for instance, productivity and competitiveness now are crucially based on the generation of knowledge and information processing. This is signalled for him by the steep growth in the 1990s of the information technology sector, the rise of the Internet industry's revenues and of Internet-related employment, the high ranking amongst corporations of new technology giants, and informationalism's pivotal role in the collapse of the Soviet Union, an event with great geo-political significance (see Chapter 3).

The rapid spread and declining costs of technology often are viewed as great democratizing forces, contributing towards greater transparency and citizen access to knowledge. In addition, such new technology is commonly seen as having a 'flattening' effect on global inequality. Thus, Thomas Friedman (2005) enthuses over the arrival of what he calls 'globalization 3.0', a coming 'flat world' which provides unprecedented empowerment of individuals and whose benefits can no longer be confined to the West, with technology promising an end to the constraints of place.

In the face of the sometimes-wild optimism and technological determinism contained within much commentary on the implications of new technology, we want to raise a couple of critical points. First, against technological determinism, as Nederveen Pieterse (2004: 10) says, 'technology itself is socially embedded and shaped. ... What matters is not technology *per se* but the way it is harnessed by economic, political, and social forces'. Third, it is well to recall some of the sceptical responses to theories of the arrival of postindustrial, knowledge, or information societies, responses that accent *continuity* with the older industrial capitalism in terms of the technological and knowledge dimensions. Second, it seems vital to note the unevenness of the diffusion of this new technology. Castells (1998), for instance, points to the heavy concentration of science and technology in a small number of developed countries, with just ten countries accounting for 84 per cent of all research and development. Similarly, the 20 per cent of the world's population living in developed countries control 74 per cent of world telephone lines and make up 93 per cent of Internet users. Overall, only 9.57 per cent of the world's population are Internet users with, for example, just 1.6 per cent of the Arab world able to access the Internet (Global Policy Forum, 2003; Blanford, 2003). It is clear, then, that there is an enormous 'digital divide' globally between the information rich and the information poor.

Trade and multinational corporations

In Chapter 1, we noted the importance in the earlier Dutch- and British-led globalization of the state sponsored chartered companies, widely seen as early versions of the multinational corporation. We also drew attention to the deepening of globalization in the 'age of imperialism', with a significant expansion in the volume of international trade, and the increasing tendency towards monopoly or corporate capitalism in Germany and America. It was, though, especially after World War Two that international trade really began to grow again and that a period of multinational capitalism was ushered in, dominated by America. In this section, we will examine further some of these issues, focussing on the multinational corporation (MNC) and 'deterritorialization'.

The growth of international trade, Castells (1996) argues, is not as significant as that of financial markets, but it has still risen substantially in the last 30 years; and, according to Grimwade (2000), it has grown faster in the past 50 years than in any other period. For instance, world exports rose from $61 billion in 1950 to over $6 trillion in the late 1990s (Khor, 2001; Steger, 2003). And international trade's share of total world output between 1987 and 1997 rose from 27 to 39 per cent for developed nations, and from 10 to 17 per cent for developing nations (Short, 2001); meanwhile, the ratio of trade to domestic GDP between 1985 and 1997 grew from 16.6 to 24.1 per cent for developed nations and from 22.8 to 38 per cent for less developed nations (Cohn, 2003).

Over time, the share of primary products in trade volumes has declined, and the place of manufactures has increased, with rises in office and telecommunications equipment, consumer goods, motor vehicles, and other machinery and transport equipment (Grimwade, 2000). Increasingly, trade in services has expanded, growing by 17.3 per cent per year between 1984 and 1994 – especially in the advanced economies, which dominate trade in services (where services tend to make up over half of GDP and a majority of total employment) – and reaching over 20 per cent of total world trade by the mid-1990s, up from 12.1 per cent in 1973 (Grimwade, 2000; Castells, 1996; Anderson *et al.*, 2000). The main services traded are tourism and travel, communications, information and legal services, and entertainment (Anderson *et al.*, 2000). This is some confirmation of the theoretical arguments that posit the advent of a 'postindustrial' or 'knowledge' capitalism, decisively signalled by the moment in 1992 when Microsoft's market value overtook General Motors' (Axford, 1995).

Measurement of capital flows is one method of judging the internationalization of economic activity. A major type of borrowing and lending that goes on in international economy is what is called foreign direct investment (FDI). FDI is 'Overseas investment by companies to set up a new overseas subsidiary or acquire a controlling interest in another company' (Grimwade, 2000: 111). During the last two to three decades, there has been a substantial growth of FDI, from 4.5 per cent of world output in 1975, to 12 per cent in 1997 (Dutt, 2004), from $57 billion in 1982 to $1.271 trillion in 2000 (Burton and Nesiba, 2004). Most FDI (95 per cent) originates in just 20 developed countries, including the US, Japan, France, UK, Netherlands, and Switzerland (Held and McGrew, 2002). The US was for some time the largest investor and recipient of FDI – the source, for instance, of 42.9 per cent of outward stocks of FDI in 1980 (Grimwade, 2000; Cohn, 2003). Nevertheless, this situation has changed. In 1998, America was the source of only 24.1 per cent of outward stocks of FDI (Cohn, 2003), with developing countries' share of FDI (mostly inflow rather than outflow) jumping from 20 per cent of the total in 1990 to 34 per cent in 1995–96, and in 2002 China became the world's largest recipient of FDI (Anderson *et al.*, 2000; Held, 2004b; Khor, 2001). This increasing movement of FDI is related to the post-Second World War trend towards relaxation of controls on capital movement (Grimwade 2000; ILO, 2004).

FDI is associated with MNCs as major actors in the global economy. Cohen and Kennedy (2000: 121) summarize the characteristics of MNCs in the following way: MNCs

- Control economic activities in two or more countries
- Maximize the comparative advantage between countries, profiting from differences in factor endowments, wage rates, market conditions and political and fiscal regimes
- Have geographical flexibility, that is an ability to shift resources and operations between different locations on a global scale
- Operate with a level of financial, component and operational flows between different segments of the MNC greater than the flows within a particular country
- Have significant economic and social effects at a global level

MNCs are associated with the growing internationalization of production and with the reconfiguration of the international division of labour. Since the 1970s, there has been an increasing 'deterritorializing' of corporations (Short, 2001), in contrast to the period of economic nationalism when the big corporations were seen as 'national champions' embedded within particular social orders (Munck, 2002). That is, MNCs have increasingly relocated production and outsourced to developing countries in the hope of benefitting from the differential costs of labour, raw materials, and transport. As a result, many products today are highly internationalized, such as automobiles which contain components produced in various countries (Held and McGrew, 2002; Cohen and Kennedy, 2000).

In 2000, there were around 60,000 MNCs, with 820,000 foreign subsidiaries, and global sales of $15.6 trillion (Held and McGrew, 2002). In total, MNCs account for about 70 per cent of world trade, 70 per cent of total FDI, 25 per cent of world production, and 80 per cent of international exchanges of technology and managerial skills, and their sales are equivalent to almost half of world GDP (Held and McGrew, 2002).

MNCs are overwhelmingly based in OECD countries. While there are an increasing number of MNCs from oil producing and East Asian nations, of the largest 500 MNCs, 179 are American based, 148 are EU based, and 107 are based in Japan (Held and McGrew, 2002; Castells, 1996). The largest and most prominent MNCs are involved in such sectors as the exploitation of petroleum, car manufacturing, trading, banking, pharmaceuticals, and information technology. In terms of market value, the largest MNCs include General Electric, Exxon Mobil, Microsoft, Pfizer, Citigroup, Wal-Mart Stores, BP, Bank of America, Royal Dutch/Shell, Johnson and Johnson, the Vodafone Group, Proctor and Gamble, IBM, and Toyota.

Many commentators have noted the concentration of power within MNCs over the past few decades, with numerous mergers and acquisitions. According to Scholte (2000), for instance, the number of mergers and acquisitions since the 1980s has doubled, with 24,600 in the period 1990–97. Therborn (2001) sees this concentration of capital as exemplified in the American case, where in 1905 the 50 largest US corporations had assets equal to 16 per cent of US GDP; while in 1999 the 50 largest had assets equivalent to 37 per cent of US GDP. Thus it is that a handful of corporations now largely dominate many sectors: the largest ten companies control 60 per cent of the automobile industry, 70 per cent of computer sales, 85 per cent of pesticide sales, 86 per cent of telecommunications; and the largest three control 80 per cent of the banana trade, 83 per cent of the cocoa trade, and 85 per cent of the trade in tea (Anderson *et al.*, 2000; Scholte, 2000).

It has been noted (see Steger, 2003) that 51 of the largest economies in the world today are corporations and only 49 are countries. This is calculated by comparing corporate sales with countries' GDPs. For some, this is an inadequate basis for comparison, and it distorts the realities of the situation so that MNCs appear more powerful than they really are (see Legrain, 2002). However, the comparison is indicative of the size and power of MNCs, and even using a more conservative comparison of GDP against value added, Wal-Mart stores rank above Pakistan, Peru, and Algeria, Exxon ranks above the Czech Republic, New Zealand, and Bangladesh, and General Motors ranks above Hungary (Held, 2004b).

For enthusiasts of global free trade, MNCs are enormously beneficial, providing consumer goods, technology, and new skills, and acting with states (whom they provide with revenue in the form of company taxes) to advance economies and provide jobs. However, for critics MNCs exercise far too much power, are largely unrestrained, and exhibit far too little social responsibility, exploiting workers, diminishing the state's sovereignty, and undermining democracy in general (Cohen and

Kennedy, 2000). One of the major criticisms of MNCs in this regard is that they can simply relocate their facilities to overcome barriers to profitability. These barriers might include decent wages or environmental protection regulations. Nike provides a good case study of this. Nike originated in Phil Knight's plan to introduce low-cost Japanese-produced athletic shoes into the US market in the 1970s (Short, 2001). As labour costs rose, Nike moved production to South Korea and Taiwan in 1972, then, as workers organized, into Indonesia, China, and Thailand in 1986, and, finally, into Vietnam in 1994 (where in 1998 workers earned as little as $1.60 a day) (Short, 2001; Anderson *et al.*, 2000; Steger, 2003). Nike now subcontracts 100 per cent of its goods production to 75,000 workers in China, South Korea, Malaysia, Taiwan, Vietnam and Thailand (Anderson *et al.*, 2000; Steger, 2003).

The movement of capital away from the US and Europe after the 1970s involved attempts to secure new markets, gain greater profits, and utilize cheap, unorganized labour (Cohen and Kennedy, 2000). In the 1950s, the major part of manufacturing employment in the world was found in North America and Europe (Short, 2001). Since the 1970s, the centre of gravity of manufacturing has shifted towards the so-called 'newly industrializing countries' – first Japan, Hong Kong, Singapore and Taiwan, and more recently, Indonesia, Philippines, and China. Thus, between 1970 and 1983, the third world's share of global industrial exports more than doubled (Hobsbawm, 1995b), and the period from 1963 to 1988 saw rises in export to GDP ratios for the following newly industrializing countries: Hong Kong – 39 to 51.1 per cent; South Korea – 2.3 to 35.4 per cent; Singapore – 124.5 to 164.2 per cent; and Brazil – 6 to 9.5 per cent (Cohn, 2003). On the other side of this, between 1973 and the late 1980s, there was a decline by about 25 per cent in manufacturing employment within the six old industrial nations of Europe (Hobsbawm, 1995b). A major factor in this decline was the disciplining of the relatively powerful organized working class of the developed nations (Cohen and Kennedy, 2000). For instance, in 1994 General Motors built a facility for the production of its 'Suburban' SUV in Mexico, where a Mexican worker received $1.54 an hour, compared to the $18.96 an hour received by an American worker (Anderson *et al.*, 2000).

One way in which MNCs have optimized their profitability since the 1960s is through relocating production, or contracting production to companies in 'export-processing zones' or 'free trade zones' (FTZs), within developing countries. These FTZs have special incentives to attract foreign firms, such as tax privileges, cheap labour, and limited environmental regulations (Cohen and Kennedy, 2000; Scholte, 2000;

Perrons, 2004). Many of the industries in these FTZs produce goods such as toys, garments, and other cheap consumer commodities (Cohen and Kennedy, 2000). In 1998, there were 2,000 such zones employing around 27 million workers (Perrons, 2004).

It is often claimed that these zones are the first step towards development, creating new industries and jobs, and attracting foreign investment. Critics are, though, sceptical about such claims. For instance, Jauch (2002) points out that many of the positions created are poor quality and lack prospects. In addition these jobs can be created at the expense of other jobs outside of the zones.

Although there is much variation across FTZs, working conditions are often appalling – inadequate health and safety regulations, poor wages, and little job security or prospects for upward movement (ILO, 2000). While wages are sometimes higher than wages outside the zones, these positions often require longer hours (12–14 hours a day is common) and more intensive work (Jauch, 2002). For example, in a silk screening factory (which contracts to companies such as Nike, Tommy Hilfiger, and Osh Kosh) within the Inhdelva FTZ in Honduras, night shifts operate from 6 p.m. to 6 a.m. with one 30 minute break (National Labor Committee, 2003). Workers are under extreme pressure to reach their production goals, on their feet for the bulk of their shifts, and working in temperatures that can reach 94–100 degrees. The basic wage is $33.15 a week, and the general manager has told workers that a union will not be acceptable to the company. In general, it can be dangerous to organize workers within such factories, and monitoring and enforcing national standards of safety and health is difficult (Jauch, 2002). One important factor in this low level of organization and the low pay is that over 60 per cent of workers in FTZs are women, seen as docile and nimble fingered, and less likely than men to be given opportunities of training and promotion (Jauch, 2002; ATTAC, 2003). Within some zones there is evidence of widespread sexual harassment of female workers, and in 1996 and 1998 Human Rights Watch reported use of pregnancy testing and mistreatment of pregnant workers in Mexican factories producing clothing, electronics, and appliances for the US market (ATTAC, 2003).

The overall thrust of the argument here is that MNCs show very little social responsibility, particularly in the less developed world, and one prominent case of Western-based MNCs' misdeeds in the developing world can be taken as exemplary in this regard – Shell's activities in Nigeria. In the late 1990s, Royal Dutch/Shell was subject to an international boycott campaign because of its activities in Nigeria. The case was brought to world attention by the execution of Ken Saro-Wiwa, leader of

Box 2.3   Short-term Hiring for Long-term Jobs

Indonesia

Since the economic crisis of 1998, the use of short-term contracts has increased significantly. New legislation in 2003 clarified and limited the legitimate uses of such contracts and allows only one renewal. But the limits are not effectively enforced. One network of Indonesian NGOs and unions is documenting just how widespread their misuse has become. Initial findings from six factories in West Java revealed between 15 and 95 per cent of workers were repeatedly hired on short-term contracts, three to 12 months at a time. They are making sports shoes, garments, and metal products – work which is neither temporary nor seasonal by nature.

South Africa

The Confederation of Employers of South Africa, COFESA, shows member companies how to cut labour costs through a legislative loophole: turn employees into 'independent contractors'. This instantly cuts labour costs by 30 per cent and makes employers exempt from obligations under the Labour Relations Act. For garment workers, the switch may mean doing the same work but without the employee protections of a minimum wage and over-time limits, paid leave, or medical and unemployment benefit schemes. COFESA's founder estimates that their advice has helped to turn one and a half million of South Africa's workers into independent contractors – and that the practice will keep spreading. 'The system can work in any industry', he said. 'We can always work out something'.

Colombia

Labour law reforms in 2002 lengthened the workday, cut overtime pay, reduced severance payments, and introduced more flexible contracts. CACTUS, an NGO supporting women working in the flower industry, is concerned that their use may spread throughout the sector. 'With these policies, labour conditions will get worse', said Ricardo Zamudio, Director of CACTUS. 'According to the government, these policies of cutting costs for enterprises are intended to create jobs, but they don't guarantee new posts, they just deepen poverty'.

Honduras

The government's proposed labour reforms would permit garment factories to hire up to 30 per cent of their workers on temporary contracts. If passed, the reforms would save employers US$90 million over three years. For workers, that would mean a loss of job security, paid leave, social security, and the annual bonus. An alliance of national unions and NGOs are campaigning to stop this change in the law so that women workers do not lose the support and benefits that they need. 'The majority of people who will be affected by this law will be single mothers, poor people, and migrants', said Maria Luisa Regalado of CODEMUH, an NGO in that alliance. 'If they are dismissed, they will be totally unprotected'.

Source: Oxfam (2004a)

the Movement for the Survival of the Ogoni People, who had denounced Shell for the social and environmental damage it had caused in Nigeria. Shell began oil production in Nigeria in 1957 and the Nigerian government had become reliant on the oil industry, forging close ties with oil companies (Frynas, 2003). When local peoples' calls for compensation from oil companies for environmental damage and funding for community projects went unheeded, there was a rise of resistance activity against the companies (Frynas, 2003). Protestors were responding to environmental destruction through exploration (clearing of land, drilling) and construction of infrastructure (such as pipeline), as well as to land confiscation for oil exploration (Frynas, 2003). The Nigerian government used oppressive measures – killings, beatings, arrests, and rapes – against the protestors and, in one incident, Shell requested the aid of the brutal Mobile Police in the face of what it alleged to be an imminent attack (for which there was no evidence), leading to the massacre of 80 people and the destruction of 500 homes (Frynas, 2003). It was also claimed that a number of oil companies had provided financial and logistical support to security forces (Frynas, 2003). Despite Shell's attempts to respond to international pressures and address environmental and social concerns, the company recorded 340 oil spills in 2000 alone (Frynas, 2003).

Less dramatically perhaps, the example of the biggest pharmaceutical companies illustrates the potential social damage caused by the power and relentless pursuit of profit (and consequent downgrading of other values) by MNCs. Major pharmaceutical companies such as Pfizer, Merck, Novartis, GlaxoSmithKline, and Johnson and Johnson have higher profit margins than any other industry, and the top five drug companies have a combined worth that is twice the GDP of the whole of Sub-Saharan Africa (New Internationalist, 2003b). The critical argument here focuses on these companies' lack of concern for the world's most pressing health issues and their apparently overwhelming drive for profits, with top selling drugs including anti-depressants, and those aimed at reducing cholesterol and tackling high blood pressure or ulcers (New Internationalist, 2003b). Meanwhile, only 10 per cent of global health research (private and public combined) is devoted to diseases that account for 90 per cent of the world's disease burden (New Internationalist, 2003b). At the same time, drug companies spend an enormous amount of money on lobbyists, marketing, advertising, and administration (almost two-and-a-half times more than on research and development), and promotion to health care professionals (about $18 billion a year) (New Internationalist, 2003b).

In sum, then, there is good evidence to suggest that MNCs exercise too much power in global terms. Governments submit to their wills, hoping for investment and fearing corporate withdrawal to other locations. Local capital has trouble competing, and countries can become unable to maintain significant self-reliance and develop local industry. Furthermore, MNCs have enormous marketing power – with global advertising expenditure ballooning from $45 billion in 1950 to $413 billion in 1998 (Worldwatch, 1999) – enabling them to manipulate consumer behaviour, sometimes in destructive ways. And, in the search for profits, MNCs frequently dispose of wider social concerns, such as labour rights or environmental protection (discussed in the next section).

Questioning the globalist case

We should, at this point, track back to consider some of the traditionalist arguments against the case that there is, today, a fully-fledged global economy in operation. For a start, there is a terminological question about the issue of multinational and transnational corporations. We have deployed the term 'multinational corporations' rather than the often-used 'transnational corporations' for a reason. 'Transnational corporations' imply that these organizations are disembodied from any national base, and that they would produce and market in a genuinely international manner (McGrew, 2000). On the other hand, MNCs would still be significantly bound to their home country (Cohen and Kennedy, 2000; Held and McGrew, 2002). Critics argue that, in reality, it is difficult to find many examples of genuine TNCs (Cohen and Kennedy, 2000; Held and McGrew, 2002). For Hirst and Thompson (1996), the absence of truly transnational corporations, the continuing centrality of the domestic economy, and the continuing efficacy of state intervention show that many claims about the extent of economic globalization are greatly exaggerated. For these writers, the strong globalist case unwittingly aligns itself with neoliberalism in implying that globalization is already fully present, that it is unstoppable, and that resistance to this onwards march will simply fail or lead to economic woe. What we see today, instead of globalization, they insist, is *internationalization*. In fact, Hirst and Thompson suggest that the world economy today might be *less* integrated than it was before the First World War, the age of imperialism.

Another sceptical argument has been that rather than genuine globalization, what we see, in global terms, is trilateral regionalization. This means that the international economy is characterized by the development of regional trading and investment blocs. Burton and Nesiba (2004), for instance, mention over 100 regional trade agreements since 1995. In particular, the 'triad' of regional trading around the US, the EU and Japan, are seen as vital evidence of regionalization rather than globalization, the triad containing 15 per cent of the world's population, and accounting for 75 per cent of the world's GDP in the late 1990s, 66 per cent of world trade flows, and 65 per cent of the world stocks of FDI (Castells, 1996). For an enthusiast of globalization such as Philippe Legrain (2002), such regionalization is very real and makes a mockery of the noble aims of free world trade. Castells (1996) argues against the thesis of growing regionalization rather than globalization, noting that regionalization happens *alongside* globalization, and that global trade has expanded significantly through the 1990s, in scope and importance. And Held (2004b) and Cohn (2003) note that regionalization has frequently facilitated and encouraged economic globalization, because priority in such regionalization is often given to the liberalization of national economies. Nevertheless, as Castells reminds us, the strong globalist case is softened somewhat by remembering that domestic markets are still important in a country's GDP, that many countries continue to shelter segments of their economy from the forces of the world market, and that public services and government account for a third to a half of all jobs in many countries.

We believe that Castells' argument that we are witnessing growing and significant economic globalization encompassing regionalization is persuasive. The economic restructuring from the period after the 1970s (deregulation of domestic economic activity, privatization, liberalization of trade and investment), and interactions between markets, governments, and international financial institutions have allowed a significant expansion of trade and finance towards a global economy, even if there is significant unevenness in this world interconnectedness. This spatial and social unevenness is signalled by the predominant role played in growing economic globalization by the G8 countries and international institutions such as the IMF. This unevenness is also clear in the substantial inequalities that globalization has, in some cases, entrenched and expanded, both between countries and within nations – with, for example, comparatively little FDI flowing to countries in Sub-Saharan Africa. We will turn to examine this inequality in a subsequent section. In the section that follows, we examine the argument that the global economy, trade liberalization, and economic expansion have had adverse impacts upon the environment.

Environmental commodification

There can be little doubt that humanity faces severe environmental challenges at present and increasingly into the future, challenges that threaten life on the planet. Such environmental issues, as Yearly (1995) says, can be considered both illustrative of, and caused by the 'shrinking world' entailed by globalization. These challenges include pollution, the depletion of resources, extinctions and loss of biodiversity. For instance, carbon dioxide emissions have increased dramatically in recent years, from 5.3 billion tonnes a year in 1980 to 6.6 billion tonnes a year in 1998 (UNDP, 2000). This and other pollutants, linked to the growth in world energy demand – which is expected to rise by 65 per cent by 2020 (New Internationalist, 2000) – are connected to effects such as depletion of the ozone layer, global warming, and acid rain. Meanwhile, forests, which absorb carbon dioxide, are being lost at an alarming rate. During the 1990s alone, global forest cover declined by more than 4 per cent (Worldwatch, 2003), with 17 million hectares of tropical forest (four times the area of Switzerland) cleared annually (Brennan, 2004). The impact of the resulting climate change is widely expected to have severe deleterious effects – for instance, on agricultural patterns and in terms of species extinctions.

The loss of forest cover is threatening large-scale species extinction and a loss of biodiversity. Five to 10 per cent of forest species may face extinction in the coming 30 years (Brennan, 2004). At the same time, 27 per cent of the world's coral reefs, another major source of biodiversity, are believed to be badly damaged, up from 10 per cent in 1992 (Worldwatch, 2003), and 75 per cent of global fish stocks are now fished at or beyond their sustainable limit (Worldwatch, 2004), with a doubling of the global fish catch over the last 35 years (Brennan, 2004). It is estimated that one quarter of the world's mammals, 12 per cent of the world's birds, and 30 per cent of fish are in danger of extinction (Worldwatch, 2003).

These are merely a selection of the problems we now collectively face. The vital question here concerns the link between these environmental threats and globalization. For some neoliberal enthusiasts of globalization, the critical argument that economic globalization brings with it growing dangers to the environment is incorrect. While these enthusiasts are likely to acknowledge that we face substantial environmental problems, they are also likely to deny that globalization is the cause of these problems. In fact, they may suggest that globalization provides strong impulses towards greater awareness and care of the environment. Thus, Thomas Friedman (1999) contends that globalization allows the emergence of what he calls 'super-empowered individuals' to promulgate their causes, making people aware, say, of the ecological threats faced by humanity, and bringing polluters to global public account for their actions. In addition, the market is often seen as precisely the mechanism that might enhance environmental causes, with companies having to adjust their practices in the face of global concern over environmental harm, so as to compete for consumers.

While there is clearly some truth to these arguments, we would argue that critics come closer to the mark with respect to the connection between environmental problems and globalization. The global gap in power between rich and poor countries, the strength of MNCs against ordinary citizens, the inexorable drive towards growth and profitability, and the focus of export-led development, together mean that environmental concerns frequently lose out to economic concerns.

In this vein, the work of Vandana Shiva and Edward Goldsmith on the problem of environmental commodification is illuminating. For Shiva (2000: 128–9), 'The reduction of all value to commercial value and the removal of all spiritual, ecological, cultural and social limits to exploitation is a process that is being brought to completion through globalization ... [the] sanctity of life is being replaced by marketability of life. With no ethical, ecological, or social limits to commerce, life itself is being pushed to the edge'.

Box 2.4   Vandana Shiva

Vandana Shiva (b. 1952) is an Indian physicist, philosopher, and environmental activist. Shiva's activism began with her participation in the Chipko movement in the 1970s. The Chipko movement emerged in the Utterkhand region of India, led by a group of women opposed to commercial deforestation in the region. The group became famous for its tactic of hugging trees to prevent them from being cut down, giving rise to the term 'tree hugger' in reference to environmentalists. In 1982 Shiva founded the Research Foundation for Science, Technology and Ecology in Dehradun, India, and in 1999 she helped initiate the Living Democracy Movement. The two movements reflect Shiva's belief that corporate globalization has two primary yet interconnected consequences: the destruction of the natural environment and the erosion of democratic freedoms and political participation. Shiva argues that the combined effects of these consequences lead to the spread of unsustainable ecological and political values and practices, which have a disproportionately negative effect on the world's poor and especially upon women and people of colour. Shiva also is a leading figure in the International Forum on Globalization, an international association of researchers and activists which focuses on developing just, democratic, and peaceful alternatives to neoliberal economic globalization. Shiva has received numerous awards for her activities, including the Right Livelihood Award (or 'Alternative Nobel Prize') in 1993 and the International Award of Ecology in 1997. Her books include *Water Wars* (2001), *Tomorrow's Biodiversity* (2000), and *Biopiracy: The Plunder of Nature and Knowledge* (1997).

The rich countries are the winners in the global economy as resources are extracted from the poor countries, and as environmental costs are shifted to the South from the North, the countries of which produce 90 per cent of the world's hazardous industrial waste (Hedley, 2002). In addition, the energy-intensive, export-oriented, and free-trade obsessed model of development presently being pursued means a loss of self-sufficiency for poorer countries (Goldsmith, 1999). The emphases on unsustainable consumerist lifestyles (Goldsmith, 2001a) and on export result, for example, in the average commodity travelling 1000 km from producer to consumer in the US (Brennan, 2004), in the process generating enormous amounts of pollution (Shiva, 2000). Goldsmith's (1999, 2001b) environmental answer to the pressing environmental and social issues connected to globalization is localization, to 'recreate local communities and economies'.

Giant corporations are frequently implicated in these environmental threats. Friends of the Earth, for instance, have charged that Exxon Mobil alone has produced 20.3 billion tonnes of carbon dioxide in its 120 years of existence, 13 times the volume of annual emissions by the US (Suri, 2004). In like fashion, big MNCs are on the leading edge of the commodification of life, where, for instance, plants and seeds are genetically modified and patented, so that growers must purchase seed each year or pay royalties. This, as well as attempts to engineer sterile seed, threatens the food security of many in the developing nations, reduces biodiversity – just 20 plants supply 80 per cent of humanity's food (New Internationalist, 2000) – and it gives companies an incredible capacity to control the world's food supply.

Overall, then, the critical argument has it that economic globalization generates or exacerbates many environmental problems: it encourages greater consumption of energy intensive products such as cars and paper (Brennan, 2004); it is characterized by an energy-inefficient and export-led economics; it is characterized, too, by the obsession with economic growth and profitability which 'provides a systematic incentive to firms to lower their costs by causing pollution' (Yearly, 1995: 162); the concentration of power and control in a relatively small number of MNCs threatens biodiversity and local self-sufficiency, resulting in agribusiness favouring mass produced, pest-resistant, high yield, and uniform crops and stock (Hedley, 2002); and commodification of life spreads to the detriment of people and their environment.

Such concerns are centrally linked to economic inequalities – between rich and poor countries, between ordinary citizens and giant corporates who are able to commodify and control ever more areas of life, and who are focussed on profit making to the exclusion of other values. We will now move on to consider such inequalities more explicitly.

Global stratification

While capital is increasingly movable and international – signalled by the mobility of MNCs and the speed of movement of capital flows – the majority of labour remains local. It has been noted that this situation provides stark contrast to the age of imperialism, when it was the labour movement that was cosmopolitan, while the capitalist class was nationalistic and parochial (see Anderson, 2002). Thus, Bauman (1999a) depicts our globalized period as witnessing the emergence of a transnational elite, a new stratum of 'absentee landlords' who are free to escape the consequences of their actions, while the bulk of people are condemned to remain as locals. This disparity in life chances reflects the differentials in terms of the new stratifying factor of mobility and is a sign of global inequality, to which we now turn.

Stratification is about patterned inequality. For Marx, of course, the major dimension of such inequality was class inequality, the division between those who owned and controlled the means of production (the capitalist class) and those that had no such ownership and control (the working class). Numerous Marxists have, as shown in Chapter 1, attempted to extend Marx's model to take into consideration the inequalities between different nations. For neoliberal enthusiasts of globalization, Marxist theories of inequality are of little value today. They argue that economic world integration and interdependency will, in the long-term at least, benefit everybody. Free global trade will result in rising productivity and wealth for all, eliminating the distortions of state intervention and protectionism, which prevent countries and people doing what they are best at (see Martin, 2000). For Thomas Friedman (1999), globalization issues in a set of constraints that he calls 'the golden straightjacket of capitalism', which mean that economies must be kept open to international competition. This straightjacket does, for him, imply an accompanying demise of politics (in that there are few alternative political courses of action), but this is not a real problem because the best formula for prosperity and freedom supposedly has been discovered: these neoliberal constraints will issue in greater wealth and choice. For Friedman, such constraints are not an elite strategy but instead something that emerges from the level of the street, from ordinary people's desires for freedom and choice. Here, the argument is that inequality worldwide is decreasing or will decrease the closer we approach a truly global economic order. However, numerous critics have charged that globalization has meant growing inequality, both *between nations*, in terms of the gap between the rich and the poor world, and *within nations*, as the rich get richer and the poor poorer. We will focus on these dimensions of inequality in turn.

As mentioned in Chapter 1, there are substantial inequalities between nations. At present, around 1.2 billion human beings live on less than $1 a day, and 2.8 billion people worldwide live on less than $2 a day (Perrons, 2004). Further, around 840 million people are malnourished, although 80 per cent of the malnourished in the developing world live in countries with food surpluses (New Internationalist, 2000), and 1.3 billion people lack access to clean water (Shalom, 1999). This inequality is not evenly distributed across countries. In 1998, the per capita GDP of OECD countries stood at $20,357, compared to Latin America's $6,510, Eastern Europe's $6,200, $4,140 for the Arab states, $2,112 for South Asia, and $1,607 for Sub-Saharan Africa (Kennedy, 2002). While those in the West (955 million people) enjoy about 86 per cent of the global product, 79 per cent of world income, consume 58 per cent of world energy, and own and control 74 per cent of world telephone lines, the poorest 1.2 billion people have only 1.3 per cent of the global product, consume only 4 per cent of world energy, 5 per cent of world fish and meat consumption, and own only 1.5 per cent of world telephone lines (Held, 2004b). The richest 1 per cent of the world receive as much income as the poorest 57 per cent (Perrons, 2004), and the wealthiest three people in the world have assets greater than the combined GNP of the 48 least developed countries and their 600 million people (O'Hara, 2004). While there has been some success in reducing the number of people living on less then $1 per day, largely as a result of the rising fortunes of India and China (Elliott, 2003), there has been, in other respects, a growing polarization of wealth over the last few decades. While in 1960, the income of the richest 20 per cent of the world was 30 times that of the poorest 20 per cent, by 1997 it was 74 times as great (Held, 2004b). Meanwhile, the ratio of income of the world's richest 10 per cent against the poorest 10 per cent has grown from 51:1 in 1970 to 127:1 in 1997 (Burton and Nesiba, 2004).

While China and India have fared reasonably in the period of globalization, in terms of rising GDPs, the same cannot be said for many countries, particularly countries in Sub-Saharan Africa, South Asia, and Latin America and the Caribbean. Shalom (1999) notes that more than

80 countries had lower per capita incomes at the end of the 1990s than they did in 1970, and some of the worse off, contrary to what neoliberals predict, were the most open to the global economy. For instance, exports account for close to 30 per cent of GDP in impoverished Sub-Saharan African countries, compared to less than 20 per cent for industrial nations; but Sub-Saharan Africa – where 39 of 47 countries are dependant on just two primary commodities for over 50 per cent of export earnings – has experienced a fall in the terms of trade, as non-oil commodity prices have fallen, leading to a large loss of income (Shalom, 1999; Khor, 2001; Burton and Nesiba, 2004). Along these lines, one major issue for many poorer countries is their dependence on a very small range of export products/crops, and their susceptibility to price instability. For instance, in 1998–2000, 70 poor countries received more than half of their export earnings from just three or fewer commodities, including: Chad, 99 per cent from cotton and meat; Yemen, 99.4 per cent from oil; Niger, 97.6 per cent from coffee, tea, and tin; and Sudan, 97.2 per cent from cotton, livestock, and sesame (New Internationalist, 2004b). Meanwhile, the UN estimates that human development – a combination of income, life expectancy, and literacy – declined in 21 countries during the 1990s, this being a particularly dismal decade for Sub-Saharan Africa and Latin America (Elliott, 2003; Hout, 2004). One aspect of this global inequality is that, as Held (2004b) says, it frequently has a woman's face. Seventy per cent of those subsisting on less than $1 a day are women (Held, 2004b). Of the 854 million illiterates in the world, 544 million are women. And, globally, women earn only 75 per cent of what men do (UNDP, 2000).

While more than 30,000 children (overwhelmingly in the developing world) are estimated to die each day of poverty-related causes, 100 million children live on the streets, half a million women die during pregnancy or in childbirth every year, 34–46 million people are infected with AIDS, one million a year die of malaria and two million of tuberculosis; total debt for developing countries stands at a shocking $2 trillion, preventing any chance of addressing many of these issues (Sane, 2004; ILO, 2004; Oxfam, 2004b; UNDP, 2000; Anderson *et al.*, 2000). Thus, Mozambique spent twice as much in 1996 on debt repayments as it did on health and education (Anderson *et al.*, 2000). Meanwhile the rich nations spent more than $1 billion a day on domestic agricultural subsidies, over six times what they spend on overseas aid every year (New Internationalist, 2004b; Catholic Agency for Overseas Development, 2004; Oxfam, 2004b).

Clearly, the outcomes of globalization are not consistently distributed. While the economies of some countries are growing and there has been a reduction in the number of people living on less than $1 per day, the nations of sub-Saharan Africa, in particular, are in a state that Arrighi (2002) describes as tragedy. Thirty of 34 countries classed as exhibiting 'low human development' are in sub-Saharan Africa (Elliott, 2003). In 1975, the GNP of the region stood at 16.6 per cent of world per capita GNP; by 1999, it stood at just 10.5 per cent (Arrighi, 2002). Thus, it is estimated that by the end of the twentieth century, the average African household consumed 20 per cent less than it had 25 years earlier (Rapley, 2004). Debt, AIDS, illiteracy, low life expectancy (49 years), and malnutrition plague the region. Arrighi rejects explanations of the post-1975 decline which focus on internal causes such as protectionism or poor governance, and stresses instead the region's dependency on foreign capital, the world slowdown in trade and production, low population density (an effect of the colonial legacy), structural adjustment policies of the 1980s, the lack of an established entrepreneurial stratum, and changing US priorities (moving towards East Asia). In general, with respect to the connection between globalization and inequality, and against the naïve optimism of enthusiastic neoliberals, as Held (2004b: 47) notes, 'Integration into trade and financial markets has different consequences for countries at different stages of development'. Simply opening up a country's economy to global forces is not automatically a recipe for growth and increased wealth. Held argues that, in fact, excessive speed in opening economies can be damaging, and he points out that poorer countries have generally opened their economies far more rapidly than rich countries. He concludes that there is no single route to economic development.

According to critics of globalization, the last three decades have also seen an increasing polarization of wealth and rises in inequality *within* countries. The UNDP's *Human Development Report* for 2005 notes 'a clear trend over the past two decades towards rising inequality within countries' (55), with inequality rising in 53 of the 73 countries with available data. Poverty and income inequality increased in most developed countries, for instance, through the 1980s and 1990s, as unemployment and insecure employment grew, union power declined, and neoliberal restructuring saw states seeking to reduce welfare spending (Faux and Mishel, 2000): there was, for example, an increase in poverty of 60 per cent in the UK, and 40 per cent in Holland, and an increase in inequality of more than 16 per cent for the US, the UK, and Sweden

(Castells, 1998; UNDP, 2000). By the mid 1990s, there were over 100 million people below the poverty line in industrialized countries, eight million malnourished, and five million homeless (Castells, 1998; UNDP, 2000).

There has, in general terms, been a shift of wealth within nations from the less well off to the rich, especially to the wealthiest 5 per cent (Faux and Mishel, 2000). This growing inequality has been marked in countries such as the UK, Sweden, Denmark, the US, Australia, Germany, France, and Norway. For instance, in America in the mid-1960s, the ratio between the income of a CEO and the company's average worker was 39 to 1, whereas in 1997 it had risen to 254 to 1 (Faux and Mishel, 2000); and there was a 20 per cent fall in wage rates between 1975 and 1995 for high school-educated men (Short, 2001). The richest 1 per cent of Americans now earn as much as the poorest 100 million combined, compared to 1977 when the top 1 per cent earned as much as the bottom 49 million (Shalom, 1999). Within many of the countries of the former socialist block, meanwhile, 'transition' saw falling production, growing inflation, dislocation, corruption, and sharp rises in unemployment, poverty, and inequality – with the top decile in Russia possessing 40 per cent of total income in 1993, compared to just 20 per cent in 1988, with wages falling by two thirds in the first years of transition, and with 100 million people in poverty by 1991 (Shalom, 1999; UNDP, 2000; Perrons, 2004; Marangos, 2004; Munck, 2002).

In light of this radical inequality, Castells (1998) speaks of the emergence within the global economy of a new 'fourth world'. That is, we see the emergence of a mass of people – 'millions of homeless, incarcerated, prostituted, criminalized, brutalized, stigmatized, sick, and illiterate persons' (Castells, 1998: 165) – across every country who are excluded from the benefits of globalization and are marginalized in terms of participation in the new economy.

To shift to a more theoretical register, for Zygmunt Bauman (1998) poverty takes on a different significance today in a globalizing world. We have moved from a social order in which people were engaged primarily as workers (where work was the centre of life and identity), where the work ethic was a central force of social control, and where the non-working population existed as a reserve army of labour. Ours is now a consumer society. People are engaged within social orders primarily as consumers: 'The role once performed by work in linking together individual motives, social integration and systemic reproduction, has now been assigned to consumer activity' (Bauman, 1998: 27). Here, possessive individualism grows and social solidarity shrinks (marked by the decline of the welfare state), unemployment becomes permanent for many, and instability of employment increases for a mass of people, because there is no longer a need for a reserve army of labour. For Bauman (1998: 1), 'It is one thing to be poor in a society of producers and universal employment; it is quite a different thing to be poor in a society of consumers, in which life-projects are built around consumer choice rather than work, professional skills, or jobs'. The main figure of the poor today, then, is as 'flawed consumer'. In Bauman's analysis of the neoliberal world, the poor today have *no* function, and they tend to be blamed for their condition. Their plight is no longer viewed as a collective social problem; rather, it is linked with criminality in that the poor are regarded as a 'nuisance and worry'. The only role left to the poor is invisibility, to behave as if they did not exist.

Work

An important dimension in approaching global inequality is the transformation of work over the past two or three decades. In Chapter 1, we discussed theories of social transformation that posit a shift from Fordism to postfordism, or from organized to disorganized capitalism, a shift widely viewed as following new methods in production pioneered in Japan (Hobsbawm, 1995b; Waters, 1999). One of the central facets of this transformation has been the growing importance of flexible specialization, linked to flexibility in products, marketing, and organization, but also to the creation of a functionally and numerically flexible labour force, with an increase in employment insecurity and instability. These issues will provide the central part of this section.

We have already commented upon the reconfiguration of the international division of labour, with deindustrialization in the advanced economies involving a halving of the numbers employed in industry in the UK between 1978 and 2002, for instance (Perrons, 2004), and a relocation of manufacturing in response to promises of cheaper, disorganized labour, to the developing world. As Therborn (2001) notes, industrial employment overall declined as a proportion of world employment from 19 to 17 per cent between 1965 and 1990, and among the developed world from 37 to 26 per cent. That is, while we see rises in the manufacturing workforce across the G7 countries between 1920 and 1970, the picture is very different from 1970 to the 1990s, with reductions across the board towards deindustrialization (though varying in speed and degree) (Castells, 1996). In the European

Union, the percentage of people employed in industry fell from 30 in 1970 to 20 in 1994, and in the US in the same period from 28 to 16 per cent (ILO, 2002). By the mid-1980s, two thirds of workers in the West were classified as service workers: there was a shift towards service work between 1960 and 1996 of 56.2 to 73.9 per cent in America, 41.3 to 58.9 per cent in Japan, 39.1 to 56.7 per cent in Germany, and 39.9 to 70.2 per cent in France (Grimwade, 2000).

This period of deindustrialization and neoliberal restructuring also saw significant rises in the numbers of people engaged in part-time, limited-term contract, and casual work – the 'flexibilization' of employment. This flexibility has a number of dimensions, including numerical flexibility, 'externalization' (for instance, 'subcontracting'), internal numerical flexibility (variable working hours), functional flexibility (changes in employment tasks in response to employer needs), and wages flexibility (Munck, 2002). These changes in the West have sometimes been characterized as the 'Brazilianization' of labour, a tendency to more insecure and informal labour, with smaller workforces, fewer rules, weaker unions, and wages linked to economic expansion and contraction (Munck, 2002). Part-time workers increased as a proportion of the workforce in the EU, for instance, from 10.7 per cent in the mid-1980s to 16.9 per cent in 1998; and temporary workers in the EU in the same period increased from 8.9 to 12.2 per cent of the workforce (Torres, 2001). From just 1990 to 1998 there was a rise in part-time employment, from 22.6 to 25.9 per cent in Australia, from 19.1 to 23.6 per cent in Japan, and from 20.1 to 23 per cent in the UK (ILO, 2002). In the developing world, this trend is extremely pronounced, with workers without contracts or with new, less secure contracts making up 30 per cent of the total in Chile and 39 per cent in Columbia, for example (UNDP, 1999).

It is often noted that there has been a corresponding 'feminization' of work, with 70 per cent of developed and 74 per cent of developing countries seeing rises in women's employment activity rate between 1975 and 1995 (Smart, 2003; Perrons, 2004). Of the 29 million new workers entering the workforce between 1960 and 1990 within EU countries, 20 million were women (Munck, 2002). In the South, there has also been a feminization of the labour force – for instance, in the electronics industry in South Asia and Mexico (Munck, 2002). And there is a connection between flexibilization and feminization (Munck, 2002), with women making up over 60 per cent of all part-time workers in all OECD countries (ILO, 2002), and 80 per cent of homeworkers worldwide (Munck, 2002).

Part of this tendency towards flexibilization is the growth of the numbers of the unemployed, sitting at about 185.9 million people worldwide, the highest level on record, with youth unemployment particularly high (14.4 per cent, against an average unemployment rate of 6.2 per cent) (ILO, 2004). Munck (2002) makes the important point that, against arguments that posit a coming 'end of the working class', what we see from the 1970s is massive proletarianization, with a doubling between 1975 and 1995 of the working class to 2.5 billion. Unemployment, nevertheless, grew enormously in the industrial countries from the 1970s, from a very low rate of about 1.5 per cent of the labour force in Western Europe in the 1960s, and was particularly pronounced in the 1980s and early-mid 1990s, now averaging 6.6 per cent for OECD countries (Hobsbawm, 1995b; OECD, 2005). Average unemployment is especially pronounced outside of the advanced countries, sitting at 9.5 per cent in the transition economies, 9 per cent in Latin America and the Caribbean, 12 per cent in the Middle East and North Africa, and 10.6 per cent in Sub-Saharan Africa (ILO, 2004).

One effect of this unemployment has been a growth in the informal employment sector. As Munck (2002) notes, 'Informal work is usually defined as any work which takes place outside the formal wage-labour market, such as clandestine work and illegal work, but also including various forms of self-employment' (111–12). He suggests that 'The only unifying factor across the range of work and workers are a certain general instability of employment, an avoidance of most labour laws, and a tendency to remain outside normal cap rules of contract, licensing and taxation' (113). It is estimated that the informal sector makes up between 2 and 15 per cent of work in the advanced countries, and between a third and three quarters of non-agricultural employment in developing countries – 48 per cent in North Africa, 51 per cent in Latin America, 65 per cent in Asia, and 72 per cent in sub-Saharan Africa (ILO, 2004; Munck, 2002). It appears that the informal employment sector is on the rise, with one report estimating that 90 per cent of urban Africa's new jobs over the next decade will come within this informal economy (M. Davis, 2004).

For Castells (1996: 268), the old mode of work, 'based on full time employment, clear-cut occupational assignments, and a career pattern over the lifecycle is being slowly but surely eroded away'. The move towards such flexibilization in employment, with a growing individualization of work – subcontracting, outsourcing, offshoring, consulting, downsizing, customizing, and casualization (Castells, 1996) – is seen by some as a necessary response to the rigidities of the labour market, and resulting economic difficulties, prior to the 1980s (Munck, 2002). Some suggest that such flexibilization will bring generalized benefits – enhanced overall economic performance, multi-skilling and autonomy for workers who will, in growing numbers, be empowered cyber- or knowledge workers (Munck, 2002). And, of course, this is the case for some flexible workers today. However, as Munck (2002) points out, for every upmarket, flexibilized worker there are three downmarket, flexible workers, and greater insecurity and harder work are the results of flexibilization for many people.

Tourism, global cities, and slums

Critical theorists point out that the cultural and the economic are ever more interpenetrated. Many of the concerns, therefore, that are raised in Chapter 4 on cultural globalization could have as easily been placed in this chapter, and it may appear that considerations addressed here on transformations in urban spaces fall most easily into a chapter on culture. We have, though, chosen to raise these issues in this chapter, because of their very intimate relationship with transformations in work, the international division of labour, and stratification. We will begin with an exploration of the growing importance of the tourist industry and some of the consequences that follow on from this. We then move to other questions of changing urban spaces, turning first to the notion of 'global cities' and then, at the other pole of the urban experience, to the phenomenon of slums.

Leisure has increasingly become important and available into the twenty-first century, at least for those in the developed countries, and a major part of leisure activity is tourism (Cohen and Kennedy, 2000; Cater, 1995). With growing wealth, cheaper travel, and more emphasis on consumption, there has been something of a 'democratization' of tourism (Cohen and Kennedy, 2000; Cater, 1995). Thus, the number of international tourist arrivals ballooned from 25.3 million in 1950 to 702.6 million in 2002, and receipts grew from $2.1 billion in 1950 to $474.2 billion in 2002 (World Tourism Organization, 2005), with international arrivals expected to double by 2020 (Worldwatch, 2002). Tourism has, then, become a major player in the global economy. According to UNESCO (2005), tourism is now the world's leading category of international trade, ahead of automobiles and chemicals. Europe and America dominate as destinations for visitors, but Asia, Latin America and the Caribbean have seen a rapid expansion in tourist numbers in recent years (Worldwatch, 2002).

The development of mass tourism, some critical theorists argue, has encouraged us all to become 'global performers', putting on presentations designed to project our own cultural heritage as commodities for tourist consumption (Cohen and Kennedy, 2000: 212). That is, to attract tourists and businesses into their areas, cities, regions, and countries are increasingly pushed to package and promote their identity, to underscore the uniqueness of their place – a 'frantic forging of signs of identity', in Lanfant's words (quoted in Cohen and Kennedy, 2000: 222). We should note here the rising emphasis on the importance of place in a globalizing world that is often seen as bringing an 'end to geography' (Doorne, 2000). Critical theorists point to the potentially negative consequences of this selling of place: as lacking authenticity, as commodifying culture (the branding of places and cultures), as presenting 'bogus history', and as tending to paper over the ways in which places are experienced and contested, marginalizing struggle and competing narratives, on behalf of the tourist's gaze and narrow economic gain (Cater, 1995).

This has perhaps especially been the case in cities that are being reconstructed, as industry declines in importance and as the urban spaces are reconfigured around lifestyle culture (nightlife, shopping, entertainment, eating out) (Valentine, 2001). That is, the emergence of the cultural economy in deindustrializing urban spaces brings with it a transformation of place towards the interests of wealthy consumers, a 'credit card citizenship', while the poor (what Bauman calls the 'flawed consumers') are marginalized as a nuisance and pushed further from the urban centre (Valentine, 2001; Doorne, 2000).

To examine this reconfiguration of urban spaces, the cultural economy, and the commodification of culture, we will turn to the example of Wellington, New Zealand's capital city. The Wellington City Council have in recent years sought to promote Wellington as 'the arts and culture capital of New Zealand'. The environment is promoted as 'green', as having a 'famous café culture', and as containing a variety of places, 'from funky urban squares to tranquil reserves to beaches and coastline'. Wellington is also promoted around the brand 'Creative Wellington', as a centre of business and arts creativity and innovation, including cinematic special effects, Internet technology, earthquake engineering, software development, optics, and multimedia and education.

One of the major points around which the notion of Wellington's uniqueness has been articulated has been the recent filming in the area of the hugely popular and profitable trilogy *The Lord of the Rings*.

Visitors are invited to 'Experience Middle Earth in all its diversity while you are in Wellington', taking tours of the places where filming took place and where cast and crew spent their spare time: 'Eastbourne: The Dominion Post Ferry will take you across the harbour to Eastbourne where Sir Ian McKellan lived during filming. He reportedly loved the ferry ride to the city'.

Doorne (2000) contends that since neoliberal restructuring in 1984 and increased integration within the global economy, Wellington's economic base has been transformed – for instance, from 1985–94, the value of trade via the Wellington port decreased by over 59 per cent. New economic bases have thus been sought, and tourism has become a focus, with Wellington promoted as New Zealand's 'cultural hub' (Doorne, 2000). The $280 million development of the National Museum of New Zealand, Te Papa, is interesting in this light, a development envisaged as a vehicle for asserting both the nation's and Wellington's identities (Doorne, 2000). For critics, Te Papa illustrates the negative consequences of the commodification of culture and the obsession with selling places. In particular, it is suggested that the theme-park style displays convey little more than glossy, dehistoricized, bite-sized chunks of history – 'infotainment' (Doorne, 2000). This presentation tends to skip too lightly over past and present conflict, remaining inanely upbeat, positive, focussed on promoting a sense of resolution and harmony, and addressing identity as centred on individuals and consumption (Neill, 2004; Doorne, 2000). This is linked to the overweening emphasis on Te Papa as a 'commercially positive' venture (Doorne, 2000). As Robinson (1999) says, the threat is that with the expansion of the cultural economy and the tourist industry, 'Instead of getting rich and authentic cultural insights and experiences, tourists get staged authenticity; instead of getting exotic culture, they get kitsch'; or, as Patin (1999) puts it, 'If the law of the market is applied indiscriminately, it may lead to jazzed-up heritage supermarkets which have been standardized and adapted to meet consumer demand'.

We will now turn to other questions of urbanization and inequality, focussing on the idea of 'global cities', on the one hand, and the growth of slums, on the other. For the vast majority of human history, life was based in the rural world. Even as late as 1800, 97 per cent of the world's population lived in rural areas of less than 5,000 people. Today, the urban population outnumbers the rural population, and cities are rapidly expanding in size.

Saskia Sassen (1998) has argued that the growth of world interconnectedness has fostered the rising importance of what she calls 'global cities'. Her argument is that the global dispersal of modern economic activity creates a need for greater central control and co-ordination; and globalization and new technology have meant not an 'end of geography' but, rather, the heightened importance of certain cities as centres of power and specialist production: 'the spatial dispersal of economic activity made possible by telematics contributes to an expansion of central functions insofar as this dispersal takes place under the continuing concentration in control, ownership and profit appropriation that characterizes the current economic system'; furthermore, 'National and global markets as well as globally integrated organizations require central places where the work of globalization gets done' (Sassen, 1998). These global cities include key cities of the North such as London, New York, and Tokyo, but also cities such as Sao Paulo, Buenos Aires, and Taipei. These cities, says Sassen (1998), are important in the following ways: they '(a) concentrate command functions; b) are postindustrial production sites for the leading industries of our period, finance and specialised services; c) are national or transnational marketplaces where firms and governments can buy financial instruments and specialised services'. And within such global cities, one finds a 'new geography of centrality and marginality' – highly educated and paid workers in leading sectors, and, on the other side of this, a proliferation of low status and pay service work (Sassen, 2002).

At the other end of the global urban spectrum are slums. According to social critic Mike Davis (2004), much of the rural population who have become urbanized in the last 20 or so years have gone not to the big metropolises but to smaller cities and 'citized' towns. The agricultural deregulation of the 1980s (eliminating subsidies and thus affecting rural smallholders) imposed on the third world has meant an exodus of rural labour – world agrarian employment fell between 1965 and 1990 from 57 to 48 per cent of total world employment (Therborn, 2001) – to urban slums, while cities have ceased to be neatly linked to expanded employment opportunities since urbanization became decoupled from industrialization. Much of the urban world, Davis contends, is rushing back to the age of Dickens, creating a 'planet of slums' characterized by decaying housing, overcrowding, locations on dangerous terrain, absolute poverty, and criminality.

There were 921 million slum dwellers in 2001, and slum dwellers constitute 78 per cent of the least developed countries and a third of the global urban population (Davis, 2004). Today, there may be as many as a quarter of a million slums globally. Without employment, 'informal survivalism' is the new mode of livelihood for many slum dwellers.

Box 2.5   The Global Challenge of Slums

- Asia has about 550 million people living in slums, followed by Africa with 187 million, and Latin America and the Caribbean with 128 million. There are approximately 54 million urban dwellers in high-income countries living in slum-like conditions.
- Sub-Saharan Africa has the highest rate of slum-dwellers with 72 per cent of the urban population living in slums, followed by South Central Asia with 58 per cent, East Asia with 36 per cent, Western Asia with 33 per cent, Latin America and the Caribbean with 32 per cent, Northern Africa with 28 per cent, and Southeast Asia with 28 per cent.
- Although the concentration of slum dwellers is highest in African cities, in numbers alone, Asia accounts for some 60 per cent of the world's urban slum residents.
- Some 1 billion people, or 32 per cent of the world's total urban population and approximately one-sixth of the world's population, live in slums; some 43 per cent of the urban population of all developing regions combined live in slums; some 78 per cent of the urban population in the least developed countries live in slums; some 6 per cent of the urban population in developed regions live in slum-like conditions.
- The total number of slum-dwellers in the world increased by about 36 per cent during the 1990s and in the next 30 years, the global number of slum-dwellers will increase to about two billion if no concerted action to address the challenge of slums is taken.
- More than 41 per cent of Kolkata's (Calcutta) slum households have lived in slums for more than 30 years.
- In most African cities between 40–70 per cent of the population lives in slums or squatter settlements. Many African cities will be doubling their population within two decades. In a city like Nairobi, 60 per cent of the population lives in slums which occupy about 5 per cent of the land.
- About one out of every four countries in the developing world has laws that contain clauses that impede women owning land and taking mortgages in their own names.

Source: United Nations Human Settlement Programme (2003).

Conclusion

We have covered a variety of questions around economic globalization, from neoliberal restructuring, to global finance, to multinational corporations, to transformed work arrangements, to urban spaces. It is clear that economic globalization touches a wide range of issues, and these are frequently highly complex. For instance, Perrons (2004) points out that a simple North-South polarity is no longer useful, given the unevenness of economic fortunes in the past two to three decades.

At the same time, we think that some general conclusions can be arrived at. We believe that economic globalization has often proven detrimental, tending towards environmental damage, polarization of life chances, economic uncertainty, and commodification. There are qualifications to be made on all of these issues, and plenty of counter instances, but one of the major problems with globalization, in our opinion, is that profitability and economic growth have come to weigh so much more heavily than considerations of equality and social justice. This is in line with the contemporary predominance of neoliberalism as economic common sense, a hegemonic shift that represents a clear defeat for those not able to enjoy the benefits of what Bauman calls the 'tourists' of contemporary globalization. A major dimension of this neoliberal common sense is the presentation of contemporary globalization as inescapable and spontaneous. For us, this approach is both unfounded and destructive. There are clear winners and drivers of corporate-led globalization, and the notion of globalization as a set of processes that move by themselves represents a powerful ideology that clearly benefits the already wealthy and powerful, and that presents threats to democracy itself. In our final chapter, we take up in more detail the ways in which such neoliberal ideology is being confronted and contested.

Further reading

Amin, S. *Capitalism in the Age of Globalization* (London: Zed Press, 1997).

Black, J. K. *Inequality in the Global Village: Recycled Rhetoric and Disposable People* (West Hartford, CT: Kumarian Press, 1999).

Clark, D. *Urban World/Global City* (London and New York: Routledge, 2003).

Gassler, R. S. 'Globalization and the Information Economy', *Global Society*, 15 (2001) 111–18.

Gray, J. *False Dawn: The Delusions of Global Capitalism* (New York: The New Press, 2000).

Hoogvelt, A. *Globalization and the Postcolonial World: The New Political Economy of Development* (Basingstoke: Palgrave Macmillan, 2001).

Munck, R. *Globalization and Labor* (London: Zed Books, 2002).

Sassen, S. *The Global City* (Princeton: Princeton University Press, 2001).

Shiva, V. *Water Wars: Privatization, Pollution and Profit* (Cambridge, MA: South End Press, 2002).

Soros, G. *The Crisis of Global Capitalism: Open Society Endangered* (New York: Public Affairs, 1998).

3
Globalization and Politics

Introduction

Perhaps the most common claim associated with the literature around globalization is the assertion that globalization entails the demise of the nation-state, summarized in notions such as an emerging 'borderless world' and a 'hollow state' (Cohen and Kennedy, 2000). The power and mobility of global finance and multinational corporations, the cultural fragmentation of national populations, the emergence of powerful agents of governance at supra-national and local levels, citizen disaffection from electoral politics, and the growth of global civil society, are all viewed as wearing away at the power or efficacy of the state. In addition, a crucial problem pointed to by critics of globalization is that, as Martin and Schumann (1998: 211) put it, economics appears to be devouring politics. At the same time, many commentators find signs that growing world interconnectedness is bringing with it new and encouraging political tendencies that promise to invigorate democracy and cosmopolitanism. The questions of the fate of the political and of democracy in a globalizing world are, then, the pivotal considerations of this chapter.

The nation-state

Today, the world is organized politically into nearly 200 nation-states. Such nation-states appear very durable and, as Walby (2003) notes, we still tend to equate modern societies with nation-states. Held and McGrew (2002) usefully summarize the four major innovations and characteristics of the state form that emerged with modernity and were subsequently globalized: 1) territoriality; 2) monopoly over the means of violence; 3) impersonal structures of rule; and 4) claims to legitimacy based on representation and accountability. However, the solidity of the nation-state is put in question by the dramatic changes to the world map over the last 60 years, with the number of states more than doubling between 1945 and the late 1990s (Held and McGrew, 2002). And it would appear that we are seeing a contemporary political shift with globalization that entails major alterations to the role and power of the state.

The genesis of the modern state can be located in Western Europe in the eighteenth and nineteenth centuries, and is linked to industrial, economic, and military changes, to an increasingly firm demarcation of national borders, and to the spread of rationalization and bureaucracy (Giddens, 1990). The French Revolution of 1789 is often viewed as a key moment in the development of the modern nation-state. This Revolution brought the centralization of the French state, the citizen army, and that key modern dynamic, nationalism. Tied to the French Revolution and to nationalism is the notion of citizenship, of being a person with certain legal rights and responsibilities derived from membership in a national community. T. H. Marshall's famous lectures of 1949 on the topic of 'Citizenship and Social Class' have become a central reference point for thinking about citizenship. For Marshall, the rights of citizenship had come in three waves, corresponding to the eighteenth, nineteenth, and twentieth centuries: first, civil rights or 'rights necessary for individual freedom' (such as freedom of speech); second, political rights that provide citizens with the opportunity to participate in 'the exercise of political power' (such as the right to vote); and third, social rights that provide citizens with a minimum social standing (such as rights to education) (Delanty, 2000). As we will see later in the chapter, globalization forces upon us a reconsideration of citizenship, tied as it is to a territoriality that is perhaps being unsettled.

The social rights referred to by Marshall are closely associated with the development of the welfare state, and a crucial dimension of state involvement in the life of its citizens in the twentieth century. In the face of the failures of free market capitalism and a growing and increasingly organized working class in the twentieth century, numerous states intervened, in the name of democracy, to restrain the forces of free capitalism: 'It [the state] pursued economic stabilization and steady growth through an active macro-economic policy. It regulated the more self-destructive tendencies of markets, especially banks and financial markets. It empowered trade unions and put a floor under labour, and later created environmental standards. It provided social income in various forms of social insurance. It financed the education and training of schoolchildren and workers' (Kuttner, 2000: 152–3). These types of interventions emerged in their initial forms in a number of countries in the late nineteenth century, but were expanded and deepened by social democratic parties after the Great Depression. In the post-Second World War period, this 'social democratic consensus' reigned as the political-economic common sense in the West, and even Right-leaning governments pursued such interventionist policies.

At the beginning of the 1970s, with spiralling costs, growing popular demands, alterations in class structure, and economic slowdown, pressures towards change began to be felt. In political terms, these pressures are often theorized by recourse to the notion of a multiplicity of crises faced by the state in the last quarter of the twentieth century. This multidimensional crisis, it is widely suggested, resulted in a weakening of the state, as increasingly audible neoliberal voices rejected the constrictions and distortions they alleged were generated by pervasive state economic involvement and redistribution policies, as government services were opened to competition or privatized, and as the viability of the welfare state was put in question.

Takis Fotopoulos (1997) theorizes this movement towards neoliberalism as an important signal of the global 'crisis of statism', a crisis that required substantial political and economic reorganization so that profitability could be re-established. Thus, just as free market capitalism went into global decline around the 1920s – with the emergence of the first communist revolution, fascism, and New Deal social democracy – so statism, both in its social democratic and communist forms, has gone into decline since the 1970s in the face of a multidimensional crisis and has been replaced by a new regime of accumulation and profitability.

For some, this crisis and decline of statism is regarded as a positive development – enhancing individual choice, freeing economic growth, and spreading democracy. In this vein, numerous commentators have noted the apparent growing universalization of representative or liberal democracy since the collapse of 'really existing socialism'. Thus, according to the United Nations *Human Development Report* of 2000, through the 1980s and 1990s, some 81 countries took significant steps towards democracy, and 140 of 200 countries now hold multiparty elections. Further, the number of authoritarian regimes worldwide fell from almost 70 in 1980 to fewer than 30 in 2000. For Francis Fukuyama (1992), the decline of such statism and the universalization of liberal democracy should be read as a sign of our arrival at the end point of ideological evolution, 'the end of history'. We can no longer imagine, Fukuyama claims, any future other than liberal democracy in the political sphere ('rational recognition') and free market capitalism ('rational desires') in the economic sphere. There is nowhere else to go politically but in a liberal democratic direction, which leads to the global expansion of capitalism. Thus, for Fukuyama the end of history amounts to the end of ideology.

Manuel Castells's (1998) conceptualization of the end of statism differs from Fotopoulos's, but the former, too, contends that our glob- alized age has seen a fundamental shift in both political and economic terms, and that neither social democracy nor communism can emerge from these changes unscathed. In Castells's argument, statism refers only to those countries of former 'really existing socialism', where the social system was organized around the appropriation of the economic surplus by elites within the state apparatus. This *power maximizing* – as opposed to capitalism's *profit maximizing* – social order went into decline from the mid-1970s because it was ill-equipped to make the transition towards an information society. This 'informationalism', Castells claims, is simply not compatible with the control of informa- tion by the state and with the narrow connection of technology with warfare found in statism. As flexible networks became ever more central in terms of power (with a shift from the 'flow of power' to the 'power of flows'), productivity and social organization, the hierarch- ical-bureaucratic structure of 'really existing socialism' was ever more unworkable and unresponsive.

Castells acknowledges the enormous implications of the collapse of statism. This variety of social order had been pivotal to twentieth century history, with 'really existing socialism' casting an immense shadow over international relations and over any idea of social trans- formation. Global politics had been, until the 'post-communist' period, crucially shaped by the split into rival blocs; and, even for many of the USSR's Left-wing critics, 'really existing socialism' still stood as an alter- native to Western capitalism, providing options for those in rebellion against Western imperialism. Arguably, today, the political horizon is much transformed, marked perhaps by what Fredric Jameson (1984) has called a blockage of the utopian imagination, a sense of a future without societal alternatives (see Chapter 5).

Before moving to explore in more detail the challenges faced by the nation-state today, we will briefly discuss certain features of the inter- state system because globalization entails crucial changes on this dimension too. The basis of the interstate system is often viewed as having its origins in the Peace of Westphalia (1648), which followed the Thirty Years War, when Europe's monarchs agreed to recognize each other's right to rule their own territories, free from external intervention (Steger, 2003; Held and McGrew, 2002). The Westphalian model of the international system gave primacy to sovereign territorial nation-states, which place their own national interests above all others, subject to no higher authority (or moral requirements), and thus justified in pursuing their interests by force if deemed necessary. For Held (1995), however, recent transformations in international relations have meant a movement away from these Westphalian principles, with a progressive undermining of exclusive territoriality, the strict division between domestic and international affairs, and the previously haphazard relationships between states. We need to explore this contention in greater depth.

The destruction and dislocation brought by the First World War gave rise to attempts to establish an international order of states committed to settling disputes through legal means. The League of Nations was formed at the Paris Peace Conference of 1919 – which produced the Treaty of Versailles that officially ended the First World War – as a supranational organization initially consisting of more than 40 states, to serve as a forum for international consensus on issues of peace and security. However, the League became increasingly ineffective into the late 1930s due to American isolationism, its lack of enforcement power, and its inability to prevent the aggression leading up to the Second World War. The League was disestablished in 1946 and its services, mandates, and property were transferred to the United Nations.

The post-Second World War period saw a changed set of coordinates, with the rise of independence movements in Asia, Africa and Latin America, a globe now divided between Eastern and Western blocs, and the threat of nuclear weapons (Whittaker, 1997). The United Nations was envisaged as a way of dealing with these and other issues. In June 1945, representatives from 51 nations came together in San Francisco to set up the United Nations system. The organization is aimed at maintaining peace and security, fostering amicable relations between nations, developing international cooperation, establishing enforceable norms, forming a forum for discussion and decisions, and functioning as an agent of improved international standards (Whittaker, 1997).

For Held *et al.* (1999), the UN system, in so far as issues of peace and security become globally shared concerns, represents a step forward and a movement away from the Westphalian system. There is, however, much debate as to just how far the UN represents a viable

Box 3.1   Purposes and Principles of the United Nations

Article 1

The Purposes of the United Nations are:

1. To maintain international peace and security, and to that end: to take effective collective measures for the prevention and removal of threats to the peace, and for the suppression of acts of aggression or other breaches of the peace, and to bring about by peaceful means, and in conformity with the principles of justice and international law, adjustment or settlement of international disputes or situations which might lead to a breach of the peace;
2. To develop friendly relations among nations based on respect for the principle of equal rights and self-determination of peoples, and to take other appropriate measures to strengthen universal peace;
3. To achieve international co-operation in solving international problems of an economic, social, cultural, or humanitarian character, and in promoting and encouraging respect for human rights and for fundamental freedoms for all without distinction as to race, sex, language, or religion; and
4. To be a centre for harmonizing the actions of nations in the attainment of these common ends.

Article 2

The Organization and its Members, in pursuit of the Purposes stated in Article 1, shall act in accordance with the following Principles.

1. The Organization is based on the principle of the sovereign equality of all its Members.
2. All Members, in order to ensure to all of them the rights and benefits resulting from membership, shall fulfil in good faith the obligations assumed by them in accordance with the present Charter.
3. All Members shall settle their international disputes by peaceful means in such a manner that international peace and security, and. justice, are not endangered.
4. All Members shall refrain in their international relations from the threat or use of force against the territorial integrity or political independence of any state, or in any other manner inconsistent with the Purposes of the United Nations.
5. All Members shall give the United Nations every assistance in any action it takes in accordance with the present Charter, and shall refrain from giving assistance to any state against which the United Nations is taking preventive or enforcement action.
6. The Organization shall ensure that states which are not Members of the United Nations act in accordance with these Principles so far as may be necessary for the maintenance of international peace and security.
7. Nothing contained in the present Charter shall authorize the United Nations to intervene in matters which are essentially within the domestic jurisdiction of any state or shall require the Members to submit such matters to settlement under the present Charter; but this principle shall not prejudice the application of enforcement measures under Chapter VII.

Source: Charter of the United Nations (26 June 1945)

and democratic global governing body. Some see it as fairly impotent and dysfunctional, especially in criticisms of the functioning of the General Assembly: for instance, in that both large and small nations have equal votes. Others contend that it is too easily used and abused by the powerful states, especially because of the secrecy and use of veto power within the Security Council, which is composed of the 'big five' permanent members – France, China, the US, the UK, and Russia. Here, critics maintain, countries clearly are not treated as equal members (Whittaker, 1997). One common Marxist argument is that, from the beginning, the UN has been a means for the US to pursue its national interests – opening up European empires by way of the principle of self-determination, vesting real power with the Security Council, and, today, using the defence of human rights as a pretext for regime change (Gowan, 2003).

In response to some of this criticism, a number of initiatives have been suggested towards reforming the UN. For example, a proposal was forwarded by the United Nations Development Programme in its *Human Development Report 1994* for the creation of a UN Economic Security Council (consisting of 11 permanent members, who would be without veto power), to review threats to global human security, and to function as an observer of international and financial institutions. More recently, UN Secretary General Kofi Annan, in his 2005 report titled *In Larger Freedom: Towards Development, Security, and Human Rights for All*, proposed a broad range of reforms to the UN system. These include streamlining the procedures in the UN General Assembly and creating deeper relationships between the UNGA and global civil society; expanding membership of the Security Council so as to make it more representative of the international community today; and creating a standing Human Rights Council that would be directly elected by the UNGA. According to Annan (2005: 5), these (and even broader) reforms are driven by 'rapid technological advances, increasing economic interdependence, globalization and dramatic geopolitical change'. As Annan (2005: 53) notes, 'At no time in human history have the fates of every woman, man and child been so intertwined across the globe'.

The decline of state power?

Already, in this consideration of the changes to interstate relations, some of the arguments about the transformations entailed by intensifying globalization come into view. The globalist argument has it that political power or governance has been, or is progressively being altered in a movement of politics from a primarily national scale towards an increasingly transnational or global scale. Global politics is no longer, they argue, first and foremost about states, and older conceptual distinctions between domestic and international or territorial and non-territorial are losing intellectual traction (Held *et al.*, 1999; Short, 2001). As Ulrich Beck (2002: 53) puts it, 'National spaces have become de-nationalized, so that the national is no longer national, just as the international is no longer international. This entails that the foundations of the power of the nation-state are collapsing both from the inside and the outside'. There are a number of strands to this type of argument: nationalism is now challenged by transborder allegiances based on a range of factors; states are forced, more and more, to submit to the dictates of powerful, mobile capital interests, especially given that many face substantial deficits; substate actors are seeking greater independence and are bypassing the state; regionalization – such as NAFTA and the EU – and transworld governance – such as the WTO or the UN – are on the increase; and new actors within global civil society have emerged – for example, Save the Children, World Vision International, and *Medécins sans Frontières* (Scholte, 2000; Castells, 2000).

The powerful forces of the global economy today arguably prevent states from pursuing independent economic or social policies. The spread of neoliberal common sense and the powerful forces exerted on states by financial markets, MNCs, and international organizations such as the WTO and the IMF mean states are increasingly forced to develop policies that leave the market as free as possible: lowering taxation, privatizing and deregulating, and cutting spending, especially spending on social services. According to Castells (2000: 254), because of the close linkages between exchange rates, budgetry policies, and monetary policies, as well as government dependence of global capital markets and foreign lending, states do not have the control that they once had over their economic policies: 'the nation-state is increasingly powerless in controlling monetary policy, deciding its budget, organizing production and trade, collecting its corporate taxes, and fulfilling its commitments to provide social benefits'. This suggests that the substantial state economic intervention once pursued as a means to the goal of national development can no longer stand.

Crucially, it is often argued that economic globalization threatens the welfare state. Thus, Scholte (2000) notes a substantial reduction in welfare provision in many countries, and Page (2004: 31) views the current key trends as 'a move away from universal forms of state protection towards means-testing, higher eligibility requirements, inward private-sector involvement, and greater decentralisation'. For Castells (2000), the prospects for the welfare state in the immediate future look grim. There will be less and less room, as globalization deepens, for a variety of welfare state forms. Such constraints, Castells argues, are potentially deeply politically disruptive, given that the welfare state has played such a pivotal role in the legitimacy of the state at large.

The above is a very common argument about the political ramifications of our era in which economics seems to be firmly in control. As Martin and Schumann (1998: 211) contend, 'the state and politics are visibly in retreat. ... Economics is devouring politics'. Corporate power has grown, it is increasingly concentrated but also highly internationalized and extremely mobile, and, with the spread of pro-business/neoliberal common sense, it is so legitimized that national governments – desiring investment, dependent on corporate taxes and on loans – are left largely helpless. Given this, Ralph Nader (1998) has argued that, 'The essence of globalization is a subordination of human rights, of labour rights, consumer, environmental rights, democracy rights, to the imperatives of global trade and investment. This is world government of the EXXONs, by the General Motors, for the DuPonts'. This situation appears, then, to be confirmation of the Marxist thesis of the primacy of the economic within capitalism, and of the epiphenomenal, secondary place of politics. Marxists, here, might contend that it is the world capitalist system, rather than the Marxist reading of it, that is economically determinist.

The general argument about the decline of state power is fairly compelling. However, it is important to note that it does not necessarily imply the strong globalist argument that nation-states are withering or utterly powerless, that the state, as Ohmae (2000: 208) puts it, 'is increasingly a nostalgic fiction'. Neither does it imply that such political changes are simply the result of the growth of MNC power and the growing centrality of global financial markets. The position taken by Castells or Held is far more nuanced. For these critics, the most crucial trend is towards a *reconfiguration of power or governance*, rather than simply the coming end of the state in the face of the expansion of capitalism. Thus, Castells (2000: 268) speaks of the contemporary situation as involving an 'irreversible sharing of sovereignty in the management of major economic, environmental, and security issues', and he contends that, increasingly, states will function as 'nodes of a broader network of power' (2000: 304). His summary position is that states have moved from being sovereign subjects to strategic actors:

'They [states] marshal considerable influence, but they barely hold power by themselves, in isolation from supranational macro-forces and subnational micro-processes' (Castells, 2000: 307). For Held (1996), 'Political power ... is being repositioned, re-contextualized and, to a degree transformed by the growing power of other (less territorially based) power systems'; thus 'state power is [now] one (albeit important) dimension of power'. Similarly, Scholte (2000: 135) argues that we are seeing the demise of sovereignty in the Westphalian sense – 'supreme, comprehensive, unqualified, and exclusive rule over its [the state's] territory' – but states are not on the way out, and this demise of sovereignty is not undifferentiated.

In this vein, Held (1995) argues that a new mode of global governance is emerging, as governments struggle to control the flows of ideas and commodities, as transnational processes expand, and as multilateral treaties and international organizations increase in number. We are, then, seeing an emerging transnationalization of politics, as state power is reconfigured and it is increasingly 'enmeshed in global processes and flows'. We need to unpack this a little. In Chapter 2, we have already looked at the growing power of multinational corporations and organizations such as the IMF, the World Bank, and the WTO. A suprastate body such as the EU, which began life in 1950 around regulation of German and French steel production, is also viewed as foreshadowing coming changes to governance. In addition, there has also been a rise in the number of intergovernmental organizations, non-governmental organizations (NGOs), and multilateral treaties. In the case of intergovernmental organizations (such as the World Health Organization or the IMF), the numbers have multiplied, from just 37 in 1909 to 6,743 in 2000 (Held and McGrew, 2002). While there were 1,083 international NGOs (organizations such as Amnesty International or Greenpeace) in 1914, there now are approximately 40,000 (nearly one-fifth of these formed in the 1990s) (Held and McGrew, 2002; Page, 2004). Last, the period 1976–95 saw 1,600 multilateral treaties come into existence (Held and McGrew, 2002).

It is clear that globalization entails not only the intensification of interactions and interconnections that have led to the 'shrinking' of our world, but also the emergence of a system of global governance that seeks to regulate and manage various areas of transnational activity. With global governance comes increased intergovernmental interaction and transnational networks, new centres of political power alongside the state, and the growth of transnational civil society (such as NGOs). This 'pluralization of global governance' is theorized by

Anthony McGrew (2000) as made up of three layers: (1) the supra-state layer, which includes intergovernmental agreements and international institutions created by intergovernmental agreement (for example, the EU, the G8, NAFTA, and APEC); (2) the sub-state layer, where the tendency, in recent years, has been towards devolution and expansion of power at local levels; (3) the transnational layer, which consists of arenas in which people across the world are able to make themselves heard (for example, The International Red Cross, and the WWF). A useful description of global governance is offered by the Commission on Global Governance (1995: 2–3):

> Governance is the sum of the many ways individuals and institutions, public and private, manage their common affairs. It is a continuing process through which conflicting or diverse interests may be accommodated and co-operative action may be taken. It includes formal institutions and regimes empowered to enforce compliance, as well as informal arrangements that people and institutions either have agreed to or perceive to be in their interest. ... At the global level, governance has been viewed primarily as intergovernmental relationships, but it must now be understood as also involving non-governmental organizations (NGOs), citizens' movements, multinational corporations, and the global capital market. Interacting with these are global mass media of dramatically enlarged influence. ... The enormous growth in people's concern for human rights, equity, democracy, meeting basic material needs, environmental protection, and demilitarization has today produced a multitude of new actors who can contribute to governance.

This description involves a number of important claims, in particular that the movement towards global governance initiated by the creation of the United Nations and the Bretton Woods institutions at the close of the Second World War has gradually become less state-centric, as the capacity of states to effectively govern the range of issues that extend beyond yet intersect their territorial boundaries has declined. In addition, a host of non-state actors including NGOs, activist groups, the mass media, and economic institutions have become increasingly influential in traditional political forums, and have also helped to shape global decision-making and policies through transnationally-networked forms of organization that operate outside of and supplement formal state and interstate functions and settings. This is not to suggest that the state is disappearing or becoming irrelevant, then, but rather that it is now enmeshed within horizontal and vertical networks of multiple supra-state, sub-state, and non-state actors whose roles and contributions to global governance can no longer be confined or limited to the boundaries and dictates of the nation-state. Consequently, global governance refers to a potentially more inclusive, non-coercive process of regulation resulting from the disaggregation of governmental and intergovernmental powers and functions onto non-state sectors for the purpose of devising and implementing global norms, principles, rules, and institutions (Slaughter, 1997, 2004).

John Gerard Ruggie (2003: 95) argues that in the process of more inclusive forms of governance spreading across the globe, 'a global public domain is emerging, which cannot substitute for effective action by states but may help produce it'. This global public domain is commonly referred to as 'global civil society' and is widely regarded as playing a central role in fostering global governance. Civil society can be defined as 'the realm of organized social life that is voluntary, self-generating, (largely) self-supporting, autonomous from the state, and bound by a legal order or set of shared rules' in which individuals act collectively and publicly 'to express their interests, passions, and ideas, exchange information, achieve mutual goals, make demands on the state, and hold state officials accountable' (Diamond, 1996: 228). In the context of globalization, it is often said that civil society has assumed a significant global dimension on the basis of transnational networks of non-state actors, especially NGOs such as Amnesty International, Greenpeace, Oxfam International, and *Medécins sans Frontières* whose memberships, common purpose, and organizational activities have spread across national borders. Global civil society has served as a source of governance through dissemination of information, formation of open forums for dialogue and debate, and advocacy of greater democracy, transparency, and accountability in governmental and multilateral institutions. In this way, global civil society or

> global public spheres can help to prevent the powerful from 'owning' power privately. Global publics imply greater parity. They suggest that there are alternatives. They inch our little blue and white planet towards greater openness and humility, potentially to the point where power, whenever and wherever it is exercised across borders, is made to feel more 'biodegradable', a bit more responsive to those whose lives it shapes and reshapes, secures or wrecks. (Keane, 2003: 174)

This expanding transnational or civil society layer has often been greeted enthusiastically, as enhancing democracy and providing a counterbalance to the power of markets and transnational institutions. Those enthusiastic about global civil society reject, then, the simple thesis that globalization entails a straightforward shift of power to markets and corporations, and argue instead that global governance has become pluralized, and that global civil society can be a real, and progressive, force in transformed governance. For instance, today more than $7 billion in aid to developing countries flows through international NGOs, such as CARE International, Oxfam, and Save the Children (UNDP, 2000). Advocates of global civil society would point to the tangible impact of 'people power' today. For instance, Amnesty International has been able to mobilize people across the world – with around 2 million members and supporters in 150 countries – and contribute to a global political discourse around the importance of protecting and extending rights (McGrew, 2000).

Similarly, the 'Stop the MAI' campaign is perhaps evidence of 'governance from below' entailed by the expansion of global civil society. The Multilateral Agreement on Investment was organized by the OECD between 1996–99 with the aim of establishing a treaty governing rules on international investment by MNCs. This treaty would, critical commentators noted, greatly diminish the power of national governments against MNCs – for instance, by eliminating government restrictions on foreign ownership of industries. Campaigners mobilized globally against the MAI, accenting national sovereignty and democratic accountability as key issues, and this mobilization, together with disagreements within the OECD, led to the collapse of the MAI negotiations in 1999. More recently the July, 2005 G8 summit in Gleneagles, Scotland – ostensibly dedicated to reducing the loan debts of African countries and to addressing the problem of global warming – drew an estimated 250,000 protestors from around the globe. While protestors ultimately were disappointed with the results of the summit, the British government did seek to highlight the issue of African debt and included a number of NGOs in summit deliberations, due at least in part to the pressures exerted by activist campaigns such as Make Poverty History and G8 Alternatives, as well as the series of global Live8 concerts timed to coincide with the summit. In general, then, the presence of global civil society may underscore a move towards people power, reflexivity, and popular scepticism and contestation (McGrew, 2000).

Against this argument about a shift towards a pluralization of governance and the emergence of a situation of power-sharing, stands the traditionalist case that nation-states are still the most vital players in domestic and international affairs. For such sceptics, it is not the case that states cannot any longer determine economic or social policy. Hirst and Thompson (1996, 2002), for example, maintain that the state is and will remain central in terms of the exercise of power. They contend that rather than pluralized governance, the world is divided into regional trading blocks dominated by nation-states. Against arguments that posit a coming race to the bottom as far as the welfare state is concerned, critics such as Philippe Legrain (2002) insist that states remain capable of choosing the sorts of policies they want: globalization is not, for instance, forcing governments to eliminate the welfare state. In line with this, Huber and Stephens (2001) note that, while we see a decline in welfare spending through the 1980s across developed nations (largely in response to the fiscal pressures of growing unemployment), the basic institutional features have been maintained and cutbacks have, for the most part, been modest. Similarly, Goran Therborn (2000, 2001) has rejected that the last four decades have seen a clear diminution of the state's capacity to pursue successfully its policy targets – the control of inflation being a major example. He insists that 'the welfare state still stands tall', that public spending is at a highpoint, as are government receipts, and that few welfare or East Asian 'development states' have opened themselves fully to the global market. Therborn (2001) concludes that 'A state, then, can still assert itself, and implement its own policies, under current conditions of globalization – provided that its economy can compete on the world market'.

These sceptics will frequently point out that states have often been extremely active in transnational, globalizing activities, thereby themselves laying the important foundations for globalization. In addition, Steger (2003) notes that governments have generally retained control over education, infrastructure, and, most notably (especially post-September 11, 2001), over immigration control, putting lie to the notion of a 'borderless world'. And, Scholte (2000: 132), viewing death notices for the state as 'recklessly premature', notes increases in state capacity in the realms of environmental, consumer, and data protection, as well as the state's increasing powers of surveillance.

Some Left-wing sceptics would point to the importance of one state in particular – the US – as evidence against both the argument that nation-states have lost their power and the case that posits a progressive pluralization of global governance. For instance, Gowan (2001) contends that while state sovereignty has eroded in the case of most states, this is not true for America. America, as the only surviving superpower, has a hefty say in world politics. This signals an era very different from the period of bipolar world politics in which the communist bloc, and especially the Soviet Union, counterbalanced this influence and hindered the unimpeded spread of American cultural, political, and economic power. Similarly, Marxist historian Perry Anderson (2000) has pessimistically commented that our period is marked by both the victory of neoliberalism and complete American hegemony in international affairs.

For many radicals or Marxists, then, 'global governance' is largely an ideological veil that covers the reality of US or, more widely, Western global dominance, a dominance won through the growing reach of corporate capitalism (Held and McGrew, 2002). Globalization is, in essence, all about economic globalization, a globalization that is propelled by and works for the benefit of financial and commercial elites, particularly in the developed world. On this view, a radical break is required towards an alternative system of global governance that would privilege 'people over profits, and the local over the global' (Held and McGrew, 2002: 64). Against the reality of Western state and corporate power, global civil society then would be viewed as fairly toothless, exercising a 'soft' rather than 'hard power' (Held and McGrew, 2002; Cohen and Kennedy, 2000).

From this perspective, US superpower hegemony remains the key to understanding the direction of global governance. The key, in turn, to this hegemony is massive US military supremacy: the US defence budget in 2004 was $379 billion, more than the next 14 spenders combined (Callinicos, 2003), and the budget for 2005 exceeds $400 billion (which does not include 'extra' costs for the military activities in Afghanistan and Iraq, estimated to be more than $50 billion per year). While this substantial spending has been justified as needed in order to conduct the global 'war on terror', it also reflects official US foreign policy as articulated in the so-called 'Bush Doctrine'. One of the main aims of the Bush Doctrine is to 'build and maintain' US military strength 'beyond challenge'. As the Doctrine puts it, 'Our forces will be strong enough to dissuade potential adversaries from pursuing a military build-up in hopes of surpassing, or equalling, the power of the United States' (www.whitehouse.gov/nsc/nss9.html). In addition to the Bush Doctrine's emphasis on the deployment of an overwhelming US military presence across the globe, is an explicitly imperial outlook on America's special position in the world (as 'the indispensable nation') and the necessary defence and promotion of this position.

Thus, following his victory in the 2004 presidential elections, George W. Bush portrayed his re-election as a mandate to pursue America's 'special responsibility' for asserting world order in spite of the nation's vulnerability as the 'heart' of civilization. This conception of America's 'special responsibility' fosters what Michael Ignatieff (2003: 2) refers to as 'empire lite', a global sphere of influence or 'hegemony without colonies' producing an empire 'without consciousness of itself as such'.

For the MIT linguist and political activist Noam Chomsky (1988, 2003, 2005), it is America, with its 'culture of terrorism', that is running the world. Only the US (and sometimes its clients), Chomsky contends, is able to act as a rogue state, unilaterally and unaccountably pursuing its interests with contempt for international law, equipped with formal or informal veto power in many situations, compelling other countries to endorse its imperial domination, and utilizing international institutions as mere instruments to promote its narrow interests. Similarly, Rahul Mahajan (2003) views the present as marked by the zenith of America's political dominance, based on unipolarity, the preemptive use of force, regime change, military transformation and expansion, and convergence of US and Israeli strategic interests in the Middle East. For Mahajan, the two US-led wars against Iraq confirm this new imperialism in a striking way. Here, the US was able to create the 'need' for, and have others finance, the first Gulf War (explicitly contravening international law), use the UN to disarm and impose appalling sanctions on Iraq (causing the death of over 500,000 Iraqi children), and then establish control over the country without Security Council agreement, deploying a host of ideological supports (including rhetorical references to protecting Iraqi human rights).

This is a forthright and controversial thesis and we will now explore it further, by comparing two quite opposed Marxian-influenced readings of globalization: James Petras and Henry Veltmeyer's (2001) analysis of globalization as imperialism; and Michael Hardt and Antonio Negri's (2000) analysis of Empire.

According to Petras and Veltmeyer (2001), globalization is not an inevitable process but a class project and an ideological device. The term 'globalization', implying the interdependence of nations and shared economies and interests, is best replaced with the concept of 'imperialism', which alerts us to the reality of domination and exploitation of less developed nations by the governments, MNCs, and banks of powerful states. What we have with 'globalization' is, most vitally, the deepening and extension of capitalism and the growing power of the capitalist class against the working class, despite some

---

Box 3.2   Globalization or Imperialism?

Globalization or US imperialism? That is the question. At the end of one millennium and the beginnings of another a definitive answer can be given: the world economy is increasingly dominated by US economic power. The dominant view in the 1980s and early 1990s was of a world of 'global corporations' that transcended national boundaries – what some called a 'global village' and others referred to as independent states linked by international corporations. But this perspective is no longer tenable. Systematic analysis of the composition of the international economy conclusively demonstrates that US multinational corporations are far and away the dominant force and becoming more so over time. Ideas of a 'bipolar' or 'tripolar' world, of a more diversified world economy based on the emergence of the Asian miracle economies, are a mirage. ... To the extent that globalization rhetoric persists, it has become an ideological mask disguising the emerging power of US corporations to exploit and enrich themselves and their chief executive officers to an unprecedented degree. Globalization can be seen as a code word for the ascendancy of US imperialism.

Source: Petras and Veltmeyer (2001: 62)

---

shifts in contemporary capitalism such as the internationalization of capital, flexible production methods, and a new international division of labour.

Petras and Veltmeyer reject the idea of the decline of the nation-state, pointing out that the state has been central in globalization in terms of trade treaties, subsidies, deregulation, military intervention, welfare state cutbacks, and ideological efforts promoting free trade. In fact, these authors contend that there has emerged a 'new statism' in recent decades. Moreover, contrary to globalist contentions, there is an identifiable centre of this new imperialism – US economic power; and the case of Latin America illustrates that this imperialism does not move by itself, it has clear agents. The debt crisis, restructuring, and privatization have, in Latin America, extended American control, and brought a 'new authoritarianism' – limited individual freedoms combined with a deeply authoritarian process of decision-making. Privatization, in particular, represents a clear attack on civil society and democracy in the interests of elites, leaving NGOs to contain the resulting ill effects. More generally, the globalization of capitalism is not inextricably tied – as optimists say it is – to the spread of democracy. Democracy is always contingent upon the preservation of property, power, and privilege; and democracy will be jettisoned when market relations are challenged, an important example being the 1973

US-backed overthrow of the democratically elected Allende government in Chile, in favour of the authoritarian Pinochet regime.

Providing a very different reading of the politics of globalization, but
also situated within the broad radical-Left tradition, Hardt and Negri's
two recent books, *Empire* (2000) and *Multitude* (2004), have prompted a
remarkable debate; and we will return again to their work in Chapter 5
because it has been viewed as, in part, theorizing the anti- or alternative-globalization movement. What is of interest here is Hardt and
Negri's reading of questions of sovereignty or the structure of rule
within the global capitalist order.

For Hardt and Negri (2000), the central conjuncture of events
marking the emergence of Empire is situated in the period between the
first Gulf War and the war in Kosovo, a moment crystallized when US
President George H. W. Bush declared the advent of a 'New World
Order'. By 'Empire' Hardt and Negri have in mind a new logic and
structure of rule, of sovereignty, that has emerged in conjunction with
globalization. Hardt and Negri (2000) argue that the power of the
nation-state has gone into serious decline, and a series of national and
supranational forms are being consolidated under a single logic of rule.
While 'imperialism' means the expansion of nation-state sovereignty
beyond national borders, Empire, by contrast, is decentred and deterritorializing, and it progressively incorporates the entire global realm
within its frontiers. Today, no nation-state is at the centre of rule.
Today, too, the object of rule has changed: rule is now the rule over
social life as a whole ('biopower'). Finally, however, Empire also offers
new possibilities for liberation, and we should not be entirely pessimistic about the new global order.

The movement away from state sovereignty and autonomy, from the
applicability of inside/outside distinctions, towards informationalism,
decentralization, and immaterial labour (flexible, service/cultural work)
in the direction of Empire, say Hardt and Negri (2000), has been driven
by the 'multitude's' struggle for liberation. In fact, they say that the
multitude (a successor to the masses or the proletariat, which underscores difference and multiplicity against the old Marxian emphasis on
sameness) called Empire into being. This Empire seems to be about the
expansion of capitalism everywhere, but it is also seen as a step
towards emancipation. We can, though, no longer imagine that there
is, as they put it, a Rome in this new Empire, or a Winter Palace to
storm: there is, in short, no place of power today. In particular, for
Hardt and Negri (2000: 384), 'the coming Empire is not American and
the US is not its centre'. Thus, while America has hegemony over the

global use of force, it acts not as an *imperialist* interest but as an *imperial* interest.

We will examine Hardt and Negri's work again below and in Chapter 5, considering some key objections raised by critics. Here, though, it seems to us that while the analysis in *Empire* can appear to underplay the unevenness of the contemporary workings of power, the argument that responds by equating globalization with a narrow US imperialism is far less convincing. We have, for instance, already discussed (in Chapter 1) the world-systems analysis of the period labelled globalization as evidencing America's decline as leader of the world-system. Arrighi (2005a), for example, points out that, while the US economy still carries great weight and America stands unchallenged as a military power, the current quagmire in Iraq and the rise of East Asian economic power point to a more complex situation than those positing America as the unassailable global hegemon allow: 'To be sure, whatever the outcome of the Iraqi war, the United States will remain the world's dominant military power for some time to come. But the chances are that, while its difficulties in Vietnam precipitated the "signal crisis" of US hegemony, in retrospect US difficulties in Iraq will be seen as having precipitated its "terminal crisis"'. From a very different perspective, Nye (2004) contends that power in the contemporary period is structured in a complex three-layered fashion, with unipolarity on the military dimension, multipolarity on the economic dimension, and a wide dispersal of power within the dimension of transnational relations. Moreover, in *Multitude*, Hardt and Negri (2004: 61) further clarify some of their claims in *Empire*, arguing that perhaps the US has been, more recently, somewhere between imperialism and Empire so that, crucially, its decisions and actions 'must always be set in relation to the entire network of global power' (2004: 61). Nevertheless. they still contend that the most important tendency is towards the construction of a deterritorialized Empire. This appears to us a compelling position.

Challenges to the state

We have surveyed theories that accent the alteration in sovereignty entailed by globalization, and those who reject that anything significant has changed in relation to the exercise of power and governance capacity. While overstating the degree to which change has occurred is flawed, it also seems to us that it is profoundly unconvincing to maintain that, politically speaking, nothing has altered. It is clear that there have emerged with globalization a number of profound challenges to the sovereignty of the state. Waters (1999: 100–2), for instance, has noted the following sorts of factors as exerting pressure on states today, leading in the direction of what Hedley Bull (1977) described as a 'new medievalism':

- the regional amalgamation of states
- the near collapse of states provoked by ethnic conflicts
- international terrorism
- a decreased capacity of states to deal with problems on a national basis
- global technological unification
- spreading consciousness of deepening environmental problems that single states are unable to solve
- a growing level of 'expertise, education and reflexive empowerment in the adult citizenry that makes them less susceptible to state authority'.

The new medievalism thus refers to the blurring of lines between inside/outside, the diffusion of state power, and 'a system of overlapping authority and multiple loyalty' (Bull, 1977: 254). In this section, while wanting to promote a critical transformationalist position, we will explore a number of pressing challenges that states have had to face in our globalizing period. We will begin with questions of human rights, which will broaden into a discussion of the challenges that globalization poses to conventional understandings of citizenship. We will then consider global environmental change. Finally, we will briefly discuss the challenge of global crime, before examining an important sub-category of such crime – 'global terrorism'.

Human rights, citizenship, and cosmopolitanism

We have already noted David Held's contention that the principles of the UN have signalled a shift from the Westphalian system of governance. A linked issue and one of the very powerful examples of the way in which global concerns can transcend state boundaries is the question of human rights. Among the most important developments in the last half of the twentieth century has been the emergence of a new law and politics of human rights. Indeed, a statement often repeated in recent years, both in scholarly circles and in the mass media, is that we now live in an 'age of human rights' (Bobbio, 1996). The reasons for this statement are simple: in a relatively brief period of time, a large number of declarations, treaties, organizations, institutions, commissions, and networks created for the purposes of promoting and defending the rights of individuals have sprung up across the globe. The swift progress of human rights in global politics has raised hopes for a better world; the expectations are that human rights will promote political liberties, lead to the enhancement of the social bases of human welfare and increased security, as well as to international relations characterized by peaceful co-operation and constructive interdependence.

The contemporary international human rights regime has developed concurrently with and under the auspices of the United Nations system and constitutes a set of norms, institutions, and procedures that most states now accept as binding at least to some degree. Although the UN Charter refers to human rights in several places it does not define what those rights are. Thus one of the first tasks the UN assumed was to produce a document that would specifically stipulate international human rights norms. The Commission on Human Rights (CHR) chaired by Eleanor Roosevelt was established for the purpose of drafting an international bill of rights (Glendon, 2001). The work of the CHR resulted in the Universal Declaration of Human Rights (UDHR) which was presented according to its preamble as a 'common standard of achievement for all peoples and all nations'. The UDHR was unanimously adopted by the UN General Assembly on 10 December 1948. Because the UDHR is a resolution and not a treaty, it is not legally binding. However, over time it has become a part of customary international law. In addition the UDHR has been supplemented by two treaties that give human rights binding force in international law, both of which were adopted by the General Assembly in 1966 and entered into law in 1976: the International Covenant on Civil and Political Rights (ICCPR), and the International Covenant on Economic, Social and Cultural Rights (ICESCR). Since the adoption of the UDHR more than 200 regional and international human rights treaties have been approved.

Since the end of the Second World War, the promotion and protection of human rights has rapidly assumed increased global salience. This has affected not only the domestic and international conduct and policies of states, but also the practices and influence of a constantly expanding range of nongovernmental organizations, advocacy groups, research institutes, and social movements committed to an assortment of human rights causes. This complex network of governmental and non-governmental human rights groups constitutes a genuinely transnational social movement committed to universal human rights principles (Risse *et al.*, 1999). It is no exaggeration to suggest, then, that since its adoption the UDHR has become 'the moral touchstone for all claims at the international level' (Franck, 1985: 232) and that, consequently, there is now 'not a single nation, culture or people that is not in one way or another enmeshed in human rights regimes' (Morsink, 1999: x).

The transnational human rights movement has helped to expose numerous human rights violations around the world and to promote fundamental human rights and freedoms, often by publicizing critical issues and problem areas and thereby raising the profiles of both specific human rights causes and the global human rights regime. Recent examples of efforts to address gross human rights violations in the forms of genocide and crimes against humanity include the former Yugoslavia and Rwanda. Between 1991 and 1999 civil war, ethnic cleansing, and other human rights abuses tore apart the republics of the former Yugoslavia. Throughout Croatia and especially Bosnia and Herzegovina, millions of people were forcibly displaced from their homes. Brutal fighting and repression including violent expulsion, mass rape, and genocidal murder resulted in the deaths of more than 250,000 people. In Rwanda approximately one million people were systematically slaughtered between April and July 1994. We discuss this genocide in more detail in Chapter 4.

Both of these cases resulted in the creation of *ad hoc* criminal tribunals. The International Criminal Tribunal for the former Yugoslavia (ICTY) located in The Hague, was established by UN Security Council Resolution 827 of 25 May 1993, making it the first ever international war crimes tribunal. The International Criminal Tribunal for Rwanda (ICTR) located in Arusha, Tanzania was established the following year by UN Security Council Resolution 955 of 8 November 1994. The ICTR is the first international court charged specifically with prosecuting crimes of genocide, although both tribunals are mandated to prosecute crimes against humanity and war crimes as well. The ICTR has issued indictments against more than 70 individuals and on 4 September 1998 sentenced Jean Kambanda – Prime Minister of the government during the genocide – to life imprisonment for genocide and crimes against humanity, the first such criminal sentence in history. The ICTY has indicted more than 80 individuals for war crimes, crimes against humanity, and genocide. Among those prosecuted was Bosnian Serb General Radislav Krstic, commander of the forces that attacked Srebrenica, who was found guilty of genocide and war crimes on

2 August 2001. Slobodan Milosevic, former President of the Federal Republic of Yugoslavia, was until his death in 2006 in the custody of the court and being tried for war crimes, crimes against humanity and genocide. More recently the former president of Serbia, Milan Milutinovic, surrendered to the ICTY on 20 January 2003 and faces charges of war crimes and crimes against humanity.

Building on these developments, on 17 July 1998, 120 states voted in favour of the Rome Statute of the International Criminal Court, establishing the world's first permanent international criminal tribunal. On 11 April 2002 the sixtieth country ratified the Rome Statute, and the Statute entered into force on 1 July 2002. The ICC is an independent treaty-based institution separate from although affiliated with the UN system, including the Security Council. As stated in Article 5 of the Rome Statute, the Court has jurisdiction over war crimes, the crime of genocide, crimes against humanity, and the crime of aggression, effective as of 1 July 2002. The scope and exercise of the Court was and still remains a matter of some controversy. The United States, in particular, has been vehemently opposed to the notion of an international criminal court with universal jurisdiction and an independent prosecutor. Indeed, after coming to power the George W. Bush administration moved quickly to withdraw US support for the ICC and on 6 May 2002 formally retracted the US as a signatory to the Rome Treaty. Nevertheless, as commentators such as Held would point out, the development of international war crimes tribunals as well as a permanent international criminal court goes against the old Westphalian principle that states had the absolute right to govern subject populations as they saw fit, free from external interference.

The spread of a global discourse of human rights is widely cited as evidence of a growing global consciousness, of the power of global civil society, and as signal of fundamental alterations in terms of the sovereignty of states. For enthusiasts of human rights discourse, such rights are important trumps against repressive regimes, allowing citizens to appeal to global principles in the face of persecution, and having the effect of deepening democracy and human freedom. After all, the notion of humanity appealed to in these rights transcends national borders. This assessment runs counter to the orthodox Marxist discourse that has often portrayed rights as merely individualistic, formal, and to be viewed, first and foremost, as linked to private property rights. The Marxist critique of rights does importantly alert us to the way in which rights discourse can be cynically deployed – for instance, by both the superpowers during the Cold War as means of getting leverage over each other, and, more recently, in the US government's 'military humanism' (Gowan, 2003). In this vein, Žižek (2005) contends that 'what the "human rights of Third World suffering victims" effectively means today, in the predominant discourse, is the right of Western powers themselves to intervene politically, economically, culturally and militarily in the Third World countries of their choice, in the name of defending human rights'. This said, the connection of rights merely to property rights and the assertion that they remain simply individualistic and formal is unconvincing. That is, as Claude Lefort (1988) has argued, rights are able to be, and have been, extended and deepened into social, cultural, and political entitlements of individuals and groups, and denial of such rights tends to do great damage to the social fabric. Therefore, to deny the importance of the growth of a global, popular discourse around rights appears very problematic.

Rights (along with duties such as paying taxes, obeying the law, and doing military service) are linked to citizenship in the context of the modern state. As Delanty (2000) and Urry (1999) point out, though, within a globalized world notions of citizenship are being unsettled with state withdrawal from welfare provision, breakdown of national economies, issues such as immigration and dual citizens, and arguments about emerging types of citizenship (such as ecological, consumer, and mobility citizenship). Consequently, numerous commentators have spoken of the emerging importance of a postnational or 'postWestphalian' conception of citizenship, which does not necessarily replace state citizenship, but complements it by recognizing the overlapping nature of identities and loyalties today, operating on multiple social levels from the local to the global and within and across communities ranging from the actual to the virtual. To reformulate, while the rights and duties of citizenship throughout modernity have been directed solely towards the state, rights, duties and participation are now becoming increasingly globally oriented.

In recent years, cosmopolitanism has emerged as a challenge to conventional ways of thinking about citizenship, rights, and democracy. This cosmopolitan challenge is explicitly focussed on the reality of an interconnected world, where we must face issues with an orientation that moves beyond narrow national interests. That is, today, says Delanty (2000), citizenship and nation have become decoupled. Cosmopolitan citizens of the future would be part of a world community, not solely of any state.

A number of cosmopolitan thinkers have attempted to delineate what a cosmopolitan democracy of the future might look like. The

---

Box 3.3   Cosmopolitanism

Cosmopolitanism means 'world citizenship' and implies membership on the part of all individuals in a universal community of human beings. Cosmopolitanism is a dynamic concept that has acquired different nuances and emphases over the course of time. It was Diogenes of Sinope (c. 400–323 BC) who possibly pronounced what has come to be regarded as the most representative statement of the cosmopolitan sensibility. When asked where he came from Diogenes is reputed to have replied, 'I am a citizen of the world'. There are three elemental characteristics to the core of cosmopolitanism which help to demarcate its guiding principles with regard to contemporary social and political theory: 1) Individual human beings are the ultimate units of moral and political concern; 2) All human beings possess equal moral status; and 3) Persons are subjects of concern for everyone, that is, human status has global scope. For cosmopolitans, our fundamental rights as well as our obligations towards others know no borders. Cosmopolitans accept and embrace the fact of human diversity yet argue that such diversity exists within and across communities that expand ultimately to the widest circle of humankind. Consequently, cosmopolitans argue that race, nation and ethnicity do not determine in a strong sense the worth of each person's life and experiences.

---

theory of cosmopolitan democracy developed by David Held, Daniele Archibugi and others outlines a project for multiple layers of democratized governance (from the local to the global) that, among other goals, attempts to resolve the shortcomings of global governance, in particular, the perceived deficit of democratic legitimacy. Archibugi, an advocate of what he calls 'cosmopolitical democracy', explains:

> Above all, what distinguishes cosmopolitical democracy from other such projects is its attempt to create institutions which enable the voice of individuals to be heard in global affairs, irrespective of their resonance at home. Democracy as a form of global governance thus needs to be realized on three different, interconnected levels: within states, between states and at a world level. (Archibugi, 2003: 8)

Archibugi as well as Held and Anthony McGrew agree that there is a general consensus about the existence of democratic deficiencies in the current international system. Global governance is often regarded as distorted in so far as it reflects a hierarchy of power at the international level that too frequently promotes the interests of the most powerful states and global social forces at the expense of the majority of the world's inhabitants (Archibugi, 2003: 8). Indeed, the agenda for international action and co-operation is often set by those very global powers with few other motives than the advancement of their own immediate interests. Distorted global governance therefore is 'a product of the mutually reinforcing dynamics of the inequalities of power between states; the structural privileging of the interests and agenda of global capital; and the technocratic nature of the global policy process' (Archibugi, 2003: 8). As such, any role that global governance can have in achieving human development through poverty reduction and the provision of both welfare and human rights is often marginalized by the self-interested considerations of powerful elites within the current system.

The failures of the current system of global governance are compounded by a persistent democratic deficit. The new supranational layers of governance created by nation-states seeking to promote or regulate the effects of globalization generally have few mechanisms of accountability accessible to the general population; these global institutions are for the most part accountable only to states and operate according to non-democratic principles (disproportionately to any population size) (Singer, 2002: 75–7). Other influential global actors, whether from the private sector (MNCs) or from civil society (NGOs), are frequently also unaccountable to or unrepresentative of a variety of members of international society. This democratic deficit of global governance has far reaching consequences, notably in terms of its impact on economic development where a system of elite governance detached from responsibility to the general population frequently rules in its own favour leading to increased poverty and inequality. As Archibugi (2003: 9) notes, 'This is the true deficit of democracy: the existence of organized transnational interests far removed from any popular mandate'.

Under these circumstances, Archibugi and Held assert the need for the creation of a global democratic polity and culture, the only framework in which the ideals of autonomy and democracy can be fully realized. The cosmopolitan model of democracy seeks to expand the levels of participatory politics and means of accountability through an adaptive 'system of diverse and overlapping power centres, shaped and delimited by democratic law' (Held, 1995: 234). Despite the deficiencies of the existing system of global governance, Held is cautiously optimistic about the prospects for cultivating cosmopolitan democracy, especially considering that some cosmopolitan ideas are already in the centre of post-Second World War legal and political developments, especially those of human rights and humanitarian assistance.

In a more philosophical register, Jacques Derrida (1997) has also insisted that globalization means we need to conceive of a democratic relationship beyond the bounds of particular nation-states. Derrida – the father of 'deconstruction', an influential and controversial strand of poststructuralism – was at the time of his death in 2004 probably the world's most prominent (and, for some, notorious) philosopher. The major thrust of Derrida's work is the rejection of linguistic, social, and political closure: he argues that meaning and identity are created relationally rather than existing 'in themselves', and thus they can never be finally fixed or fully known in advance.

Derrida is deeply sceptical of those political aspirations that limit themselves to any preconstituted and supposedly self-contained 'us'. He suggests that this 'us' – whether a community, nation, or class – is always dependent on others for its identity (in so far as an 'inside' cannot be defined except against an 'outside'); and such pure identity

---

Box 3.4   Derrida, Democracy, and Globalization

What's the situation today of democracy? 'Progress' in arms-technologies and media-technologies is incontestably causing the disappearance of the site on which the democratic used to be situated. The site of representation and the stability of the location which make up parliament or assembly, the territorialization of power, the rooting of power to a particular place, if not to the ground as such – all this is over. ... What the acceleration of techni-cization concerns today is the frontiers of the nation-state, the traffic of arms and drugs, everything that has to do with inter-nationality. It is these issues which need to be completely reconsidered, not in order to sound the death-knell of democracy, but in order to rethink democracy from within these conditions. ... Since no locality remains, democracy must be thought today globally, if it is to have a future. In the past one could always say that democracy was to be saved in this or that country. Today, however, if one claims to be a democrat, one cannot be a democrat 'at home' and wait to see what happens 'abroad'. Everything that is happening today – whether it be about Europe, the GATT, the Mafia, drugs, or arms – engages the future of democracy in the world in general. ... In the determination or behaviour of each citizen or singularity there should be present, in some form or other, the call to a world democracy to come, each singularity should determine itself with the sense of the stakes of a democracy which can no longer be contained within frontiers, which can no longer be localized, which can no longer depend on the decisions of a specific group of citizens, a nation or even of a continent. This determination means that one must both think, and think democracy, globally.

Source: Derrida (1994)

claims are potentially dangerous in their neglect of difference. Derrida (1997) approaches globalization through close analysis of concepts like 'friendship', 'hospitality', and 'democracy', which are currently associated with notions such as brotherhood, family, roots in territory, and the nation-state. With growing world interconnectedness, says Derrida, limited models of friendship, hospitality, and democracy are being deconstructed in the world. What we need to do, then, is to think of another type of friendship and another type of democracy. He thinks about this through the idea of a 'democracy to come'. This democracy to come is linked to a promise, namely, one implicit in the ideas of equality, freedom, and respect for singularity. It will never be fully realized, but it allows for an endless process of improvement. As an open promise, an expansive and inclusive notion of friendship and a concomitant concept of democracy demands that we think beyond just other citizens to non-citizens too. For Derrida, this thinking beyond demands new international laws, practices, institutions, values, and ideals. That is, the changes in the world require that we break open the older conceptions, recognize that they are exclusionary and antiquated, and imagine opening these up and rethinking politics away from constricting territorial foundations.

The environment

Environmental problems, similarly, force us to think beyond the nation-state. Pollution, for instance, does not respect borders, and depletion of natural resources worldwide has much wider implications than a focus on the national level alone allows. Today it is generally understood that it is not acceptable to simply do what one wants, environmentally-speaking, within one's own territory, because of the very tangible global effects of atmospheric pollution, deforestation, and species extinctions (all detailed in the previous chapter). In recognition of this, certain places have been allocated as 'global commons' outside the sovereignty of nation-states – for example, the oceans and Antarctica (Waters, 1999).

As a result of a number of global environmental threats becoming increasingly evident over the past three decades, a transnational environmental movement has emerged. During this same period, management of the global environment has arisen as a major concern in world politics, and environmental matters have assumed a growing importance for numerous scholars and practitioners (Vogler and Imber, 1996). The manifestation of environmental globalization can be regarded as a consequence of the 'thickening' of environmentally-centred linkages between state and non-state actors around the world, which has occurred largely as a result of mounting concerns about the very possibility of sustaining human life in the face of severe threats to the planet's environment (Held *et al.*, 1999; Clark, 2000).

The transnational environmental movement and the importance attached to global environmental problems have occurred mainly as a result of the recent emergence of a number of well-publicized global environmental threats. Environmental organizations in both developed and less developed countries have increased the profile of these threats and have helped to move them onto political agendas by putting pressure on influential actors and institutions. For this reason, global environmental change is best understood as a social rather than physical phenomenon. This is because what has occurred is not simply dramatic change in the natural environment but more significantly the growth of an environmental consciousness, which realizes the limits of human exploitation (of both the earth and other human beings) and seeks to preserve the environment as the support system necessary for human existence (Lipschutz and Meyer, 1996: 20). The emergence of environmental consciousness is, then, very much the result of the 'rediscovery' of human dependence on our natural surroundings, which has been masked by the modern scientific and technological illusion that nature can be mastered in a process of unlimited human expansion – what the Frankfurt School theorists referred to as the notion of 'instrumental rationality' (Falk, 1995: 252; Horkheimer and Adorno, 1989).

Largely as a result of the emergence of the transnational environmental movement and its shared global ethic, environmental globalization is rapidly occurring. As William C. Clark (2000) argues, if environmental globalism consists of 'the existence of a rich network of environmentally mediated linkages among actors at multicontinental distance', then it is unequivocally a feature of global society. He suggests as well that if environmental globalization is the 'thickening' of the linkages of environmental globalism then this process is well under way (Clark, 2000: 101–2). Clark outlines three groups of environmental linkages that have noticeably increased in the past few decades, namely, the flows of materials (such as hazardous materials, toxic wastes and greenhouse gases) and biota around the globe, environmental ideas, and environmental governance. He cites increases in the variety, strength, and density of long distance relationships among actors, the number of actors involved in those relationships, and the velocity of change in society that these relationships help to induce as persuasive proof of environmental globalization.

Given the growing awareness of the extent of interconnectedness in the global environment as well as the emergence of pressing environmental problems at the global level, it is not surprising that there is widespread demand for global environmental policy and management to ensure that environmental degradation is minimized and reversed as much as is possible. Consequently, collaborative efforts between state and non-state actors to advocate good environmental practices, as well as a substantial amount of international research, monitoring, and assessment have taken place in order to develop consistent policies on addressing global environmental threats.

A good example of the transnationalization of political activity in relation to environmental issues is the Kyoto Protocol. The aim of the Kyoto Protocol is to 'stabilize and reduce greenhouse gas emissions (GHGs), mitigate climate change, and promote sustainable development' (http://www.cop3.org/). GHG emissions (such as carbon dioxide, methane, hydrofluorocarbons, and sulphur hexafluoride) come primarily from industrial and transportation sources, and the 'continued accumulation of GHGs could lead to an increase in the average temperature of the earth's surface and cause a variety of changes in the global climate, sea level, agricultural patterns, and ecosystems that could be ... detrimental' (Energy Information Administration, 2002). In 1988, the Intergovernmental Panel on Climate Change (IPCC) was established by the World Meteorological Organization and the United Nations Environmental Programme to assess issues in climate change (Energy Information Administration, 2002). The Framework Convention on Climate Change was adopted at the UN in 1992, with the goal of stabilization of GHGs (Energy Information Administration, 2002). As a follow up to this, in December 1997, in Kyoto, Japan, representatives of more than 160 countries met to negotiate binding limits on GHG emissions for developed nations (who are seen as needing to take the lead here) relative to their 1990 emissions, with these countries expected to reduce emissions by an average of 5.3 per cent by 2008–12 (Simonis and Bruhl, 2002; Energy Information Administration, 2002). The agreement includes a number of flexible mechanisms such as international emissions trading and a clean development mechanism through which nations can earn credit by spending on clean technologies for less developed countries (Reuters, 2005). 141 countries have now ratified the pact. However the US, the world's biggest polluter, has pulled out, with the Bush administration arguing that Kyoto is too expensive and that it should not omit developing nations (Reuters, 2005). Unfortunately, many countries are doing poorly on their targets – for instance, in 2002

Spain was 40 per cent up on its 1990 levels, and there have, overall, been significant increases in the levels of carbon dioxide in the atmosphere between 1990 and the present (Fotopoulos, 2005; Reuters, 2005). In addition, many critics see the targets as far too low to significantly avert the threat of detrimental climate change (Fotopoulos, 2005).

Although systems of global environmental governance have not yet made major progress in solving environmental problems, important building blocks have been put in place in the organization of the transnational environmental movement. The most encouraging aspect of this movement is its contributing role in the emergence of global civil society in which networks of actors spanning different levels and different sectors of society are linked by their shared concern for the environment and human development, which results in local groups taking action based on globally embedded ideas. For instance, an example of one mode of the postnational citizenship discussed above is the conception of 'world environmental citizenship'. World environmental citizenship arises from an ethical concern for the social, political, and economic problems associated with the environment and humanity's dependence upon it, and from a recognition of our global responsibilities for the human condition in light of humanity's interconnectedness with the environment. Thus, world environmental citizenship is concerned about the common good of the human community and places particular emphasis on the fact that we are all citizens belonging to both local environments and a single global environment.

The values and aspirations contained in the conception of world environmental citizenship may have found their fullest expression yet in the Earth Charter, which was officially launched at the Peace Palace in The Hague on 29 June 2000. The Earth Charter is the culmination of a decade-long consultative process that involved prominent political figures, individual experts, national committees, intergovernmental organizations, and domestic and international NGOs. It is therefore the result of global civil society as a constructive partner in global governance. The impetus for the Earth Charter came from the 1987 United Nations World Commission on Environment and Development report *Our Common Future*, which called for the creation of a new global charter that would set forth the fundamental principles of sustainable development. Following the 1992 Earth Summit, calls for the drafting of a new charter increased, and in 1997 an Earth Charter Commission was formed with an Earth Charter Secretariat established at the Earth Council in Costa Rica. Ultimately, the mission of the Earth Charter initiative led to the adoption of a platform of global environmental justice in order to 'establish a sound ethical foundation for the emerging global society and to help build a sustainable world based on respect for nature, universal human rights, economic justice, and a culture of peace'. The Preamble to Earth Charter concludes by declaring:

> To realize these aspirations, we must decide to live with a sense of universal responsibility, identifying ourselves with the whole Earth community as well as our local communities. We are at once citizens of different nations and of one world in which the local and global are linked. Everyone shares responsibility for the present and future well-being of the human family and the larger living world.

Crime and 'global terrorism'

As noted, it is now widely acknowledged that it has become increasingly difficult for states to monitor and dictate what goes on within their territories. One much commented upon dimension of this has been the alleged struggle that states today have when faced with an explosion of global criminality. Information-related crime, the drugs trade, illegal gambling, trafficking of people and human organs, illegal immigration, the illicit arms trade, and kidnapping are some examples of transnational criminal activity (Castells, 1998). For instance, the retail value of the illicit drugs trade in 2003 was estimated at $321 billion, higher than the GDP of 88 per cent of the countries in the world (United Nations Office on Drugs and Crime, 2005a). Trafficking in people is another aspect of global criminality with obviously important implications for states, reaching what the UN Office on Drugs and Crime has called 'epidemic proportions': it is thought that each year in the US 45,000–50,000 women and children arrive under false pretences to work as 'prostitutes, abused labourers or servants'; and UNICEF note that up to 200,000 children are enslaved by cross-border smuggling in West and Central Africa alone (UN Office on Drugs and Crime, 2005b). And conventional weapons, particularly small arms and light weapons, are the major items exchanged in the global arms market, which is subject to minimal control and provides for massive illicit weapons trafficking. The illegal arms trade is an enormous industry, with clearly destructive and destabilizing consequences. It is estimated that there are 639 million small arms and light weapons in circulation globally – one for every 12 people in the world (UN Chronicle, 2001) – and up to 41 per cent of small arms transfers

are illegal (Graduate Institute of International Studies, 2002). It is estimated as well that between 500,000 and 700,000 people are killed by
small arms fire each year, roughly the equivalent of one death per
minute. In this context it is worth noting that global military expendi-
tures amounted to approximately $794 billion in 2002, a figure that
eclipses the $57 billion in Overseas Development Assistance provided
by all of the developed countries combined that same year (SIPRI,
2003).

Perhaps the most prominent dimension of global criminality in
recent years, though, has been that of 'global terrorism'. The attacks of
September 11 ushered in the discourse of 'a war on terror', and led to
the invasions of Afghanistan and Iraq. The threat of global terrorism
has also been used by the government in Israel to support its policies
against the Palestinians and by the Putin regime in Russia to justify its
continued military presence in Chechnya. In the aftermath of the
September 11 attacks, governments around the world have drafted
wide-reaching anti-terrorism legislation and stepped up surveillance to
combat terrorist activity.

September 11 has widely been viewed as ushering in a new era. As
British Prime Minister Tony Blair (2004) contends, 'It [global terrorism]
is a challenge of a different nature from anything the world has faced
before'. Arguments about the nature of the novelty of the attacks vary.
For Beck (2002: 48), for instance, the terrorist threat today means that
'no nation, not even the most powerful, can ensure its national security by itself'. According to Bauman (2002: 81), the events signal 'a
symbolic end to the era of space', where there are no longer any strictly
territorial solutions and nothing remains 'outside'. Habermas (2003),
meanwhile, suggests that 'what was new was the symbolic force of the
targets struck', the fact that the events unfolded before a global public,
and the intangibility of the terrorist threat today. The emergence of a
new 'global terrorism' is a common theme to many discussions of
September 11. This global terrorism is viewed as differing from the
older terrorism in a number of ways: in organizational terms (with the
move to decentralized networks); in terms of the use of new media; in
terms of funding, with the move from state sponsorship to illicit commercial activity; and in terms of the smaller, cheaper, and more easily
available instruments of destruction (Kaldor, 2003; Nye, 2004).

September 11 has also frequently been couched in the rhetoric of
evil and as a sign of a fundamental cultural divide between the West
and Islam. According to US President George W. Bush, for instance, the
new global terrorists 'have no justification for their actions. There's no

religious justification, there's no political justification. The only motivation is evil'; furthermore, 'they hate what they see right here in this chamber – a democratically elected government. Their leaders are self-appointed. They hate our freedoms – our freedom of religion, our freedom of speech, our freedom to vote and assemble and disagree with each other' (quoted in Johnson, 2002: 221, 216). In this vein, for philosopher Louis Pojman (2003), this terrorist act brings a change in the world, in warfare, and a 'new dimension of evil'. Poverty and oppression are contributing causes to such terror, Pojman (2003: 141) notes, but the 'overriding impetus is a culture that endorses and reinforces violent responses against certain types of persons and property'. Muslim fanaticism, 'which opposes Western liberal values, including women's rights, tolerance of different lifestyles, and abortion', is vital in this (Pojman, 2003: 142). But, more generally, the culture of the Middle East is implicated by Pojman. Here, he alleges, the rule 'destroy or be destroyed' reigns supreme: 'Warring tribes confront each other with no impartial arbiter to enforce mutually agreed-upon rules, so that the only relevant concern is survival, which entails that the enemy must be destroyed by whatever means necessary' (Pojman, 2003: 137). Consequently, many political leaders argue that the new terrorist threat can only be dealt with by a range of measures, including refusal to negotiate with terrorists, bringing terrorists to justice, pressuring states that support terrorism, bolstering counter-terrorist capacities, scrutinizing immigration control policy, and promoting national service (Pojman, 2003).

Critical theory can offer crucial interrogation of such notions, unsettling the terms of the debate in important ways. A first question concerns the definition of 'terrorism'. As the cliché goes, one person's terrorist is another's freedom fighter. The US State Department defines terrorism as 'premeditated, politically motivated violence perpetrated against non-combatant targets by subnational groups or clandestine agents, usually intended to influence an audience' (in Sterba, 2003: 206). Despite the apparent exclusion of state actors, though, the US recognizes state-sponsored terrorism as a major problem. This is still, though, a misleading emphasis, because the main actors in violence against non-combatants worldwide are governments. Furthermore, while many participants in the dominant discourse around the terrorist threat would be happy to label governments such as Syria, Iraq, and Libya 'terrorist', the suggestion that Western governments, or governments friendly to the West, regularly engage in terrorism is frequently considered unconscionable. Kapitan (2003), in contrast, insists that, by most definitions, we cannot escape the conclusions that the US engaged in terrorism in its support of the Contra rebels in Nicaragua in the 1980s, which cost over 3,000 lives; that US actions against Iraq, including the bombing of Baghdad in 1991 and the punitive sanctions that ballooned into a major humanitarian crisis, are an instance of terrorism; and that Israel's 35 year occupation of the West Bank and Gaza Strip, complete with extrajudicial murders, tortures, deportations, destruction of property, and widespread intimidation, is terrorism. However, these examples are regularly excluded from mainstream discussions about the terrorist threat. Instead, focus and condemnation is concentrated on substate groups such as Hamas, Hezbollah, the Tamil Tigers, and the Real IRA.

We would, then, tend to agree with Badiou (2004a) that, today, 'terrorism' is an intrinsically propagandistic term, and with Kapitan (2003) that the constant reference to 'terror' obscures the issues at stake, particularly the nature, origins, and causes of terrorist actions. The 'terrorist' label automatically discredits and dehumanizes, placing these actors and actions outside of 'reasonable discourse' as amoral, psychopathic and beyond dialogue (Kapitan, 2003). For instance, Tony Blair has argued that 'There is no compromise possible with such people, no meeting of minds, no point of understanding with such terror. Just a choice: defeat it or be defeated by it' (quoted in Johnson, 2002: 223). Particularly obfuscatory and pernicious is that way in which terrorism is contrasted with 'Western values', which as Badiou (2004a) notes is preposterous, given, for example, the brutality exhibited by Western powers in the wars of decolonization of the post-Second World War period.

The consequences of the post-September 11 period are also relevant for this chapter in terms of the issue of state surveillance. For Castells (2000), the non-fulfilment of the Orwellian prophesy of the 'big brother' state, deploying technology to completely control the population, is yet another sign of the 'emptying out of the state'. This sort of statism has, Castells maintains, completely collapsed, as new technologies are today pushing towards networking and decentralization, rather than centralizing, vertical, one-way, bureaucratic surveillance. The real surveillance trend, says Castells, is towards the gathering of information on individuals by business firms and the creation of a global market for this information.

This view could perhaps be contested after September 11. For David Lyon (2003), the attacks on the World Trade Centre reinforced and intensified existing surveillance operations, leading us further towards a 'surveillance society'. Lyon finds this trend disturbing, as such societies undermine trust and solidarity, focus on control rather than care, and create cultures of fear, suspicion, and secrecy. After the attacks, for example, the US government instituted both the Department of Homeland Security and the PATRIOT Act, and many other countries, as previously noted, have implemented anti-terrorist legislation of their own, such as the UK's Anti-Terrorism, Crime and Security Act of 2001 and Australia's Anti-Terrorism Bill of 2005. These policies increase the likelihood of detention without trial and of intrusive surveillance measures. For instance, over 500 uncharged 'illegal combatants' still languish in Guantanamo Bay, Cuba, as 'suspected members of Al Qaeda', without POW status as required by the Geneva Convention, denied access to legal counsel, and according to numerous reports, subject to cruel, inhuman, and degrading treatment – treatment which further undermines the widely deployed contrast between Muslim fanaticism and 'Western values' such as humanism, respect for the rule of law, and individual liberty.

Lyon sees all this as having a profound 'chilling effect': as alternative globalization writer Naomi Klein says, 'After September 11, politicians and pundits around the world instantly began spinning the terrorist attacks as part of a continuum of anti-American and anti-corporate violence' (in Lyon, 2003: 54). Such surveillance trends demonstrate the continuing power and centrality of the state, but they also demonstrate the globalizing tendencies of surveillance – for instance, as state/centralized and commercial/decentralized surveillance come together in places such as airports, the prime site for observing the new global citizen (Lyon, 2003). With respect to the power of the state in terms of terrorism and surveillance, Bauman's approach to globalization also seems of relevance – if perhaps a little overblown – here. For Bauman (1999a), states, though in general equipped with less and less power, are focussing ever more on the question of law and order. The effects of this are security for some (the mobile globals) and the awesome force of law for others (those who have no choice but to remain local). For Bauman, the trend in these terms is towards spatial separation, exclusion, immobilization, and the suspension of communication – a quite new disciplinary mode to the older emphases on correction, social improvement, and rehabilitation.

Finally, in an interesting analysis, Hardt and Negri (2004) claim that September 11 merely made visible a shift in the conditions and nature of war. War has now become a 'permanent social relation' (Hardt and Negri, 2004: 12). From the war on drugs in the 1980s to the war on terror today, war is increasingly 'indeterminate, both spatially and temporally' (2004: 14). Under a condition of 'permanent' war, the suspension of democracy becomes the norm, with a tendency towards authoritarianism and totalitarianism; and with the shift of emphasis from defence to security, war becomes the foundation of politics, now viewed as a central productive mechanism in global social ordering.

A changing political culture?

We now turn to a multifaceted issue that has been touched on at several points in the discussion thus far – the question of whether there is emerging a new political culture. This issue is broadly one of democracy in a globalizing world. We have already discussed some of the arguments that contend that the state as container of politics, democracy, and citizenship is being challenged, undermined, or outflanked by growing world interconnectedness. There are a number of ways that politics have been transformed in line with globalization: for instance, loss of faith in the state and political parties; the fragmentation of older party, class, and national-ethnic senses of belonging; growth of new political actors and the invigoration of global civil society; and the transformation of social democracy and the demise of the communist alternative. At a time in which liberal democracy appears increasingly to be universalized, many people across the globe seem disaffected with party politics and democracy as never before (see Box 3.5). At the same time as the lack of trust in democratic governments has grown, some thinkers point to new information technology as one possible means by which to extend and deepen democracy, when the public sphere appears to be shrinking and Western style democracy can appear ever more shallow and elite-centred.

Box 3.5   Global Crisis of Democracy

In 2002 Gallup International, on behalf of the World Economic Forum, conducted a worldwide public opinion survey of a representative sample of the world population (36,000 people across 47 countries) on the topic of 'Trust in Institutions'. The survey revealed increasing lack of trust of citizens towards their political representatives and institutions. 51 per cent of people in the world exhibited little or no trust in parliaments, and the least trusted institutions were MNCs, parliaments, political parties, and governments. The following tables present additional findings from the survey.

Box 3.5   Global Crisis of Democracy – *continued*

Trust in Parliament/Congress to
Operate in Society's Best Interests

Global Ratings (*n*=34,000 across 46 countries)

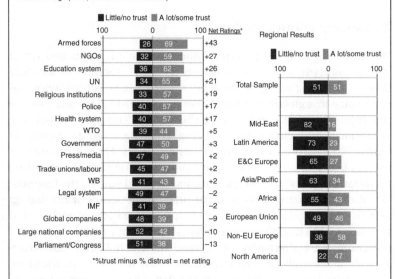

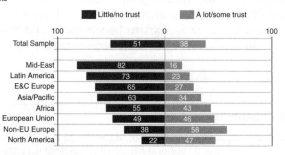

Source: World Economic Forum (2002)

One pervasive argument about the age of globalization and its associated new technologies is, then, that there has been a rearrangement of politics away from political parties and nation-states. We have seen that Castells (2000) maintains that governments no longer have the autonomy to direct economic and social policies, and that one significant result of this has been a withering of the welfare state. This is important, because the welfare state has been a crucial factor in the legitimacy of the modern state. In recent years, though, states have been devolving responsibility to local levels, partly in response to popular demands, partly as a key moment of the neoliberal emphases on anti-statist decentralization, responsibility, and accountability. This devolution further undermines state legitimacy and discourages involvement in national level politics. Many commentators have also noted a generalized post-1968 movement away from the state and from the party system. Since this time, the state has been resonantly criticized as intrusive and authoritarian, and neoliberals are often said to have cashed in on this popular mood for quite undemocratic and elitist ends. From the 1960s, this argument goes, individuals have become more assertive and better informed, more sceptical of intellectuals and experts, and more focussed on qualitative and life-style issues than on the old distributional demands.

The result, some contend, is a withdrawal from liberal democratic politics. Thus voting, in many countries, is low or has declined significantly. This has been viewed by some as a sign of satisfaction, but by others as a signal of disaffection and cynicism. Similarly, in many Western countries – France, Italy, Norway, and the US, for example – membership of political parties is half what it was just 20 years ago (UNDP, 2000). This is often understood as indicative of the neoliberal convergence of the major parties on the political spectrum where the left and the right now tend to meet in the middle, as well as evidence of disgust or sceptical distance from the 'show business' and image-obsessed trajectory of contemporary electoral politics. The Gallup poll referred to above seems to confirm this sense of alienation from electoral politics today.

This trajectory can be read in both optimistic and pessimistic lights. For thinkers positing a movement into a second or reflexive modernity, these changes announce the genesis of a positive new politics. Anthony Giddens (1991: 214), for instance, speaks of the emergence of 'life politics', signalling the growing importance of 'political issues which flow from processes of self-actualization in post-traditional contexts, where globalizing influences intrude deeply into the reflexive project of the self, and conversely where processes of self-realization influence global strategies'. This shift to questions concerning self-identity stands in contrast to the older emancipatory politics, which focussed (and will continue to focus) on freeing groups and individuals from the forms of domination that negatively affect their life chances. In like fashion, Ulrich Beck (1997, 1999) speaks of the advent of 'sub-politics'. This sub-political shift is a function of weakening state structures, loss of faith in hierarchical institutions, growing detraditionalization, awareness of risk, globalization, and mounting individualism. Politics increasingly escapes its conventional boundaries and takes place beyond the confines of the formal political system, where individuals can truly shape politics and a cosmopolitan orientation beckons.

On the other hand, more pessimistic commentators note the rising tide of negative political and social consequences in an emerging 'crisis of democracy'. Castells (2000), for instance, contends that globalization's challenge to the nation state unsettles the idea of citizenship. Meanwhile, communalism around, say, religious, local, or ethnic identity is on the rise (see Chapter 4), and is weakening the solidarity that underpins democratic politics. The resulting 'legitimation crisis' brings decentralization and further state incapacity to respond to citizens' interests and generate legitimacy. Today, says Castells (2000), in the formal political realm 'informational politics' has come to dominate. What this means is that political contestation is increasingly organized around the media. Political marketing, relentless opinion polling, media spinning, personalization, and image management of the kind Tony Blair's New Labour is famous for, have become the new, ever more universal modes in the conduct of politics. This informationalization brings with it, Castells (2000: 337) asserts, the growth of 'scandal politics', the emergence of corruption as an inescapable facet of politics globally. Thus it should come as no surprise that at a moment in which liberal democracy has apparently attained complete victory, we see widespread disaffection, disorientation, and cynicism amongst citizens. Democracy is now but an 'empty shell'. However, Castells finds sources of hope for politics into the future, especially around the regeneration of politics at local levels, greater mobilization around 'non-political' (for example, environmental and humanitarian) causes often linked to NGOs, and in the possibilities presented by new information and communication technologies (ICTs).

We will address below this last set of issues around ICTs, the public sphere, and democracy. First, we will consider a similar account to

Castells', provided by Colin Crouch (2004) who sees the political terrain of our period as demonstrating what he calls 'post-democracy'. As Crouch (2004: 19–20) explains: 'The idea of post-democracy helps us describe situations when boredom, frustration and disillusion have settled in after a democratic moment; when powerful minority interests have become far more active than the mass of ordinary people in making the political system work for them; where political elites have learned to manage and manipulate popular demands; where people have to be persuaded to vote by top-down publicity campaigns'. Here, political rivalries have become more and more 'bland and vapid' (Crouch, 2004: 21); rational dialogue disappears in favour of advertising and personality-based campaigning; and crime and tax cuts become the only real issues. Globalization is important in the arrival of postdemocracy, for Crouch, as capitalism (the firm) and the consumer come to take precedence over politics and citizenship. Class fragmentation is another important and related factor, with parties no longer appealing to interests and programmes, and political action sinking into a mass of causes and lobbies, with most of the successful ones representing the already rich and powerful. For Crouch, Silvio Berlusconi's 'Forza Italia' is an exemplar of this postdemocratic state: a firm rather than a party; not representing any particular interests or identity projects; built on personality rather than programme; media-created and racked with corruption; and driven by private rather than public interests.

Bauman (1999c) offers a comparable analysis of the current malaise of Western politics. This malaise is centrally linked to globalization and to its accompaniment, an increasingly powerless state. It is signalled further by the resignation associated with the neoliberal common sense that 'there is no alternative', and the sense many people have that no-one is in control. In this situation, the public sphere has gone into serious decline. Today, the public space is predominantly a sphere in which private troubles and concerns are displayed. In contrast, the conception of the *agora* from classical antiquity, the civic forum of debate, dialogue, and commerce between citizens where 'private' and 'public' concerns were brought together, provides another path, away from both totalitarian politics and from the effacement of the public sphere as the market, privatization, individualization, and consumption take control. For Bauman, this conception might best be approximated in a reinvigoration of the republican alternative to liberalism. The republican tradition reaches back to classical Rome and to Renaissance Italy, and is based on the notion of a free polity and society emerging from the existence of an active, informed citizenry (not just a voting majority) who participate in self-government and contest any abuses of state power (Pettit, 1997).

For Bauman and others, the contemporary political situation can be measured by its distance from the classical meaning of the term democracy as 'popular rule or sovereignty'. Democracy properly understood entails that people should be suitably informed, responsible, concerned about, and involved with, the governance of their political community – not just cajoled, bribed, and entertained. For Cornelius Castoriadis (1997a, 1997b, 2004), democracy is equated with what he called 'autonomy', meaning the lucid and unrelenting questioning of ourselves and our institutions, leading to a radical awareness that it is we – rather than God, great men or women, or History's unfolding – that are responsible for our institutions and that we might therefore again take them up and alter them.

Often, as with Bauman, this desire to reinvigorate democracy as autonomy places hopes in the regeneration of the public sphere, an issue which chimes in well with the last major consideration of this chapter: the possibility that new information and communication technology might empower people, enhance freedom, and spread democracy and critical deliberation. Frequently, an optimistic connection is made between democratic aspirations and new information and communications technologies. One aspect of this is the way communication technologies can empower those excluded from power. For instance, the beating of Rodney King by officers of the Los Angeles Police Department in 1991 was caught on video, sparking public outrage at discrimination within the force and the legal system (Taylor, 1997). Similarly, in Mexico, the Zapatista revolutionaries utilized the Internet to bypass traditional media outlets, and more directly make their cause known to the world (Castells, 2000). In addition, alternative globalization activists have made use of digital recorders, cell phones, and the internet to inform, mobilize, organize, and train citizens concerned about the deleterious impact of institutions such as the WTO, the IMF, the World Economic Forum, and the G8 (see Chapter 5).

Forty years ago, Robert Dahl argued that, 'Telecommunications can give every citizen the opportunity to place questions of their own on the public agenda and participate in discussions with experts, policy-makers and fellow citizens' (in Alexander and Pal, 1998: 13). Similarly, it is now argued that new information and communication technologies can make democracy more direct, less distant, providing opportunities for the free exchange of information and open debate. In this vein the Internet, in particular, has been seen as providing the possibility of a new public sphere in which citizens will be able to truly contribute and become informed, and within which democracy might be not only reinvigorated and deepened but also extended globally – that is, such technology might be employed so as to get closer to two-way communication and to direct participation in the democratic process, and this democratic process need not be confined to the state level.

Some proponents of the notion of digital or e-democracy are informed by German philosopher Jürgen Habermas's ideas. Habermas, like the first generation of Frankfurt School thinkers, notes the spread in modern societies of instrumental rationality – that is, the use of the most efficient and rational means to reach a desired end. This obsession with getting things done and with efficiency is, in many respects, beneficial, but it also can be distorting in that it can move us away from normative questions of appropriate goals and means. What Habermas refers to as 'communicative rationality', on the other hand, is premised on the notion of an 'ideal speech situation', a situation derived from the very act of trying to communicate in a way that is free from certain distorting influences (such as threats or bribes). For some drawing on Habermas's ideas, the public sphere that emerged with the Enlightenment, and involved people collectively questioning society's organization, might be approximated through the Internet. Lincoln Dahlberg (2001) has distilled what Habermas's theory of the ideal speech situation might entail, in order to analyze claims made for the democratic potential of the Internet. For Dahlberg, such a situation would entail the following sorts of things: autonomy from state and economic power; reflexivity, where people are able to examine their own positions critically; sincerity, in terms of making known all relevant information around a certain problem; and discursive equality and inclusion.

Dahlberg concludes that although a number of e-democracy projects have gone some way to instituting important formal procedures towards such a public space, in general the Internet does not really approximate the vanished or vanishing public sphere Habermas speaks of, since it is increasingly colonized by government and corporate power, and all too often distorted by unreflexive, insincere, irrational, and exclusionary behaviour. Here, Dahlberg sets himself against those who imagine that a mere technological change will solve complex political problems or will create a completely new political culture and set of values. Likewise, Alexander and Pal (1998: 8) suggest that 'technological developments do not automatically enhance our communicative competence', since 'In the "global village" we may be less – not more – communicatively competent. In the Information Era, we may possess a more impoverished, not a more enhanced, understanding of world issues, events, and ideas'.

Conclusion

In this chapter, we have sided with the transformationalists in arguing that, as Castells (2000) puts it, the exclusive link between territory and power has been broken, and that governance has become increasingly, though not fully and evenly, multilayered. The state remains an important actor, but it faces challenges in a way that does involve significant shifts in the exercise of power and the operation of politics. An important part of this is the growth of power of MNCs and markets (as analyzed in the preceding chapter). Another important challenge is new suprastate issues, forces, and institutions, ranging from environmental problems to organizations such as the WTO and the EU. At the same time, the local arena has been the focus of renewed political interest. And there are important signs of an at least morally powerful global civil society emerging, a signal of a more critical and, some would say, more informed citizenry, who are increasingly loath to give their unwavering support to the state or to political parties. Such political tendencies can be read in either pessimistic or optimistic ways. On the one hand, pessimists note the demise of autonomous state paths in the face of powerful elites, and the emptying out of democracy that has resulted. On the other hand, optimists have seen in the movement of politics away from the state and parties, the possibilities of new technology, and a more pluralized tendency in governance a real opportunity for more globally democratic outcomes. Some of these questions will be raised again in the final chapter, which deals with the alternative globalization movement.

Further reading

Brysk, A. and Shafir, G. (eds) *People out of Place: Globalization, Human Rights, and the Citizenship Gap* (London and New York: Routledge, 2004).

Gould, C. C. *Globalizing Democracy and Human Rights* (Cambridge: Cambridge University Press, 2004).

Dunne, T. and Wheeler, N. J. (eds) *Human Rights in Global Politics* (Cambridge: Cambridge University Press, 1999).

Evans, T. *The Politics of Human Rights: A Global Perspective* (London: Pluto Press, 2001).

Held, D. *The Global Covenant* (Cambridge: Polity, 2004).
Keane, J. *Global Civil Society?* (Cambridge: Cambridge University Press, 2003).
Linklater, A. *The Transformation of Political Community: Ethical Foundations of the Post-Westphalian Era* (Cambridge: Polity, 1998).
O'Byrne, D. J. *The Dimensions of Global Citizenship: Political Identity Beyond the Nation-State* (London: Frank Cass, 2003).
Payne, R. A. and Samhat, N. H. *Democratizing Global Politics: Discourse Norms, International Regimes, and Political Community* (Albany: SUNY Press, 2004).
Van Rooy, A. *The Global Legitimacy Game: Civil Society, Globalization, and Protest* (Basingstoke: Palgrave Macmillan, 2004).

4
Cultural Globalization

Introduction

As we have noted in Chapter 2, the contemporary period is often viewed as marked by a 'cultural turn'. Meanings, language, identity, and the proliferation of media are all seen as crucial issues that mark our postmodern, global condition. This cultural turn is signalled by Marxist Fredric Jameson's (2000) claim that today even the economic has become cultural. Clearly, cultural questions are central and pressing in discussions of globalization: as Tomlinson (1999: 1) argues, 'Globalization lies at the heart of modern culture; cultural practices lie at the heart of globalization'.

In the premodern period cultural globalization was most importantly about globalizing religions – Buddhism, Christianity, and Islam. In the modern period, with the Enlightenment and the spread of capitalism, industrialization, and democracy, cultural globalization has been predominantly about the movement of secular ideologies – nationalism, liberalism, socialism – and the diffusion of the values and practices associated with modern science. Today, cultural globalization seems most urgently centred around the impact of the growing volume of exchanges of cultural products, the rising power and visibility of the 'cultural industries', the apparent ubiquity of Western popular culture, and the consequences for identity that flow from these other forces (Held *et al.*, 1999). As a result, the combined effect of contemporary processes of cultural globalization is often understood through the notion of deterritorialization, 'the loss of the "natural" relation of culture to geographical and social territories' (Canclini in Tomlinson, 1999: 107).

We will examine a cluster of issues around cultural production and identity in this chapter. Most importantly, we will explore what Holton

(2000) sees as the three major theses on globalization's cultural consequences: first, the 'homogenization thesis', where globalization amounts to Westernization or, more narrowly, Americanization; second, the 'hybridization thesis', which points to the pervasive global intermixing of cultures that renders obsolete notions of the existence of distinct and pure cultures; and, third, the 'polarization thesis', which views globalization as producing a series of antagonistic fissures between different cultural worlds.

Cultural production and the cultural industries

Cultural goods can be defined as 'those consumer goods that convey ideas, symbols, and ways of life. They inform or entertain, contribute to build identity and influence cultural practices' (UNESCO, 2004). In the last two or three decades, there has been a remarkable growth in the global circulation of cultural goods such as printed matter, radio, crafts and fashions, television, cinema, visual arts, games, and sporting goods. Hesmondhalgh (2002: 232), for instance, refers to the contemporary 'proliferation of texts' and our exposure 'to an unprecedented amount of entertainment and information'. The value of cultural imports and exports increased by nearly six times between 1970 and 1980; and between 1980 and 1998, the level of trade in cultural goods surged to $387.927 million, a fourfold increase (UNESCO, 2004). The global trade in music alone rose from $27 million in 1990 to $38 million in 1998 (UNESCO, 2004). Overall, trade in cultural goods made up 2.8 per cent of all world imports in 1997, up from 2.5 per cent in 1980, and the growth of major copyright industries was rising considerably faster than the growth of the economy as a whole in core countries such as the US, UK, China, Germany, and France (UNESCO, 2004). For some commentators, then, cultural production, formerly the 'side salad' of world commerce, is now becoming the 'beef' (Barber, 1996: 90). One important signal of this growth is that in 1996, cultural products became the largest US export (UNESCO, 2004). The prominence of cultural consumption is also reflected in the high level of household expenditure dedicated to such goods, at least in the North: for example, UNESCO (2004) has estimated that the average French household spends 3.5 per cent of its budget on cultural products.

Both the deregulatory policies from the 1990s and the development and diffusion of information and communication technologies have been important in this growth. For example, with respect to technology, the number of television receivers per thousand inhabitants in the world increased from 57 in 1965, to 113 in 1980, to 243 in 2000 (UNDP, 2004). In addition, there has been a progressive increase in the number of channels available: there was, for instance, a doubling of broadcast programme hours in Western Europe between 1986 and 2000 (Mackay, 2000). Users of the Internet, too, have increased steadily, from 30 million in 1996 to 508.78 million in 2002 (Global Policy Forum, 2003). The speed of this spread is remarkable. It took the Internet only four years to reach 50 million users, compared to 38 years for radio and 13 years for television (Global Policy Forum, 1999).

For some, this new information and communication technology and the growing volume of cultural exchanges mean the possibility, imagined by Marshall McLuhan in the 1960s, of a 'global village'. For McLuhan, the constraints of place are overcome by time: 'Electric circuitry has overthrown the regime of "time" and "space" and pours upon us instantly and continuously the concerns of all other men ... The old Civic, state, and national groupings have become unworkable.... You can't go home again' (in Waters, 1999: 175). The optimistic reading of this thesis has it that new information and communication technology and greater cultural interpenetration will lead to the possibility of enhanced global understanding and harmony. We will see that, for some critical theorists, more likely than a 'global village' what we are witnessing in the realm of cultural globalization is 'global pillage' by the rich and powerful at the expense of an increasingly powerless mass of people.

An important feature of cultural production is the prominence and power of the so-called 'cultural industries'. The cultural industries are usually seen as 'those institutions ... which are most directly involved in the production of social meaning', including advertising and marketing, broadcasting, film, print and electronic publishing, music industries, video and computer games, and other more 'borderline' cases such as fashion, sports, and software (Hesmondhalgh, 2002: 11). The term 'the culture industry' was coined by the critical theorists of the Frankfurt School. During Adorno's and Horkheimer's exile in America, they were struck by the power, reach, and pervasiveness of cultural production diffused by corporations. For them, the industrialization of culture was disastrous. The culture industry foisted a debased and banal culture onto an increasingly passive mass of people, in a one-way communication that reproduced 'the status quo within the mind of the people', having the effect of 'anti-Enlightenment' (Adorno, 1991: 92). People's perception of choice and enjoyment around the products of this industry, they argued, should be treated with scepticism since such perception 'corresponds to the behaviour of the prisoner who loves his cell because he has been left nothing else to love' (Adorno, 1991: 35). Provocatively, Adorno suggested that 'the culture industry is not the art of the consumer but rather the projection of the will of those in control onto their victims' (Adorno, 1991: 160).

For the Frankfurt School theorists the culture industry meant a loss of personal authenticity, a decline in the demand for and appreciation of authentic artwork, a growing inability to imagine other possibilities, and a uniformity of opinion, taste, and behaviour that confirmed Marx's comment that those who controlled the material means of production also controlled the ideological means of production; in other words, the ruling ideas of the age were always the ideas of the ruling class. As Herbert Marcuse (1964: 12) argued, 'the irreversible output of the entertainment and informational industry carry with them prescribed attitudes and habits, certain intellectual and emotional reactions which bind the consumers more or less pleasantly to the producers and, through the latter, to the whole. The products indoctrinate and manipulate; they promote a false consciousness which is immune against falsehood'. Critical thought itself was in peril from such commodified 'affirmative culture', as image and reality became blurred, and dissent was increasingly absorbed.

The term was reworked after the 1960s as 'the cultural industries' to indicate a greater degree of complexity within these industries and to move away from the pervasive pessimism contained in Adorno and Horkheimer's work on the subject (Hesmondhalgh, 2002). Nonetheless, a glance at these cultural industries – condensed in signifiers such as Saathci and Saatchi, Hollywood, Disney, Sony, and Microsoft, for instance – confirms the power and reach they have attained, and it is useful to read this power in a way continuous with the emphases of the Frankfurt School thinkers. Only five Western news agencies, for instance, produce 80 per cent of the world's news. More generally, ten large multinational corporations, including AOL Time Warner, Disney-ABC, General Electric-NBC, Viacom-CBS, News Corporation, Vivendi, and Bertelsmann, control a large part of the production of information and entertainment across the globe (Kellner, 2004). These corporations have huge annual revenues, as evidenced by AOL Time Warner ($36.2 billion), Viacom ($23.4 billion), Bertelsmann ($19.1 billion), and News Corporation ($13.8 billion) (Hesmondhalgh, 2002). Frequently, too, their holdings spread across a range of cultural industries: News

Corporation's holdings, for instance, include Twentieth Century Fox, the US Fox Broadcasting Network, Harper Collins Publishers, 25 magazines, and controlling interests in American, Latin American, British, and Japanese Sky televişion (Mackay, 2000). More generally, while the large organizations within the cultural industries are not the size, say, of the automobile and oil giants, they have become increasingly prominent and, with a wave of mergers and acquisitions through the 1980s and 1990s, fewer corporations dominate larger parts of the market (Hesmondhalgh, 2002).

Ben Bagdikian's (1997) book *The Media Monopoly* puts forward the argument that the sort of concentration of power we now see in mass media is profoundly worrying. Looking at the US media market, and analyzing the number of firms together accounting for over 50 per cent of market share in newspapers, magazines, book publishing, and motion pictures, Bagdikian finds that over time the number of controlling firms has shrunk: from 50 in 1984, to 23 in 1990, to just six in 2000. For Bagdikian, the power of this new 'communications cartel' means unprecedented domination of the distribution and content of cultural production. It also means the capacity to dominate society, given the media's centrality in the way in which we understand and act in the world. This is a situation dangerous to democracy, suggests Bagdikian. The ideology of such corporates is aggressively pro-free market, advertisers are allowed to control the content of media, and only commercial ends matter. Thus, for example, children are viewed merely as a target audience for fast food, clothes, and toys; they are not seen, as they should be, above all as future responsible citizens.

For numerous critics, then, the result of this concentration of power and influence is that much cultural production is of the order of propaganda, subverting the goals of truth, democracy, freedom, equality, and international understanding. In the case of news, for instance, MIT linguist and political activist Noam Chomsky has argued that the misnamed 'free' press in America functions largely as a conduit for propaganda on behalf of the interests of corporate and government elites. Edward Herman and Chomsky's *Manufacturing Consent* (1988) develops a propaganda model of the news industry's workings based on a number of 'filters': 1. the size, concentration, and ownership of the media – many media have interlocking relationships with other industries, affecting, for instance, what and in what ways these other industries are covered; 2. advertising – that is, the main source of funding for media is advertising, and advertisers put pressure on media about the content of the news and other programming they screen; 3. the reliance of the media on government, business, and experts – that is, the media must be careful not to alienate these important sources; 4. flak – that is, the volume of complaints from powerful interests has significant impact on media representations; 5. anti-communism (perhaps, today, anti-Islam) as national ideology. These filters, then, work to produce a certain type of news that distorts people's perception of the world in the interests of the already powerful.

In summary, the argument by many critical theorists is that the size, reach, and concentration of these cultural industries is deleterious to democracy, free expression, authenticity, and justice. A few, very powerful corporations control much of what we see. As corporations, they tend to have little interest in presenting information that does not coincide with their interests as corporations, and cultural production ends up merely promoting a political common sense consonant with the interests of elites. Part of this is the promotion and generalization of a banal culture of consumerism that fosters false needs, generates conformism, and sedates and diverts ordinary people from important issues towards concerns that are trivial.

Globalization as cultural imperialism

As we have noted, the cultural industries have become more powerful and prominent over the last two to three decades. One notable feature of these cultural industries is that the largest come, overwhelmingly, from a small number of countries – most notably, the 'big four': America, the UK, Germany, and France. A particularly important strand of commentary on cultural globalization, which draws on and extends the ideas of Adorno and Horkheimer, is that much cultural production today amounts to *cultural imperialism*. It is to this issue that we now turn.

It is widely believed today that the globalization of culture will lead to greater global understanding. It will make people aware of difference, lead to rich cultural intermixing, and might even reduce the likelihood of cultural misunderstanding and conflict. Some would argue that a new global culture will emerge in the process. This could potentially lead to the demise of specific cultural values and practices, but this is not necessarily to be lamented. On the one hand, those echoing a modernization theory approach might argue that the demise of tradition and the spread of Western-led cultural globalization will lead to a generalization of individualism, choice, freedom, democracy, and greater prosperity. In this vein, some commentators will insist that this does not involve an imposition by the West; rather, those in the less developed countries tend to look towards the West as utopia, and are far from desperate to retain their own cultural values and practices (T. Friedman, 1999). In addition, it is often argued that the distancing from particular traditions that one finds with globalization – that is, the move away from tight senses of belonging and commitment to place-specific forms of life and belief – is probably a good thing. If people were less tightly wedded, say, to nationalism, would that not be a good thing, meaning the lessened likelihood of venomous conflict and resentment (Legrain, 2002)?

In contrast, it is also argued that the crucial feature of contemporary cultural globalization is the diffusion by Western cultural industries of the most vacuous and destructive Western ideas and practices out-wards, leading to the involuntary demise of other cultures. A form of imperialism, then, is the most visible process attached to today's glob-alization in the sphere of culture. This cultural imperialism is defined by Mackay (2000: 48) in the following way: 'Cultural goods flow to the rest of the world, inculcating US or Western values in those in recipi-ent nations. This process prepares the ground for the import of other Western goods'.

The discourse around cultural imperialism began in the 1960s and became popular in the 1970s and 1980s (Tomlinson, 1999; Hesmondhalgh, 2002). This notion is captured by terms such as 'Disneyfication', 'Coca-colonization', and 'Westoxification'. These terms convey that cultural power is not at all evenly distributed but is largely held by the West, or more narrowly, by America. The result of more voluminous global cultural flows, then, will be cultural homoge-nization, a 'world-wide standardization of lifestyles' (Latouche in Tomlinson, 1999: 89).

This homogenization is typically read as something to be lamented, with a convergence towards something like the social order Benjamin Barber (1996) calls McWorld. We will return later to the other side of McWorld – Jihad – but, for Barber, it is McWorld that will eventually emerge triumphant. Barber's (1996: 8) argument is that a 'bloodless economics of profit', a social order he designates 'McWorld', is coming to dominate everywhere. Here, profit making becomes the primary function of social organization and the individual is posited, above all else, as a consumer. As a result, all sense of the collective interest or a common good begins to whither, and citizenship, civil society, and democracy are emptied out.

One of the central planks of McWorld is an increasingly cultural economy centred on services, knowledge, communication, lifestyle, and entertainment. We see a shift in emphasis from 'hard goods aimed at the body' to 'soft technologies aimed at the spirit', what Barber (1996: 60) calls the 'infotainment tele-sector' whose sights are set on the human soul. Those who dominate this sector, says Barber, will be the economic powers of the twenty-first century. One example of this sector is the world of advertising, which has grown enormously since the 1950s. Worldwide, in 1950 $45 billion was spent on advertising; by 1998 the figure was $413 billion, a nine-fold increase and a rate of growth one third faster than the global economy as a whole (Worldwatch, 2005). As a result of such growth, people are exposed to an enormous amount of advertising every day – 254 adverts a day for the average American, for instance (Worldwatch, 2005). This sector, Barber notes, is dominated by America, with American-based organizations heading the list of the top 20 global advertising companies. The reach of such advertising is huge: Saatchi and Saatchi's Pepsi Cola account, for instance, saw the soft drink's images placed in 40 countries, potentially visible to one-fifth of humanity (Barber, 1996).

This expansion of advertising signals the domination of the image within McWorld, says Barber. For him, companies like Nike function more like state religions than sportswear manufacturers in their connection of products with emotions, fantasies, and ways of life. Advertising and marketing function as 'needs factories', generating with incredible rapidity new desires and wants, and attaching these to specific commodities. 'Just Do It' thus functions not only as an advertising slogan, but more significantly as the emblem for a very way of being that drives individuals' perceived needs and desires. For Barber, these wants and desires are increasingly American. American television, film, and music are everywhere. Even when a film is produced outside of America, it is still American, in that it is pervaded by what Barber calls the American 'lifestyle trinity' of sex, violence, and money.

The consequences of McWorld's visualization of culture are particularly unfortunate, Barber contends. Argumentation, patience, and imagination wane, along with the printed word; and instead of informed debate and careful analysis, critical issues are concentrated in simplified and highly politicized images. There is also a tendency for the distinction between advertising and entertainment to collapse – seen, for instance, in MTV, which is little more than one long advert, in Barber's estimation. And the uniformity of product and cultural industry monopoly ('commercial totalitarianism') utterly disconfirm neoliberal claims made about the free market expanding pluralism and choice.

Let us unpack some of these arguments a little further. First, consider Barber's notion that, more and more, people the world over are turning into mindless consumers. The argument developed by some critical theorists is that issues of the common good – addressing poverty or threats to the environment, for instance – are falling from the agenda. In place of older utopias of mutual freedom, equality, and harmony, we have a narrow utopia of individual consumption. In a similar vein, critical theorists have followed Marx in objecting to capitalism's tendency to commodify everything. That is, more and more things – including, in Barber's argument, emotions, feelings, ideas, and imagination – have a price put on them, are commercialized. Such commodification threatens personal authenticity and genuine connections between people, as 'value' is ever more equated exclusively with monetary value. A related aspect of this is the idea that commodities are turned into objects of devotion, that they are fetishized. That is, extraordinary desires and hopes of fulfilment are invested in commodities, and these commodities acquire a magic power that disguises the essential point that it is we, collectively, who have created these products, that these products have no life independent of the persons responsible for their creation. In such fetishism of commodities, then, as Marx (1987) described it, we see alienation, as the creators bow down before their creations.

Box 4.1   Commodification

Commodification refers to the process, identified by Marx, through which social relations are reduced to exchange relations. The most fundamental process of commodification in capitalist society is the labour process, in which the worker not only produces commodities, but becomes a commodity. According to Marx, in the labour process the real, material activity of labour by individual workers is reduced to an abstract value that is sold to those who can use it for the purpose of manufacturing commodities for exchange. In this way, workers themselves possess value only as another commodity to be bought and sold. Commodification also plays an important role in the cultural sphere. This is primarily through what is referred to as 'commodity fetishism', an important theme in Horkheimer and Adorno's *Dialectic of Enlightenment* (1989). According to them, in capitalist society commodities have replaced religion and politics as those things which have assumed a dominant importance in people's lives. Commodities have become fetishized insofar as they are publicly accorded more 'reality' than individuals and social relations themselves, even though commodities are merely inanimate objects. Consequently the cultural industries are able to exploit fetishization in order to evoke desires for goods that are consumable and therefore profitable. With the worldwide spread of neoliberal economics, commodity fetishism has become globalized; literally anything it seems – from international cuisine to 'alternative' music and 'authentic' indigenous arts, crafts and rituals – can be turned into a commodity.

With the advent of Western or American led consumerism and commodification the concern is that we are seeing the arrival of a worldwide monoculture, where global dreams and fantasies revolve around Western or American brands and their associated values and lifestyles – Nike, Coke, McDonald's, Star Wars, Baywatch, Britney Spears, Survivor, Gap, and so forth. Indeed, a survey of the flow of cultural goods goes some way to supporting the cultural imperialism thesis. The flow of cultural products, in other words, is highly uneven. About four-fifths of the exports of cultural products are accounted for by just 12 countries (UNDP, 2004). Exports of printed matter and literature are dominated by the US, Germany, United Kingdom, France, and Italy; exports in music are dominated by Japan, the US, Ireland, Germany, and the UK; in visual arts, the UK, the US, Switzerland, Germany, and France lead; in cinematic, photographic, and radio and television technology the picture is broadened, with the shift of production to countries such as Mexico, China, and Malaysia, along with Japan and the US; and in games and sporting goods, the field is led by China, the US, Japan, Germany, and Italy (Ramsdale, 2000). Overall, the big four – the US, the UK, Germany, and France – have for some time dominated cultural trade, with China more recently becoming part of a new 'big five' (UNESCO, 2004).

Let us survey some supporting data from elsewhere across the cultural industries, where the West clearly dominates. In the film industry, US productions account for about 85 per cent of film audiences worldwide, 35 per cent of industry revenues, and, for most countries, the US is the first or second country of origin of imported films (UNDP, 2004). In the case of the Internet, most Internet traffic is routed through US lines; in 1999, 69 per cent of all the '.com' domains were located in the United States and 77 per cent were located in the US, Canada, and the United Kingdom; and in 1997, 94 of the top 100 web sites were based in the US (Zook, 2001). In terms of transnational television channels, MTV reaches 282 million households, Discovery 222 million, CNBC 180 million, and CNN International 172 million (Chalaby, 2003). And companies such as Bertelsmann Music Group, EMI, the Warner Music Group, Sony, and Universal Music control over 80 per cent of music sales worldwide (Chalaby, 2003).

The globalization of nothing?

An integral part of the cultural imperialism thesis, developed from the Frankfurt School critique of the culture industry, points to the *growing emptiness* of cultural production and consumption. A recent reworking of this contention is George Ritzer's (2004) notion of the 'globalization of nothing'. Ritzer's argument is that *nothing* is becoming an increasingly global phenomenon. Nothing, for Ritzer (2004: 3), refers to phenomena like malls, Gap jeans, scripted employees, and ATMs – that is, 'a social form that is generally centrally conceived, controlled, and comparatively devoid of distinctive substantive content'. This globalization of nothing increasingly results in the loss of something, namely, 'a social form that is generally indigenously conceived, controlled, and comparatively rich in distinctive substantive content' (Ritzer, 2004: 7).

This nothingness is created by and large in the West and, in particular, in America. It involves a number of things: the move from place (relations, history, identity) to non-place; from things to non-things (a Big Mac, for example); from persons to non-persons (say, a McDonald's employee whose interactions with customers is centred on a script); and from services to non-services. Whereas something is unique, embodies local geographical ties, is specific to the times, is humanized and enchanted, nothing is generic, lacks local ties, is timeless, dehumanized and disenchanted.

Against those who see with cultural globalization growing cultural heterogeneity, Ritzer insists that homogeneity is the dominating trend, captured by his concept 'grobalization'. Grobalization, linked to both Marx's and Weber's analyses of modernity, denotes the central motive of growth and the concentrated power of certain nations, corporations, and organizations. In this analysis, the world is becoming more and more the same, social processes are one-way, people are left with little room to pursue alternative ways of life, and commodities and media are key. Grobalization contains three sub-processes: capitalism, McDonaldization, and Americanization. Capitalism is the central process with growing marketization and the collapse of societal alternatives. McDonaldization, as we have noted, is a concept that points to the spread of formal rationality to more and more areas of life. And Americanization is about the way in which the US has become everyone's 'second culture' (Ritzer, 2004: 90). While he recognizes that there are counter trends within globalization that, for instance, bring a globalization of something – his example is a touring exhibition of paintings by Van Gogh – the really important dynamic, notes Ritzer, is the grobalization of nothing. This is so for a number of reasons, including the less sophisticated tastes required in consuming nothing, the lower costs, and the ease of manufacture. There is simply more demand for nothing than something. While there are some positives involved in the spread of nothing – cost, convenience, efficiency – there are significant disadvantages: primarily, that it is harder to identify the local, that rich experiences are lost from the world, that consumption comes to dominate people's identities, and that there will be less room for something in the world.

Interrogating the cultural imperialism thesis

These, in our opinion, are significant and pressing arguments, but there are a number of critical responses to the cultural imperialism thesis that need to be considered. We will now turn to these. The main tenor of these responses is that globalization is issuing in 'hydridization' rather than, or alongside, homogenization.

First, it is often argued that cultural flows are not so straightforwardly one-way as the cultural imperialism thesis would have us believe. For instance, there is the 'world music' phenomenon, offering an example of cultural products travelling the other way – from the South to the North. There has also been the so-called Japanization of work practices accompanying the movement towards postfordism (Cohen and Kennedy, 2000). In terms of food, Legrain (2002) points out that Indian curries, not burgers, are Britain's most popular take-away food. More generally, the example of the internationalization and pluralization of cuisine in the West is surely a good counter to those who fear everyone will be left eating McDonald's and drinking Coca-Cola.

Second, it is important to qualify the argument about global fears of American, or, more broadly, Western domination. As Appadurai (1990: 295) says, 'it is worth noticing that for the people of Irian Jaya, Indonesianization may be more worrisome than Americanization, as Japanization may be for Koreans, Indianization for Sir Lankans, Vietnamesization for the Cambodians, Russianization for the people of Soviet Armenia and the Baltic Republics'. Cultural domination may take many forms – such as the forced assimilation of ethnic minorities – and often occurs on the local, national, and regional levels, not merely the global.

Third, there is evidence that local cultural production continues to be favoured. There are numerous examples here. Domestically produced programming and newspapers typically attract the highest audiences, and US television imports are often used as relatively inexpensive 'fillers' outside of peak screening times (Mackay, 2000; Hesmondhalgh, 2002). MTV was, for instance, forced to alter its programming in Asia to include high levels of local pop music, with one survey revealing that 95 per cent of Thai teenagers preferred Thai to Western popular music (Santana,

2003). In Italy, pizzerias vastly outnumber McDonald's (Legrain, 2002). And American football or baseball have not really travelled beyond North America, in comparison, say, to soccer or Asian martial arts (Legrain, 2002). In this mode, Held and McGrew (2002: 30) argue that 'there is no common global pool of memories; no common global way of thinking; and no "universal history" in and through which people can unite'. The idea here would be that 'global culture' is not really a culture at all, and therefore does not penetrate as deeply in terms of meaning and identity as some have argued (Smith, 1990).

Fourth, and related to some of the above, there is the argument that instead of growing uniformity, we see increasing heterogeneity in the cultural sphere and widespread cultural mixing. Critics making this argument frequently deploy concepts such as glocalization, hybridization, indigenization, and creolization. Here the notion is that new hybrid cultural forms are emerging with globalization. Rather than the replacement of local culture by a single global/Western culture, we see 'selective borrowing and transformation' (Thompson, 1997). For Roland Robertson (1995), globalization is far too complex a beast to be captured accurately by the notion of growing homogenization. The idea of 'glocalization' – a blend of the local and global producing a cultural hybrid – can help us get closer to what is really taking place. For instance, in the spread of nationalism we see both a homogenization of sorts (nationalism as worldwide dynamic) and, at the same time, an important particularism, as each nation seeks to map out its specificity. Similarly, Robertson identifies a globe-wide discourse of locality, community, home, and so on. For Robertson (1995: 35), 'the global is not in and of itself counterposed to the local. Rather, what is often referred to as the local is essentially included within the global'. Globalization links localities, and it also involves the 'invention' of locality. Robertson (1995: 38) contends that 'the overwhelming evidence is that even "cultural messages" which emanate directly from "the USA" are differentially received and interpreted; that "local" groups "absorb" communication from the "centre" in a great variety of ways.... Second ... the major alleged producers of "global culture" ... increasingly tailor their products to a differentiated global market.... Third, there is much to suggest that seemingly "national" symbolic resources are in fact increasingly available for differentiated global interpretation and consumption ... [for instance,] Shakespeare no longer belongs to England'. We will unpack these ideas further.

An example from the field of popular music is offered by Stephen Epstein (2001) in his analysis of Korean punk music. Arguably punk music emerged in Britain in the 1970s as a dramatic expression of youth alienation and social dislocation. The Korean punk scene since the mid-1990s looks and sounds similar in many ways, but Epstein contends that there are significant differences, too. Epstein sees Korean punk as a case study in indigenization. In Korea, the major themes of punk music are freedom, and a response to the stress of middle class educational expectations and difficulties with parents. It is less about overturning society, thus less political in a sense, but it takes up nationalist themes, hoping to create a new place for Korean youth, a new mode of being Korean. Epstein (2001: 385) concludes that, 'Korean youth are maintaining agency and autonomy in the face of the normalizing pressures of school, home and the state on the one hand, and the encroaching influence of global culture on the other'.

Important in these arguments is the way in which critics have troubled the assumption that we know how people are reading this or that cultural product just because they are consuming it. As Tomlinson (1999: 83–4) argues, 'The problem with the cultural imperialism argument is that it merely assumes such a penetration: it makes a leap of inference from the simple presence of cultural goods to the attribution of deeper cultural or ideological effects'. Even if people in the South are consuming cultural products originating from the West, this does not at all entail that they are no longer attached to more long-standing customs, family and religious obligations, or national identifications. As Legrain (2002) argues, we can partake of other cultures without being overwhelmed by the experience. Legrain also makes the laudable point that Left-wing critics should be the first to agree that what we are extends beyond that which we consume.

Crucial, here, is the argument that cultural products can be read and used in a variety of ways: they can mean a whole host of things. Critics of the cultural imperialism thesis will often draw on the notion of the 'active audience' from communication, media, and cultural studies. Here, the creativity and agency of ordinary people is underscored, against a top-down Marxian approach that imagines it can simply reveal the class coordinates and function of a particular cultural product. This approach attempts to get at the micro-dimension of meaning-making, emphasizing complexity, ambivalence, and contestation in cultural production and consumption (Hesmondhalgh, 2002). Part of this is that the cultural industries are perhaps not as unified as is often thought. Popular culture should not be read merely in terms of its function in maintaining the status quo, that is, as ideology or mystification that serves class interests (Barrett, 1991). It should always be read as a potential expression of popular desires and commitments. Thus, the Fox television network, owned by Rupert Murdoch, a political conservative, broadcasts *The Simpsons*, a popular show that is, on many levels, deeply critical of American society and culture (Hesmondhalgh, 2002). More generally, some critics will insist that popular culture is crammed with elements of contestation, and that ideology is precisely not an expression of the ideas of the dominant class (Hesmondhalgh, 2002; Žižek, 1997).

In addition, as Tomlinson (1999: 84) argues, 'Movement between cultural/geographical areas always involves interpenetration, translation, mutation, adaptation, and "indigenization" as the receiving culture brings its own resources to bear, in dialectical fashion, upon "cultural imports"'. An aspect of this movement, backed by empirical cultural studies work, is that people tend to read cultural products in terms of local concerns and interests (Tomlinson, 1997). In this vein, Jan Nederveen Pieterse (2004) insists that cultural and social forms transform as they travel. For him, hybridization is an inescapable feature of our period of 'accelerated globalization'. Today, 'Cultural melange and cosmopolitanism ... is not merely a precious elite experience but a collective condition and experience' (Nederveen Pieterse, 2004: 115).

Nederveen Pieterse (2004) interrogates, too, the very notions of national or ethnic cultures that provide the premises of the cultural imperialism or homogenization argument. A number of critics have argued that the cultural imperialism thesis assumes a unity, purity, and historically unvarying character for culture, or, at least, for non-Western cultures. They will retort that cultures are always divided and contested, changing, and very seldom 'pure', and that the pessimists are romanticizing non-Western cultures. While ours is a period of 'accelerated mixing', Nederveen Pieterse (2004) sees hybridization as deeply rooted in history and as quite ordinary. All nations and traditions, then, share a 'plural heritage'. Thinking about the West and the much discussed Westernization represented by the spread of fast-food outlets, Nederveen Pieterse (2004: 51) argues that 'Fast food may well have originated outside the West, in the street side food stalls of the Middle East, Asia, and Africa. American fast-food restaurants serve German food (hamburgers, frankfurters) with French (fries, dressing) and Italian elements (pizza) in American management style'.

To summarize, it seems clear that the realities of cultural production and consumption are more complex than the cultural imperialism thesis allows. Cultural texts are complex and contested, and they are always appropriated by 'specific individuals who are situated in particular social-historical contexts, and who draw on the resources available to them in order to make sense of media messages and incorporate them into their lives' (Thompson, 1997: 174). On the other hand, a simply celebratory focus on heterogeneity and cultural mixing appears inadequately to ignore the unevenness of power. We must, argues Nederveen Pieterse (2004), attend to the way in which hegemony is reproduced and reconfigured in the process of hybridization. The workings of power and hegemony are perhaps evident in what Tomlinson (1999) argues is a more plausible version of the homogenization argument that focuses on the commodification of an increasing number of cultural practices, a world dominated by the principle of consumerism. On this note, Hesmondhalgh (2002: 238) argues that 'The cultural industries have brought about an unprecedented commercialization of our everyday lives over the past 20 years'. He also points out – despite his emphasis on complexity, ambivalence, and contestation within the cultural industries – that the production of culture is still clearly dominated by a number of core countries, the concentration of power within these industries over the last 20 or so years, and the unevenness of international flows of cultural texts (Mesmondalgh, 2002). Both the homogenization approach that leaves resistance, agency, and complexity out of the equation, and a naïve optimism that neglects questions of uneven power and underscores the purely positive implications of cultural mixing are inadequate. As Featherstone (1990: 2) says, 'The binary logic which seeks to comprehend culture via the mutually exclusive terms homogeneity/heterogeneity, integration/disintegration, unity/diversity, must be discarded'.

Identity and globalization

The concept of identity and related issues of subjectivity are central to much contemporary social analysis, and are closely tied to the concerns raised in the preceding section. Identity is a concept social scientists deploy to understand the connection between our subjective experiences and the contexts (cultural, historical, social) within which we are situated (Woodward, 1999). The concern with identity is again part of the so-called 'cultural turn' which focuses on language, experience, meaning, and symbols, refusing to understand them as merely secondary expressions of more important structural factors. How we view ourselves, what we see as central in what makes us, 'us', and how we see ourselves against others, it is clear, are hardly negligible concerns. These questions do not go away by referring, for instance, to 'objective' class positions. Orthodox Marxist class analysis can be regarded as too unconcerned with what people themselves think and do, determined instead on dropping a rigid theoretical framework on top of and over real experiences and sources of individuation and community.

It can be said that in the period of high modernity or globalization, 'the acquisition and maintenance of identity has become both vital *and* problematic' (Bendle, 2002: 1), that our period entails a 'crisis of identity' (Woodward, 1999). Today, we seem to have moved a long way from the orthodox Marxian assumption that class provides the basic coordinates of identity, and that this class identity would eventually (perhaps inevitably) overcome all other identity claims and commitments. Identity now seems very unstable and fractured, involving numerous shifting factors. Globalization is often seen as fundamental in the apparent urgency of contemporary identity issues: migration changes the composition of community and brings cultural interchange and dislocation; Western culture impinges on smaller traditions and alters them; travel brings people side by side and places are altered through the impact of tourism; the reorganization of the international division of labour and neoliberal restructuring radically change the character of work and work identity; and transformations in the power, reach, and legitimacy of nation-states lead to transformations in identity.

In some accounts, the uncertain world of our global 'risk society' and the effects of de-traditionalization and social flux mean the production of a sense of self that is 'unstable and untrustworthy' (Bendle, 2002: 3). In postmodern work on the subject, identity is socially and culturally constructed 'all the way down' (Woodward, 1999). These theorists reject, then, the notion that there is, at some level, a stable core of selfhood that can be discovered and that would provide a solid ground or guarantee for knowledge or action. There is, the argument goes, nothing *essential* to being, say, an Arab, a woman, or a teenager. Identity, instead, is 'fragmented, multiple and transient' (Bendle, 2002: 5) – it is plastic. This view of identity is often linked to arguments about the growing problematization of knowledge and truth, rising individualism and emphasis on self-realization, increased social mobility, and the questioning and fragmentation of traditions and older hierarchies.

It is often said that these postmodern emphases entail a break with Enlightenment notions of knowledge and of subjectivity. The Enlightenment view of identity and subjectivity is argued to have

---

Box 4.2 Subjectivity and Enlightenment Thought

The question of human subjectivity – in its philosophical, sociological and political dimensions – has been a central concern of critical theorists. In questioning the problem of subjectivity the ideas of many Enlightenment thinkers are of paramount importance, in particular their assumption that rationality is the essence of human being. This assumption was famously advanced by the French rationalist philosopher René Descartes (1596–1650), when he proclaimed *Cogito, ergo sum* ('I think, therefore I am'). For critical theorists, the legacy of Enlightenment conceptions of subjectivity leads not only to an exaggerated view of the powers of human reason, but also to crude dualisms such as mind/body, reason/emotions, and humanity/nature in which the first term is more highly valued than the second. A key figure in the turn towards critique of the notion of the rational subject is the German philosopher Friedrich Nietzsche (1844–1900). Rather than focusing on immaterial mind and pure reason, Nietzsche portrays humans in terms of dynamic drive of unconscious, bodily forces at work in shaping and controlling the world. For Nietzsche, because the relationships of forces are constantly changing, the self is something composed within the conditions of specific circumstances, actions, passions and interests, and from particular interpretations of those conditions. These aspects of Nietzsche's thought were a precursor to the work of the Austrian psychoanalyst Sigmund Freud (1856–1939), whose own ideas about the socio-psychological formation of identity and the complex, 'non-rational', and opaque nature of psychic life had a profound influence on critical theory.

---

been centred on the coherence of identity and on the self-directing, self-knowing individual. Stuart Hall (2001) contends that there have been five major ruptures with these assumptions of stability of self, stability of meaning, and stability of knowledge. First, Marxism challenges the idea of universal essence, as subjectivity is crucially produced by the mode of production in which the actor is situated. Second, psychoanalysis discovers the unconscious (we are split, in Lacanian terms, between the ego and the 'discourse of the Other', the unconscious) against the illusions of subjective wholeness, stability, and self-directedness. Third, feminism contends that sexual difference is central in social organization, and that femininity and masculinity are not timeless and universal categories. Fourth, as Derrida's work emphasizes, the turn to language shows meaning as a function of difference and as inescapably in movement: we can not get at the object directly; there can be no 'I' outside of language; and meaning is inherently unstable. Last, as presented in Foucault's work, subjectivity is a discursive production and thus a function of complexes of power-knowledge.

Zygmunt Bauman's work on identity in the contemporary period is centred on themes such as uncertainty, plasticity, and fragmentation. While identity and meaning in modernity are projects, connoting durability and solidity, the postmodern period sees identities 'adopted and discarded like a change of costume' (Lasch in Bauman, 2001: 478). A new world of uncertainty, speed (a 'continuous present'), and surfaces means that people increasingly avoid fixation and maintain openness in identity terms. Bauman's four postmodern identity figures – the stroller, the vagabond, the tourist, and the player – all signal this new 'liquid' (as he comes to call it) world. Increasingly freed from 'ascribed, inherited and inborn determination of social character' (Bauman, 2001: 474), so that determination is replaced by self-determination, contemporary men and women are forced 'to be constantly on the run ...[promised] no rest and no satisfaction of "arriving" ...; being on the road has become the permanent way of life of the disembedded ... individual' (Bauman, 2001: 476).

A related concern for those thinking about identity today – and this concern also looks back to questions around the cultural industries and the cultural imperialism thesis – is that identity in contemporary times is increasingly centred around a *consuming self*. That is, our patterns of consumption are now ostensibly paramount in defining who we are – at least in the North. Shopping, lifestyle, and conspicuous consumption become the new sources of self-definition (Bauman, 1999a). The problem with this, for critical theorists, is the shallowness, inauthenticity, conformism, atomization, and depoliticization that this tendency is thought to bring. Bauman (1999a) contends that society no longer 'interpellates' its members primarily as producers but first of all as consumers. No more is work the key to identity, social recognition, community, and solidarity. Instead, the model of consumption spreads, say, to politics, meaning that there is nothing outside of the market. Such consumption works not by domination or ideological mobilization but through seduction. And such consumption has quickened, as fashions turn over at great speed and new desires are created, making ours a period of extreme transience, shallow attachments, and intense individualization. We have, here, a culture of forgetting rather than learning, and nothing can be embraced firmly (Bauman, 1999a).

In contrast, some social theorists insist on a more optimistic reading of the prominence of consumption in our period. Anthony Giddens (2003a), for instance, regards 'late modernity' as marked by choice, self-identity, and lifestyle. As habit and tradition retreat, we become more individualized. This can be pathological – for instance, with citizenship subsumed beneath consumption – but it also promises greater autonomy. Giddens insists that consumption is a much less deterministic process than many critical theorists assume. People are reflexive and sceptical, they resist, and their consumption patterns are complex and contradictory. Advertisers, for instance, cannot impose themselves in a straightforward way on people. More generally, we must not overplay the power of corporations, partly because the expansion of reflexivity today provides an important counter to the negative possibilities of consumer culture run amok.

'Defensive identities' and the 'clash of civilizations'

We have considered thus far some of the negative possibilities around identity in a postmodern, globalizing period: a decline in the public sphere and in the possibilities of strong solidarities, a rise in individualist and consumerist social orders. At the same time, this fragmentation and plasticity of identity could be viewed as providing possibilities towards what Castoriadis (1997a, 1997b) calls autonomy – the promise of genuine self-questioning and more inclusive, cosmopolitan politics, as tradition and the boundaries that separate people lose their hold.

On this note, postcolonial thinkers, while hardly uncritically optimistic about the politics of the present, point to some potential gains implicit in questions of identity within the contemporary era. As a theoretical field, postcolonialism has had its biggest impact in the study of literature. However, the big three thinkers of postcolonialism – Edward Said, Gayatri Chakravorty Spivak, and Homi Bhabha – develop concerns that move far beyond the speciality of literature. They employ a constantly global frame of reference for questions they address and, importantly for our discussion, they problematize the simplistic dichotomies typically employed in relation to understanding identity.

Most obviously, as Gandhi (1998) points out, postcolonialism refers to the emergence, especially after the Second World War, of political, social, economic and cultural practices that resisted colonialism and to the establishment of independent nation-states in the so-called third world. Postcolonial thinkers are wrestling with the colonial past as something that crucially marks the present, and they are sceptical about responses that romanticize the colonized or that retreat to essentialist notions of identity. Thus, Spivak (1988) critically interrogates both the colonial fantasy of the civilizing mission of Europe in the colonies and the nativist response that elevates as pure and superior the knowledges and practices of the colonized. Both discourses eradicate the real heterogeneity of those of inferior rank ('subalterns').

In place of Eurocentric ideology, and instead of any essentialist romanticization of the oppressed, postcolonial thinkers have insisted on the importance of others in the constitution of our identity, and on the mix of power, knowledge, and desire that the relationships East/West and colonized/colonizer always involve. Seeing in modern 'objective' accounts of the 'oriental' other the operation of regimes of power-knowledge, postcolonial thinkers also distance themselves, then, from a naïve and dangerous politics of identity – national, ethnic, or religious – which would provide a reactive form of solidarity for those suffering the effects of Western imperialism. Theirs is a cosmopolitan and postnational politics, jettisoning myths of pure origins and the separation of cultures and knowledge. For instance, Said (1993: xxix) contends that identities, cultures, histories, and literatures are inevitably hybrid, that they are overlapping and interdependent: 'Partly because of empire, all cultures are involved in one another; none is single and pure, all are hybrid, heterogeneous, extraordinarily differentiated, and unmonolithic'. Emphasizing tropes of exile, hybridity, in-betweeness, and unhomeliness, postcolonialism practices what Said (1994; 2001) calls 'secular criticism' – a stance always attentive to his dictum, 'never solidarity before criticism'.

Critics of postcolonialism have posited this emphasis on cosmopolitanism and ineradicable hybridity as a discourse expressing the emergence of a new cosmopolitan elite, and as a signal of a new globalized, postfordist capitalism (see, for instance, Dirlik, 1997). Against this criticism, what Nederveen Pieterse (2004) calls the 'accelerated mixing' of our globalizing period does give weight to the postcolonial argument about the impurity of culture and identity, where more and more people are now involved in more than one culture (Featherstone, 1990), generating the sense that 'No one today is purely one thing' (Said, 1993: 407). On the one hand, while enormous numbers of people have migrated at different periods, the numbers of international migrants – people living outside of their country of origin – have grown dramatically in recent decades, from 76 million in 1960, to 154 million in 1990, to 175 million in 2000. On the other, it is often argued that with globalization and its tendencies of uprooting, disjuncture, and metamorphosis, our conditions of life are increasingly scattered, mixed, in movement (Tomlinson, 1999; Gilroy, 1999). The hope here would be that, in identity terms, newer tropes of space, distance, travel, and movement might replace or soften older emphases on rootedness, temporality, and fixity (Gilroy,

1999). The pervasive hybridity of our period, potentially revealing the constructedness of identity might, then, lead in a progressive political direction: 'Hybridity unsettles the introverted concept of culture that underlies romantic nationalism, racism, ethnicism, religious revivalism, civilizational chauvinism, and cultural essentialism' (Nederveen Pieterse, 2004: 82).

Against such political commitments and hopes is the frequently restated argument that rather than a cosmopolitan and pluralistic orientation in matters of identity, the dislocations that globalization brings usher in a new era of rigid and exclusionary commitments to particular identities. Here, progressive political hopes are washed away by a reality that is more accurately characterized by terms and phrases such as 'Lebanonization', 'Balkanization', 'the rise of tribes', or 'the clash of civilizations'. Such phrases point to the broad issue of cultural globalization as marked, most centrally, by *polarization*. In the remainder of the present chapter, we will explore theories of such polarization, utilizing as a framework Castells's (2000) contentions about identity in the information age. Castells, like many others, underscores the plurality of sources of meaning and identity in our period, as well as the decline of tradition. This, though, is viewed as a contradictory and anxiety-provoking situation and not, as Giddens sees it, as an opportunity for profoundly reflexive life-planning (Castells, 2000). What tends to happen, says Castells (2000: 11), is that the search for meaning and identity building takes place in 'the reconstruction of defensive identities around communal principles', rather than on the basis of wider civil or political society. Examining instances of such resistance identities – religious fundamentalism, nationalism, ethnic identity, and territorial identity – Castells (2000: 66) reads them as 'defensive reactions' to challenges such as globalization, networking and flexibility, and the crisis of the patriarchal family, which build havens, rather than heavens, within the new network society: 'When the world becomes too large to be controlled, social actors aim at shrinking it back to their size and reach'. We will now explore three of these 'defensive identities' – nationalism, ethnicity, and fundamentalism.

Nationalism

Ethnicity, nationalism, and religious fundamentalism are articulated in various ways and, especially in the case of ethnicity and national identity, they can be very hard to separate. As Puri (2004: 179) states, 'Both nationalisms and ethnicities are understood as forms of solidarity, shared culture, and shared descent'. Ethnicity is often central in the form and content of nationalism, although ethnic mobilization does not necessarily lead to nationalism (Puri, 2004). Ethnicity is 'a form of collective identity based on shared cultural beliefs and practices, such as language, history, descent and religion' (Puri, 2004: 174). In the social sciences today, 'ethnicity' frequently replaces 'race', because the notion that human beings can be divided into physiologically identifiable and separate racial groupings is viewed as scientifically unsustainable. Just as in the case of sexual difference, social scientists tend to insist that physical differences are of far less significance than the variable meanings leant to them. It is, then, meaning and culture that are underscored. We will set aside the question of ethnicity for the moment – although it will inevitably be invoked in the discussion that follows – and focus on nationalism.

According to Benedict Anderson, nationalism emerged to fill the space left by the decline of religious modes of thought ushered in by the Enlightenment (Gandhi, 1998). The scholarly debate around nationalism is complex and highly contested. For a start, there are important challenges to the periodization of nationalism that oppose 'modernists' such as Anderson who connect nationalism to the advent of modernity – industrialization, uneven capitalist development, problems of modernity, and so on – to so-called 'primordialists' who view contemporary nationalism as built on premodern ethnicities (Puri, 2004). There is also significant debate around whether nationalism comes from above or below, and about the 'carriers' of nationalist sentiment (for instance, intellectuals or the capitalist class). Some insist on distinguishing metropolitan from anti-colonial nationalism (Puri, 2004), and nationalism can variously focus on secession, reclaiming territory from outside of the state's border, elevating the nation, or on reconfiguring the population make up within the territory (Schroeder, 1999; Hutchinson, 1994).

These sorts of difficulties give rise to a variety of definitions – psychological (attachment to symbols and beliefs accenting communality), cultural (a cultural sensibility of sovereignty), and political (rhetorical discourse to unify a nation), for instance (Arnason, 1990: 210). There are a host of complex issues involved here, and we will use the following from Puri (2004: 2) as a working definition: 'nationalism refers to relatively recent beliefs and practices aimed at creating unified but unique communities within a sovereign territory.... Nationalism is seen to unify people and provide a sense of belonging to a community that takes precedence over all else, whether family, or ethnic or local group'. Nationalism is frequently associated with factors such as historic territory, common myths and memories, a mass public culture, shared ancestry, common legal rights and duties, a sense of common purpose, common language, the underscoring of homogeneity, and animosity towards others (Bradshaw and Stenning, 2004; Alter, 1989), though not all of these are evident in the variety of nationalisms one encounters.

Marxists, in particular, have tended to be hostile towards nationalism, seeing it as involving simply the 'invention of tradition', as ideological and irrational like religion, and as a reactionary, Right-wing attachment. For a fervently anti-nationalist Marxist like Rosa Luxemburg (1970), nationalism was merely a mystification that served the interests of the capitalist class, dividing workers and diverting them from acknowledging class as the true global community of interests and destiny. And Marxists imagined a time in which these illusory ties of nation would be replaced by the real community of class. Theorists of globalization, too, have often imagined that increasing world interconnectedness would have a weakening effect on nationalist sentiments: for instance – as the nation-state loses its power, and citizenship becomes more complex; people, ideas, and goods cross borders, diminishing any sense of solid traditions and pure cultures; new communities will form at a distance through new information and communication technology. On the other hand, as Dunaway (2003) observes, there has been, in recent years, a scholarly preoccupation with increasing levels of nationalist and ethnic conflict. Thus, Hechter (2000) remarks on the existence of a virtual epidemic of nationalist violence in recent years; and Castells (2000: 27) asserts that 'The age of globalization is also the age of nationalist resurgence'. Here, we will focus on the reassertion of nationalism in the past 15 or so years evident in the revival of the fortunes of the extreme Right.

It was the startling 27 per cent gained by Jorg Haider's Freedom Party in Austria's 1999 elections (giving the party a place in the coalition government) that really galvanized opinion about the threat of a growing European far-Right. The fortunes of far-Right nationalist parties had been rising in Europe, though, for some time, so that by the end of the 1990s and into the early twenty-first century they appeared to many to be a force to be reckoned with. In 2002, Pim Fortuyn's List received 33 per cent of the vote in Holland, even though its candidates were unrecognized newcomers (collectively getting just 255,000 votes) and, by this time, their charismatic leader had been assassinated (though electors could vote for him, and 1.3 million did) (Roxburgh, 2002). In Italy, meanwhile, Berlusconi's coalition included the 'postfascist' National Alliance (12 per cent of the vote) led by Gianfranco Fini (whose candidates included Mussolini's granddaughter), and Umberto Bossi's Northern League (4 per cent of the vote). It was a similar story in France, where Jean-Marie Le Pen, leader of the National Front, received 16.86 per cent of the vote in the first round of the 2002 elections, beating the socialist Prime Minister Lionel Jospin, and getting 18 per cent (5 million votes) in the run-off with Jacques Chirac. And elsewhere, too, far-Right parties were getting robust and worrying electoral results: in Belgium the nationalist Vlaams Blok received 15 per cent of the vote in 1999, with 26 per cent of the Antwerp voters behind them; the Danish People's Party managed 12 per cent of the vote in 2001; in Norway in 1997, the Progress Party got 14.7 per cent of the national vote; in 2001, the far-Right in Portugal managed 9 per cent; in Switzerland, the anti-immigrant Swiss People's Party came second in the 1999 elections with 22.5 per cent of the vote; in Germany, membership of Right-wing extremist organizations doubled in the decade after 1990, and has been especially marked in the East; and in Britain, the British National Party made gains in the 2001 election, especially in the North, and subsequently won three council seats in Burnley in the local elections of 2002 (*Economist*, 2002; Roxburgh, 2002; *Guardian*, 2004; Merkl, 2003; Davies and Lynch, 2002).

In Australia and New Zealand, Right-wing, anti-immigrant parties – Pauline Hanson's One Nation party and Winston Peters' New Zealand First, respectively – gained high levels of support. In America, David Duke won 44 per cent of the vote in the 1990 Louisiana State House of Representatives election, and Pat Buchanan ran for president in 1992, 1996, and 2000 on an anti-immigration, anti-gay rights, and anti-abortion platform; he finished in fourth place nationwide in 2000 with 449,895 votes, or 0.4 per cent of the popular vote. Following the September 11 attacks, a burst of nationalism swept the US, with 88,000 flags sold by Wal-Mart on September 12 alone and 435,000 subsequent tip-offs to authorities regarding 'un-American activity' (Puri, 2004). In 2003, several Republican members of the US Congress and numerous restaurants across the country renamed French fries as 'freedom fries' as a symbolic assertion of American nationalism in the face of the French government's criticism of the US invasion of Iraq.

Meanwhile, nationalism was widely viewed as on the rise in the former countries of 'really existing socialism'. New laws post-1991 in

Estonia, Latvia, and Lithuania placed pressures on Russians who had arrived there in the period of communism (Roxburgh, 2002). In Russia in 1993, the ultra-nationalist Liberal Democratic Party of Zhirinovsky received 23 per cent of the vote; and, even though it was down to just 6 per cent by 1993, Vladimir Putin's platform was, for some commentators, infused with a similar aggressive nationalism, and nationalist feeling continued to run high (Roxburgh, 2002). In Poland, the anti-Semitic Self-Defence organization registered 21 per cent support in a recent opinion poll; and the Greater Romania Party received nearly 20 per cent of the vote in 1999.

In these countries, anti-Semitism and anti-Roma feelings were often strong, as well as hostility between groupings that had lived side by side with each other under communist regimes. Such nationalist sentiment has been widely connected to post-communist economic collapse ('transitional recessions'), which left one-third of former Eastern bloc nations in 1998 40 per cent or more below their 1989 economic output levels, with high unemployment, non-payment of wages, collapsing benefit systems, high numbers of poor, declining life expectancy and severe stress (Bradshaw and Stenning, 2004; Horschelmann, 2004). Border disputes, struggles over land, and the unfamiliarity with parliamentary democracy have also been seen as playing their part (Davies and Lynch, 2002; Verdery, 1996).

Elsewhere in Europe, the main targets were immigrants, even though anti-Jewish sentiments could be found within some of the parties. Roxburgh (2002) notes that 3.75 million refugees sought asylum in EU countries in the period 1992–2001. And many of these countries have substantial migrant populations: over 4 million in France, 3 million in Germany, and 1.3 million in Britain (Roxburgh, 2002). In Holland, there are reportedly 800,000 Muslims, and 10 per cent of the population is described as being non-Western immigrants (Roxburgh, 2002). Here, leaders such as Pim Fourtyn in Holland and Jurg Haider in Austria insisted that Islam, in particular, was incompatible with their nations' values: for Haider, for instance, 'The social order of Islam is opposed to our Western values. Human rights and democracy are as incompatible with the Muslim religious doctrine as is the equality of women. In Islam, the individual and his free will count for nothing, faith and religious struggle – Jihad, the holy way – for everything' (in Betz, 2003: 84). In some countries, fears of Americanization, loss of national identity with a closer European Union, crime and unemployment (both frequently blamed on immigrants), aspirations among some for independence (Vlaams Blok or the Northern Alliance), and the corruption of and lack of differentiation between the major parties are factors frequently viewed as playing important roles in the rise of the Right.

Thus, globalization has been viewed as centrally implicated in the rise of the far-Right: the collapse of communist alternatives; the shift from corporatist welfare regimes to neoliberal competition states; growing immigration and multiculturalist policies; rising unemployment and more precarious working conditions; the post-political trajectory of mainstream parties under pressure from economic globalization; and 'postmodern' dislocations as coordinates of belief and identity fragment or collapse (Betz, 2003).

There are differing opinions on the seriousness of the threat posed by the far-Right. Certainly, though, the above survey indicates that John Hall (2000) is correct in rejecting the claim that globalization means the straightforward demise of nationalism: as he notes, most polls show national identity is still strong. Rather, Hall suggests, what has disappeared is the link between nationalism and protectionism. That is, few of the far-Right parties hold to the old national socialist agenda of the mid-twentieth century fascist parties, and are often committed to free markets. In a more general sense, this Right-wing nationalist revival is clearly at some distance from the fascism of old, being perhaps better described as an 'exclusionary populism', which is particularly focussed on establishing a more restrictive notion of citizenship (Betz, 2003), though Betz still worries that the far-Right have the potential to undermine openness, solidarity, and historical sensitivity. For Bauman (2002), the picture is ambiguous, with borders under attack and states perhaps no longer able to afford the level of protection of citizens they once did. For other thinkers, the power of the far-Right is already evaporating. Castells's (2000: 31) judgement is that contemporary nationalism tends to be 'more reactive than proactive', providing 'defensive trenches of identity, rather than launching platforms of political sovereignty'.

Ethnicity

Castells (2000: 59) similarly finds today's ethnic mobilizations at some distance from those of days past: 'ethnicity does not provide the basis for communal heavens in the network society, because it is based on primary bonds that lose significance ... according to a new logic of informationalization/globalization of cultures and economies that makes symbolic composites out of blurred identities. Race matters, but it hardly constructs meaning any longer'.

For others, our globalizing period is witness to a massive rise in the mobilization of indigenous minorities and widespread ethnification (J. Friedman, 1999, 2000) that can be characterized as a 'new tribalism' – violent, irrational, threatening. This argument is supported by the following information from the Minorities at Risk Project (quoted in Dunaway, 2003: 4–5):

1. Between 1955 and 1996, there were 239 wars, regime transitions, and genocides in which inter-ethnic conflicts were the causative factors;
2. Between 1980 and 1996, 60 distinct ethnic and religious minorities were victimised in wars and geno/politicides;
3. At the end of the 1990s, there were 275 groups in 116 countries – representing nearly one-fifth of world population – at risk of (a) violent repression from their national governments, (b) initiating open rebellion against a national government controlled by representatives of another ethnic group, or (c) engaging in violent collective action against other groups;
4. At the turn of the twenty-first century, one-quarter of the population of Latin America and the Caribbean and one-third of the population of Africa and the Middle East are at risk of open ethnic conflict.

Along these lines, Friedman (2000) writes of the fragmentation of the former centres of the world system, the reversal of the homogenizing tendencies of nation-state consolidation, and a polarization between elites (who may embrace the ideology of globalization) and locals (who are left with 'lemon nationalism'). Dunaway (2003), on the other hand, contests the idea that ethnic conflict is growing, maintaining that the Cold War period witnessed higher levels of conflict, and that the incidence of ethnic conflict was no higher in the 1990s than it was in the 1980s. For Dunaway, the character of ethnic confrontation has changed too, away from separatist and anti-statist mobilization towards demands for greater shares of state resources and/or increased political participation. Concern with ethnification, with a new tribalism remains a largely Western preoccupation, while outside of the West Aids, nuclear weapons, and environmental change are the more pressing issues. Still, Dunaway does acknowledge the particular significance of such mobilization in terms of the overall stability of the world-system; for instance, since 1954, 60 million people have died in ethnic conflicts, and since 1990, 13–16 million people have been displaced within their countries by such conflict, with 20 million persons pushed across borders (Dunaway, 2003).

The salience of ethnicity and its connection to globalization are often underscored by reference to two particularly brutal conflicts during the 1990s – Yugoslavia and Rwanda. Both conflicts demonstrate Hall's point that 'Cultural identities ... have histories ... but they undergo constant transformation' (in Jackson, 2004: 189), against the predominant tropes around such conflicts that emphasize primordial hostilities and ineradicable differences of culture as central factors. While the civil war and ethnic cleansing that, between 1991 and 1999, tore apart the republics of the former Yugoslavia and resulted in the deaths of approximately 250,000 people (Kaldor, 1999), is central in the discourse around the 'Balkanization' generated or unleashed by globalization, for reasons of space we will focus on the 1994 genocide in Rwanda.

In Rwanda approximately one million people were systematically slaughtered over a one hundred-day period between April and July 1994. In the late nineteenth century, Rwanda was divided into three

---

Box 4.3   Genocide

The term genocide was coined by the Polish jurist Raphael Lemkin in 1944. A combination of the Latin, *cide* (killing) and Greek, *genos* (race or tribe), the term was used by Lemkin to describe any act or attempted act of destruction aimed primarily at a racial, religious, or social grouping as such. In 1946 the United Nations General Assembly (UNGA) described genocide as 'a denial of the right of existence of entire human groups, as homicide is the denial of the right to live of individual human beings'. Lemkin and other scholars and activists assisted in the drafting and passage of the Convention on the Prevention and Punishment of the Crime of Genocide, an international treaty that criminalizes genocide, which was adopted by the UNGA on 9 December 1948. The Genocide Convention has been ratified by 133 states as of November 2005. Article 2 of the Convention defines genocide as follows:

In the present Convention, genocide means any of the following acts committed with intent to destroy, in whole or in part, a national, ethnical, racial or religious group, as such:

(a) Killing members of the group;
(b) Causing serious bodily or mental harm to members of the group;
(c) Deliberately inflicting on the group conditions of life calculated to bring about its physical destruction in whole or in part;
(d) Imposing measures intended to prevent births within the group;
(e) Forcibly transferring children of the group to another group.

groups: the Tutsi (an upper strata of cattle-herders), the Hutu (mostly peasant farmers who formed the largest group), and the Twa (hunter-gatherers who made up less than 1 per cent of the population) (Braeckman, 2001). Hutu and Tutsi shared a religion and language and intermixed and intermarried, despite status divisions (Puri, 2004; Braeckman, 2001). After Belgium replaced Germany as colonial rulers in 1918, extant divisions were reinforced (with European racial typologies employed to demonstrate Tutsi superiority based on their more 'noble', European features), using Tutsi hierarchies and Hutu forced labour (Braeckman, 2001). Tensions boiled over in the late 1950s with violence and a Belgian turn to favour Hutus, who formed a majority government which declared independence in 1962. A subsequent Tutsi (many of whom had moved or been displaced to neighbouring states) invasion from Burundi, was followed by Hutu killings of Tutsi (Braeckman, 2001; Puri, 2004).

The recent killings were initially triggered in 1990 when the Rwanda Patriotic Front (RPF), a Tutsi-led guerrilla army, invaded Northern Rwanda, and the Hutu government of President Juvénal Habyarimana was forced into a power-sharing agreement in 1993 (Braeckman, 2001; Puri, 2004). However, the Habyarimana regime was, between 1990 and 1994, able to buy $83 million worth of arms, through the approval of a structural adjustment programme, at the same time as an economic slump brought on by a crash in tea and coffee prices, a lack of arable land, and increased reliance on international aid (Puri, 2004; Braeckman, 2001). Growing tensions, and numerous warnings of a coming massacre, were ignored by America, Britain, France, Belgium, and the UN Security Council. The genocide's ostensible cause was the death of Habyarimana, whose plane was shot down on 6 April, 1994 as it approached the Kigali airport. Militant Hutus claimed that Tutsi rebels had assassinated Habyarimana and that the assassination prompted the carnage in response. However, it became known that extremist members of the government had already orchestrated a ruthless strategy of genocide in order to eliminate threats to their power which they then systematically implemented on the occasion of Habyarimana's death. The genocide was carried out by security forces and armed militias – most notoriously the *Interhamwe* ('those who attack together') and *Impuzamugambi* ('the single-minded ones') – loyal to the ethnic majority Hutu government. Most of the victims belonged to the minority Tutsi population, but Hutu moderates including Prime Minister Agathe Uwilingiyimana were targeted as well (Power 2002: 329–90; Gourevitch, 1998). International intervention was painfully slow in coming, and by the time it did nearly one million people had been murdered. In addition, Hutus refugees were fleeing the country as the RPF marched across Rwanda: one million into Zaire and Goma in July 1994, 500,000 into Tanzania, 200,000 into Burundi, and 1.7 million displaced within Rwanda itself (Braeckman, 2001).

While this conflict is illustrative of the argument that such ethnic conflict is perhaps supplanting the great power conflicts of the Cold War period, it also reflects the difficulty of conceiving of ethnicity or ethnic identity as something fixed and immutable. Rather, critical theorists tend to point out that ethnicity is a socially constructed phenomenon, subject to manipulation, transformation, and also reification through the complex dynamics of identity politics, as opposed to existing primordially and statically. Consider the fact that in Rwanda, a 'Hutu' could become a 'Tutsi', and vice versa, simply on the basis of a change of socio-economic status. It was only with the introduction of European racialism under colonial rule that ethnic identities in Rwanda assumed a racial connotation and subsequently were treated as invariant. Yet even 'traditional' identities must be viewed critically, since there is inescapable indeterminacy surrounding the ostensible 'origin' of any ethnicity, the scope of its membership, and its status *vis-à-vis* other identities, all of which are mediated through cultural symbols, myths, representations, and socio-economic divisions that are susceptible to constant modification. It is particularly important, in our view, to resist the temptation to understand such conflict as primordial so that it appears the 'destined, natural or inevitable' result of 'ancient hatreds' (Mount, 2000: 154). Such naturalist images and tropes, connoting irrationality and savagery (Mount, 2000), are perhaps more important in illustrating the way in which Western commentators have tended to 'other' those outside the West – seeing identity here as immutable, historical, pure, and barbaric.

What is unique about this form of identity politics, however, is that ethnic claims can be not only voluntarily chosen but, more insidiously, forcibly imposed or treated as a birthright which 'cannot be acquired through conversion or assimilation' (Kaldor, 1999: 77). As Mary Kaldor notes, the demand for political rights based on identity is quite different from political movements seeking power on the basis of exclusivist religious, cultural, or national identities. While the former type of politics accepts values of reciprocity, equal recognition, and shared rights, the latter type 'At best ... involves psychological discrimination against those labelled differently. At worse, it leads to population expulsion and genocide' (Kaldor, 1999: 78). For Kaldor, the new forms of ethnic or identity-based conflict must be understood in connection to globalization, since the processes of globalization are breaking up the old cultural and socio-economic divisions that characterized politics in the modern period and, most importantly, contributing to the disintegration or erosion of many state structures. Where 'old wars' were waged for geopolitical or ideological goals and were territorially based and centralized, in particular through the form of the modern state and its monopoly of organized violence, 'new wars' are waged by inherently exclusive identity-based movements and are decentralized, involving both local and global actors: from privatized paramilitary units, local warlords, and criminal gangs to diaspora communities, international reporters, international NGOs such as Oxfam, *Medécins Sans Frontières* and Human Rights Watch, and international institutions like the United Nations High Commissioner for Refugees, the African Union, and the United Nations itself. Box 4.4 highlights the prevalence of ethnic-based conflict during the post-Cold War period of accelerating globalization.

Box 4.4   Post-Cold War Ethnic Conflicts, 1990–2002

Begin	End	States Involved	Brief Description
1990	1991	Mali	Ethnic violence (Tuareg)
1990	1991	USSR	Sporadic ethnic/communal violence
1990	1994	Rwanda	Ethnic warfare (Tutsis v Hutu regime)
1990	1997	Azerbaijan	Ethnic war (Nagorno-Karabakh)
1990	1997	Niger	Ethnic violence (Azawad and Toubou)
1990	2002+	India	Ethnic war (Kashmiris)
1991	1993	Kenya	Ethnic violence (Kalenjin, Masai, Kikuyu, Luo)
1991	1993	Georgia	Ethnic war (Abkhazians-Ossetians)
1991	1993	Bhutan	Ethnic violence (Drukpas v Nepalese)
1991	1995	Croatia	Ethnic war (Serbs)
1991	1997	Moldova	Ethnic violence (Trans-Dniester Russians)
1991	1999	Senegal	Ethnic violence (Casamance)
1991	2001	Sierra Leone	Civil/Ethnic warfare (RUF/Mende)
1991	2002+	India	Ethnic violence (Hindu v Muslim)
1992	1995	Bosnia	Ethnic war (Serbs, Croats, Muslims)
1992	1996	Zaire	Ethnic violence
1993	1993	Congo-Brazzaville	Ethnic violence
1993	2002+	Burundi	Ethnic warfare (Tutsis against Hutus)
1994	1994	Rwanda	Ethnic violence (Hutus against Tutsis)
1994	1994	Ghana	Ethnic violence
1994	1994	Yemen	Ethnic warfare (south Yemenis)

Box 4.4   Post-Cold War Ethnic Conflicts, 1990–2002 – *continued*

Begin	End	States Involved	Brief Description
1994	1996	Russia	Civil/Ethnic war (Chechnya secession)
1994	1997	Mexico	Ethnic violence (Chiapas)
1994	1998	Rwanda	Ethnic warfare (Hutus v Tutsi regime)
1996	1998	Iraq	Ethnic warfare (Kurds)
1997	2002+	Indonesia	Ethnic violence (Aceh; GAM militants)
1998	1999	Yugoslavia	Ethnic war (Kosovar Albanians)
1998	1998	Georgia	Ethnic warfare (Abkhazia)
1999	1999	Indonesia	Ethnic violence (East Timor independence)
1999	2002+	Indonesia	Ethnic violence (Moluccas; Muslim/ Christian)
1999	2000	Ethiopia	Ethnic war (Oromo separatists)
1999	2002+	Nigeria	Ethnic violence (Delta and northern regions)
1999	2002+	Russia	Ethnic war (Chechen separatists)
2001	2002+	Indonesia	Communal (Dayaks v Madurese immigrants)
2001	2002+	Rwanda	Ethnic war (attacks by Hutu guerrillas)

Source: Adapted from Center for Systemic Peace, http://members.aol.com/ CSPmgm/warlist.htm

Fundamentalism

More than any of the other 'defensive identities' we are considering, fundamentalist religious attachments are viewed, in the West at least, as the greatest threat to global peace, stability, and progress, the other side of the coming together promised by globalization. Defining fundamentalism is a politically charged affair. The *New Fontana Dictionary of Modern Thought* (Bullock and Trombley, 1999) links fundamentalism with the belief in the infallibility of holy books and with the attempt to incorporate religious law into daily practices; while Stuart Sim (2004) offers a broad conceptualization in which fundamentalism involves a lack of tolerance for outsiders and a dislike of dissent, a turn to tradition in a search for security at a moment when authority is breaking down and fragmentation and multiculturalism rule. Sim (2004: 29) contends that, 'What fundamentalism involves above all else is a desire for certainty and for the power to enforce that certainty over others'.

Such fundamentalism is usually linked to religion, and religious fundamentalism is a force in various parts of the world: seen, for instance, in India in Hindu nationalism, with the Bharatiya Janata Party's (BJP's) rise to dominance, and with the brutality in Gujarat in 2002, which left as many as 1,000 Muslims dead; and evident in America since the 1980s, with some estimating that up to a fifth of Americans could be described as fundamentalists (Sim, 2004). However, these examples are generally considered to be less pressing problems than the threat of fundamentalist Islam in the Middle East and elsewhere, especially after the attacks of September 11. As Sayyid (1997) notes, book burning, veiled and oppressed Muslim women, suicide bombers, and inflamed mobs have become stereotypical symbols of Islam, and Islam has become a metaphor for intolerant fundamentalism in general. The threat of Islam is frequently associated with the idea of an emerging clash of cultures or civilizations, as Western humanism, rationalism, liberalism, and democracy battle it out with 'backward'-looking Islam. We will explore this thesis now, before offering some critical analysis of the notion of civilizational war.

A clash of civilizations?

In 1993, the journal *Foreign Affairs* published Samuel Huntington's influential and much debated article 'The Clash of Civilizations'. As Murden (2002) notes, Huntington's contribution represented a 'new pessimism', replacing Francis Fukuyama's triumphal assertion that liberalism was inescapable, and that Islam would, like all other ideological alternatives, wither. This new pessimism saw a shift from the discourse around the notion of an 'end of history', towards one focused on the idea of a new Western-Muslim iron curtain going up (Murden, 2002).

In his article, Huntington claims that world politics is entering a new period. No longer will conflict pivot around ideology or politics as it did for most of the twentieth century, with communism, fascism, and liberal democracy fighting for adherents. Now, he argues, culture and the conflicts between civilizations will be the defining feature of global struggles. Huntington (1993) defines a civilization as 'a cultural entity, the highest grouping of people at the broad level of cultural identity', tied to language, customs, institutions, and self-identification. These civilizations can involve a very large or very small number of people, and they can include several nation-states or just one. Into the future, claims Huntington, the world will be shaped most importantly by the clashes between eight major civilizations: Western, Confucian, Japanese, Islamic, Hindu, Slavic-Orthodox, Latin American, and African.

For Huntington, the differences between civilizations are material and basic, concerning the essence of a person ('what are you?') and therefore much less mutable than, say, class identifications. Different civilizations hold to very different understandings of the relationship between God and man, the individual and the group, and men and women, and differ significantly on the importance of liberty, equality, and authority. Clashes between civilizations increase in likelihood with contemporary processes such as the rise in interactions between people of different civilizations, the growth of economic regionalism, the dislocation of local identities and the related 'unsecularization' of the world (the growth of religious attachments). Huntington's particular concern is the 'battle' between Western and Islamic civilizations. Western ideas and values – democracy, human rights, the rule of law, for instance – have had little impact, he claims, on Islamic civilization, and these widely diverging civilizational values mean conflict and competition. Finally, Huntington proposes some broad principles so that Western victory might be achieved in this civilizational clash: for instance, promoting greater unity between Western nations; limiting the expansion of Confucian and Islamic states, and exploiting conflicts among Confucian and Islamic states; and strengthening international institutions that reflect and legitimate Western interests. The September 11 attacks were widely heralded as confirming Huntington's analysis, and in an article responding to 9/11, Huntington (2001) argued that we had entered the 'age of Muslim wars': 'Muslims fight each other and fight non-Muslims far more often than do peoples of other civilizations'.

As an example of this civilization clash – seen by commentators like Scruton (2002) as particularly troublesome given large Muslim populations in the West – and as a way to move towards a critical interrogation of this notion, we will briefly consider the infamous issue of headscarves (or hijab) in France. The controversy began in 1989 when a school principal in Creil sent home three Muslim girls who wore headscarves in class. A 1989 court ruling forbade 'ostentatious' religious signs that might 'constitute an act of pressure, provocation, proselytism or propaganda' (*Economist*, 2003). The issue subsequently broadened into a national debate, culminating in a Presidential investigation. In February 2004, an overwhelming majority of the French National Assembly voted to formally ban all such religious symbols from public schools, a law effective as of September 2004. Opinion polls suggested a great deal of popular support (around 70 per cent) for the ban (BBC, 2004). The headscarf was viewed by many as an affront to the secularism, to separation of church and state, of the French republic.

A number of issues are involved here. First, part of the concern revolved around the fear of the growing Islamicization of France, a country with Europe's largest Muslim minority (between 3.5 and 5 million people). Some commentators feared the 'binladenization' of city outskirts, with France becoming an outpost of Islamic terrorist activity, and were concerned about the rise of 'communitarianism' – religious and ethnic minorities separating themselves from the idea of the nation as highest entity (Brenner, 2004; Cobb, 2004). Some of this concern has resonances with the positions of Jean Marie Le Pen's National Front, some commentators insisting that Islam rather than religion in general is the object at issue here. Conversely, some on the Left have pointed the blame at Muslims for an escalation in attacks on Jews and synagogues, and to the negative impact of Islamicization on the position of women in France (Brenner, 2004). Life for the so-called 'women of the quarters', Muslim women in poor city outskirts, can be harsh – a repressive home life, forced marriage, and violent reaction to failure to abide by strict religious etiquette (Brenner, 2004). The hijab, in this reading, symbolizes the subjugation of women within Islam (Giddens, 2004).

On the other hand, critics have attacked the 'Islamophobia' and opportunism of the new laws. Emmanuel Terray (2004), for instance, views the issue as an exercise in 'political hysteria', a fictional problem that has come to command attention and substitute for real issues such as unemployment, ghetto schools, educational failure, high imprisonment rates, and discrimination. These latter substantive issues came to the fore during the violent protests that swept across France in October and November 2005, which French President Jacques Chirac characterized as provoked by 'a crisis of meaning, a crisis of identity' (BBC News). It is often said that the 'problem' of the hijab is in reality minute – involving only around 1,200 girls country-wide, in Emmanuel's estimation – and that the laws will have little, or perhaps even a worse effect for the women of these quarters. For Giddens (2004), the issue most crucially expressed in this debate is the battle over femininity, which is no longer automatic and whose meaning is contested. For instance, while the meaning of the hijab may, in some contexts, signify the subjugation of women, it can have other meanings as well – including a feminism resistant to the male sexual gaze and an attachment to political Islam that contains a critique of Western materialism and power politics in the Middle East

(Giddens, 2004). In this vein, Sayyid (1997) asks whether it is not just as controlling of women to force the removal of religious garb as it is to insist they wear it. Meanwhile, philosopher Alain Badiou (2004b) raises crucial issues around female subjugation, the hijab, and secularism in a polemical contribution in *Le Monde*. Badiou points to the perversity of punishing these young women who are said to be oppressed; he sees as morally noxious the criticism of the hijab while, at the same time 'the prostituted female body is everywhere. The most humiliating pornography is universally sold. Advice on sexually exposing bodies lavishes teen magazines day in and day out...the law on the hijab is a pure capitalist law. It orders femininity to be exposed. In other words, having the female body circulate according to the market paradigm is obligatory'. Consequently, he turns the focus of the secularism debate around, asking 'isn't business the real mass religion?. ... Isn't the conspicuous symbol of this degrading religion what we can read on pants, sneakers and t-shirts: Nike, Chevignon, Lacoste.... Isn't it cheaper yet to be a fashion victim at school than God's faithful servant? If I were to aim at hitting a bull's eye here – aiming big – I'd say everyone knows what's needed: a law against brand names' (Badiou, 2004b).

Interrogating the 'clash of civilizations' thesis and Islamophobia

This is a good way in to some critical analysis of the ideas put forward by Huntington. First, a number of commentators have broadened Huntington's comments on clashes of civilizations to move the focus away from Islam. Stuart Sim (2004), for instance, argues that we cannot confine our analysis of the rise of fundamentalism to Islam. Instead, we need to understand that – against the notion of our period as one of secularism and an end to grand narratives – we have entered a fundamentalist world, a 'new dark age of dogma'. Islam, for Sim, is but one of the threatening fundamentalisms on offer today. A congruent alliance of political power and religious fundamentalism is to be found as well in the United States, where George W. Bush espouses his beliefs as a 'born-again' Christian with the same zeal that his administration advocates 'faith-based' policy initiatives and pursues a global war of 'good' against 'evil'. We can also see such dogma at work in 'market fundamentalism', the neoliberal economic doctrines that function as a new secular religion, ignoring the devastating social impact of its policies in favour of pure principles immune from contrary evidence. Similarly, political fundamentalism, from dogmatic Marxism to Fukuyama's triumphant liberalism, is equally evident in our period.

And nationalism – from the far-Right in Europe to the militias in the US – is another dimension of our fundamentalist world.

According to Tariq Ali (2002), the real clash today is a clash of fundamentalisms – on the one side religious fundamentalism, on the other imperial fundamentalism. By far the most dangerous fundamentalism, claims Ali, is American imperialism, 'the mother of all fundamentalisms', the fundamentalism that bears the weight of responsibility for the spread of Islamic fundamentalism. That is, for Ali the unchaining of brutal free market capitalism, the resulting deepening divide between North and South, the paucity of political and economic options for the mass of people, and Western intervention (especially Western support for reactionary Islamic forces as a bulwark against socialism) are together responsible for the rise of bin-Laden style fundamentalism. In a somewhat similar vein, Benjamin Barber (1996) views 'Jihad' – the turn towards communalism and the invocation of the past – as a dialectical response to the consumerist, individualized, homogenous, and shallow McWorld that is coming to dominate everywhere. Jihad is, then, the child of McWorld.

An even more substantial set of criticisms of the clash of civilizations thesis come from scholars who reject the easy dichotomies between the West and Islam/the Middle East. Edward Said was an important postcolonial literary critic and commentator on the politics of the Middle East. For Said (2001), Huntington's 'Clash of Civilizations' thesis is little more than a cynical rehashing of Cold War ideology. Huntington's position is deemed by Said as politically and morally obnoxious, an approach likely to generate more conflict and lead to less inter-civilizational dialogue. The function of Huntington's discourse, argues Said, is tied to the maintenance of the position of Cold War experts after the collapse of communism.

Furthermore, Said (2001) rejects the sweeping statements made about civilizations – for him, these are quite absurd generalizations advanced about one billion Muslims spread across five continents and possessing a wealth of diverse traditions and languages. Said argues, very importantly, that civilizations are never monolithic and closed. Even if Islamism has spread across the Middle East and elsewhere, there is no absence of internal debate and contestation. In addition there is, and has for a long period been, a significant volume of cultural traffic between civilizations, traffic that makes a mockery of Huntington's image of sealed-up civilizational formations.

Said's criticisms of Huntington continue the formers' early scholarly preoccupations with the relationship between the West and the Middle

Box 4.5   Edward Said

Edward Said (1935–2003) was a Palestinian-born literary and cultural critic. As a child, Said lived in both Jerusalem and Cairo before emigrating to the US, where he attended Princeton and Harvard universities. After receiving his PhD he then taught at Columbia, Harvard, Johns Hopkins, and Yale universities. Said is most famous for his critical analysis of 'Orientalism', which he describes as the discursive production of 'the Orient' in Western culture through ethnography, literature, art, and history. For Said, Orientalism depended upon a system of binary oppositions according to which 'the Orient' was constructed as a negative inversion of the West – as that which the West supposedly was not – lending support to Western claims of superiority and authority over the Orient. Said was also a prominent activist in support of the cause of a Palestinian state, yet he always supported democratic, non-violent solutions to the Israeli-Palestinian conflict and was in later years an outspoken democratic critic of Yasser Arafat's Palestinian Authority. In addition to *Orientalism*, Said's other major works include *Culture and Imperialism* (1993), *The Pen and the Sword* (1994), and *Humanism and Democratic Criticism* (2005).

East. The most important of these contributions, *Orientalism*, was first published in 1978, and has been hugely influential across a number of disciplines. In this work, Said insists on the inextricable connections between literature and politics in exploring the discourse of Orientalism, that is, the representation and rhetoric that is tied to Western domination over the territories of the 'less developed' world. Said (1978: 4) insists that 'the Orient is not an inert fact of nature' but instead a social construct, a 'western style for dominating, restructuring, and having authority over the Orient' (Said, 1978: 3). This Orientalism works to separate, and also to create in a set of representations, the Orient and the West through the establishment of a series of binary oppositions. Here, 'The Oriental is irrational, depraved (fallen), childlike, "different"; thus the European is rational, virtuous, mature, "normal"' (Said, 1978: 40). Such binaries are deeply flawed and begin to crumble upon even the most cursory examination of empirical reality. Orientalism, then, for Said (1978: 328) is both an intellectual and a human failure.

For Said, for much of its history, Orientalism is marked by a problematic European attitude towards Islam. In another early work, *Covering Islam* (1981), Said examined Western media representations of Islam, sparked by the Iranian Revolution of 1978–79. This book remains deeply relevant over 20 years later, in its consideration of the politics of representation and the construction of Islam as monolithic, threatening, and backward-looking. Islam is scarcely discussed, insists Said (1981: 23) outside of 'a framework created by passion, prejudice, and political interests'. Today Islam is imagined, in the main, by way of a small number of condensed images – chanting mobs and hostage taking in Iran, book burning and fatwas from the Rushdie affair, terrorism and suicide bombings, veiled women, honour killings, female genital mutilation, September 11, and so on.

How, then, might we better approach Islamism, against these sorts of simplified images and simple-minded dichotomies that imagine it possible to generalize about, say, the 'Islamic mind', 'the Arab street', and the compatibility of Islam and human rights, democracy, or liberalism? The most important work done in this area seeks to understand historically the rise of Islamism, rejecting that it can be viewed simply as a 'return' to older traditions or seen as automatically incompatible with and opposed to modernity.

Islamism really became prominent from the 1970s, and its rise is often tracked by reference to key events such as the Iranian Revolution; the assassination of Egypt's President, Anwar Sadat, in 1981; the emergence of Hezbollah and other groups in Lebanon and of Hamas in the Occupied Territories; and the victory of the Taliban in Afghanistan. In addition, the rise of Islamism is frequently traced to a number of explanatory factors, including: the failure of nationalist secular rulers who were unable to satisfy the hopes and expectations of the mass of people, faced with corrupt, undemocratic, and dependent states, economic failure, and looming structural adjustment; a lack of political participation and a weak civil society; the dislocation of traditional ways of life, with migration and urbanization, cultural fragmentation, and the frustration of both educated and impoverished urban dwellers; and continuing humiliation and anger over Western interference and influence in the region (Sayyid, 1997; Wallerstein, 2003; Castells, 2000).

Bobby Sayyid's *A Fundamental Fear* (1997) argues that the above factors are necessary but not sufficient in understanding the rise of Islamism. Sayyid sees Islamism as a political movement (rather than exclusively as a religious movement) – for instance, in the way it often contains a critique of the current world order – championing the dispossessed, rejecting the culture of consumerism and the interminable Israeli-Palestinian 'Peace Process'. In addition, Islamism cannot be understood as a return to tradition, and as necessarily opposed to modernity: Khomeini's discourse, Sayyid (1997) argues, mobilized people by way of modern means and categories such as revolution, the people, state, and the notion of people as political agents. The rise of Islamism, for Sayyid (1997), is to be understood as linked with the advent of postmodernism, when understood (after Robert Young) as 'European culture's awareness that it is no longer the unquestioned and dominant centre of the world', a discovery following from two world wars and de-colonization efforts (in Sayyid, 1997: 109). Here, Europe's *provincialism* is underscored – the 'West' not as universal but particular – and 'the West' and 'modernity' are disarticulated, with Islamism embracing modernity while rejecting Westernization. No more does the West exist as a hegemonic model of political, economic, and intellectual development.

Critical theorists have, then, consistently accented the modernity of contemporary Islamism, against the pervasive tropes of the barbarism, irrationalism, and anti-modern backwardness represented by Islamic resurgence. As Lechner (2000: 340) says, 'It [fundamentalist religious discourse] actively strives to reorder society; it reasserts the validity of a tradition and uses it in new ways; it operates in a context that sets non-traditional standards; where it does not take decisive control, it reproduces the dilemmas it sets out to resolve; as one active force among others, it affirms the depth of modern pluralism; it takes on the tensions produced by the clash between a universalizing global culture and particular local conditions; it expresses fundamental uncertainty in a crisis setting, not traditional confidence about taken-for-granted truths; by defending God, who formerly needed no defense, it creates and recreates difference as part of a global cultural struggle'. For Lechner (2000: 339) all this indicates that contemporary religious fundamentalism is a modern thing: 'The very reappropriation [of the sacred] is a modern, global phenomenon, part of the shared experience of "creolization"'.

In this vein, Al-Azmeh (1993, 1997, 2003) challenges both the Orientalist discourse about Islam as monolithic and anti-modern, and the discourse of Islamists themselves who view their efforts as a return to purity and authentic, essential Islamic identities. There are, for a start, many Islams, says Al-Azmeh (1993: 1), rejecting the discourse that posits Islam as 'generically closed, utterly exotic, repellently mysterious, utterly exceptionalist'. Drawing on the widespread attention from both Western critics of Islam and Islamicists, to arguments about the 'application' of Islamic law, for instance, Al-Azmeh (1993: 14) argues that 'Calls for "application of Islamic law" have no connection with the Muslim legal tradition built upon multivocality, technical competence and the existence of an executive political authority which controls the legal system. It is a political slogan, not a return to a past reality'.

The 'return' to Islam is therefore not the traditionalism of the past but a traditionalization of the present. Thus Islamism is a product of *modernity*, not of a premodern tradition. It has its origins in the 1920s and 1930s, at the same time as the West was moving rightwards, and is unthinkable without the universally-available discourse of right-wing, populist movements (Al-Azmeh, 1997, 2003). It was then nurtured in the 1950s and 1960s and came to the fore in the late 1970s with economic failure and the collapse of the Keynesian consensus (Al-Azmeh, 1997, 2003). Both the civilizational discourse of Huntington and company, and the 'post-modern delight in the pre-modernity of others' (Al-Azmeh, 2003: 41), with its notions of cultural incommensurability, are to be rejected, because what we have here is a modern movement, which must be seen as deploying the standard tools of structural social scientific explanation:

> The 'return' to Islam is in fact to a place newly created. Its different components are generated from romantic and vitalist ideological elements present in the repertoire of political ideas universally available, no matter how much the rhetoric of identity and of authenticity might deny this; they are socially crafted out of a social material which requires for its understanding a sociology of structural marginality, another of elite competition, as well as a social psychology of middle and upper class youthful radicals in situations of normative schizophrenia and structural closure, not an ethnology of precolonial Arcadia; and last but not least a sociology of subcultures and of cults. (Al-Azmeh, 2003: 35)

Our sympathies, then, to conclude this section, lie with critics of the clash of civilizations thesis. This reading – and readings accenting today's globalization as marked simply by an explosion of nationalism or a 'new tribalism' – of issues around cultural globalization puts forward *polarization* as the crucial dynamic at work within the contemporary period. As Holton (2000: 148) argues, 'The polarization thesis tells a vivid, morally loaded story, easy to translate into one or another version of the struggle between good and bad, sacred and profane, depending on the location of the storyteller in time and space'. The problem is that the story is too simplistic and also perhaps too pessimistic inasmuch as it assumes, with Huntington (1996: 130), that 'it is human to hate'.

Conclusion

As we noted in the introduction to this chapter, despite the amount of ground covered – from the cultural industries, to cultural imperialism, to identity, to nationalism, to the clash of civilizations thesis – the concerns addressed here pivot around interpretations of cultural globalization that variously emphasize homogenization, hybridization, or polarization.

Each of these broad interpretations of globalization's cultural consequences offers compelling, though by themselves incomplete, arguments. In support of arguments about homogenization, for instance, we have the very uneven flow of cultural traffic, the progressive commodification of culture, the almost universal recognition of certain cultural forms and products. Yet the homogenization thesis can appear deaf to the variety of ways in which people read and respond to culture and to the complexity of identity formation and maintenance, to the realities of agency and the significance of the moment of reception, and it is often premised on unconvincing notions of the prior existence of unified and pure cultures.

Hence the argument that underscores hybridization of cultures and identity seems both empirically and ethically compelling. At the same time, when this thesis leaves power out of the equation, or when it universalizes the condition of plasticity of identity, the result is often inanely optimistic and naïve in disregarding the enormous fissures between the plurality of hybrid peoples, flattening the realities of systemic inequalities. There are surely both positive and negative consequences to such hybridization, to the realities of cultural and identity change, dislocation, and recomposition. Here the polarization thesis does some good work, looking at the fragmenting as well as unifying consequences of globalization. Again, though, those holding this position very quickly bend the stick too far – say, in Huntington's clash of civilizations thesis – and are frequently caught in an exceedingly Eurocentric discourse that plays upon representations of the primordial forces at work outside of the North, setting in place rigid binary oppositions between peoples and their cultures.

It seems to us, then, that critical deployment of arguments from each of these positions, allowing each to rub against the others, bringing them into conversation and crisis, is the most productive way to approach questions of cultural globalization. These questions, quite clearly, cannot by resolved, but attempts to reconceptualize and reframe such debates may ensure that at the least we do not become bored with them.

Further reading

AlSayyad, N. and Castells, M. (eds) *Muslim Europe or Euro-Islam: Politics, Culture, and Citizenship in the Age of Globalization* (New York: Lexington Books, 2002).

Appadurai, A. *Modernity at Large: Cultural Dimensions of Globalization* (Minneapolis: University of Minnesota Press, 1998).

Berger, P. L. and Huntington, S. P. (eds) *Many Globalizations: Cultural Diversity in the Contemporary World* (Oxford: Oxford University Press, 2002).

Cowen, T. *Creative Destruction: How Globalization is Changing the World's Cultures* (Princeton: Princeton University Press, 2002).

Cvetkovich, A. and Kellner, D. (eds) *Articulating the Global and the Local: Globalization and Cultural Studies* (Boulder: Westview Press, 1997).

Featherstone, M. *Undoing Culture: Globalization, Postmodernism and Identity* (London: Sage, 1995).

Gunster, S. *Capitalizing on Culture: Critical Theory for Cultural Studies* (Toronto: University of Toronto Press, 2004).

Jameson, F. and Miyoshi, M. (eds) *The Cultures of Globalization* (Durham: Duke University Press, 1998).

UNDP *Human Development Report 2004: Cultural Liberty in Today's Diverse World* (Oxford: Oxford University Press, 2004)

UNESCO *World Culture Report: Cultural Diversity, Conflict and Pluralism* (Paris: UNESCO Publishing, 2000).

5
Resisting Globalization: The Alternative Globalization Movement

Introduction

In Chapter 2, we noted that social scientists regard the study of social change as one of their central vocations. This not only involves delineating and analyzing extant and emerging institutions and processes of social transformation, but also thinking about the role of social movements. In what follows, we will examine a central contemporary social movement – the alternative globalization movement (AGM). This movement has been touted by some as a 'second superpower' announcing the return of people onto the stage of history (Yuen, 2004), and interpreted by others as a threat to the gains of contemporary globalization, and as violent, irrational, and reactive. Much of the preceding chapters have dealt with claims about, and critiques of globalization offered by the alternative globalization movement, but it is important to more closely analyze the movement as a movement. Our discussion of the AGM will range across a variety of issues, debates, dilemmas, organizations, and key figures of what is in truth a complex 'movement of movements'. However, we will emphasize the return of a form of socialist contestation with the AGM, although there are some important points of differentiation between the AGM and socialism. Finally, we address the movement as an important utopian moment within contemporary globalization and, therefore, as the reappearance of utopian 'thinking beyond'.

Social movements

Social movements are vital features in social change. Buechler (2000: 213) defines social movements as 'intentional, collective efforts to transform the social order'. Social movements were not discussed explicitly in the social sciences until the 1960s, in the face of the rise of the civil rights, feminist, and other so-called 'new social movements'. Until this point, what we now view as social movements were analyzed by reference to explanations of collective behaviour (Scott, 2001). These explanations tended to gather social movements together with very different types of collective action such as panics and crowds (Buechler, 2000). This collective behaviour tended to be read as shapeless, as a reaction to stress, as psychological and individualistic, and as irrational and menacing (Buechler, 2000). After the 1960s, there was a shift in the interpretation of these movements, away from collective behaviour theory and towards understandings that focussed on social movements as enduring, patterned, rational, and political (Buechler, 2000).

The most significant early interpretation of social movements was resource mobilization theory (RMT). Social movements were treated by RMT as comparable to other sorts of organizations, interacting with other social movements and with the state (Scott, 2001). RMT asked crucial questions about the resources available to movements, about the organizational features of the movement, about the influence of the state on a movement, and about the possible outcomes of movement mobilization (Mueller, 1992). This orientation is interpreted by Meyer (2002) as an 'outside in' approach, because it analyzed social movements in terms of factors external to the movements themselves.

A prominent theorist of the RMT paradigm is Charles Tilly. Tilly (2004) contends that three elements, in particular, are essential in defining and analyzing social movements. Social movements involve:

1. sustained, co-ordinated public efforts that make collective claims – a combination of identity, programme, and standing (similarities to and differences from other actors) – on target authorities;
2. an array of claim-making performances, such as rallies, petitions, marches, sit-ins, and so forth;
3. and sustained public representations around notions of worthiness, unity, numbers, and commitment.

For Tilly (2004), such social movements are distinctly a product of modernity, emerging in the late eighteenth century in England (in particular) and the US. Central in the emergence of social movements were the following: the 'nationalization of politics, a greatly increased role of special-purpose associations, a decline in the importance of communities as the loci of shared interests, a growing importance of organized capital and organized labour as participants in the power struggle' (in Scott, 2001: 130).

The so-called 'cultural turn' in social theorizing after the 1960s, the rise and evident importance of the 'new social movements', and challenges to Marxism's relegation of these movements to the status of the 'merely cultural' (Butler, 1998) saw social movement theory moving towards an 'inside out' approach, focussing increasingly on the importance of symbols, meanings, discourse, and identity (Meyer, 2002). Thus, the social constructionist paradigm of the 1980s onwards studied social movements in terms of 'framing', exploring the significance of the making of meaning in collective action – the voicing of grievances, the assignation of blame, the development of solutions, and the engagement with tactical and strategic questions (Buechler, 2000) – in contrast to the widely perceived neglect of questions of grievances, ideologies, and collective identity in RMT (Mueller, 1992).

Many commentators on social movement theory believe that, more recently, a tendency towards synthesis is emerging, which is attempting to overcome older dichotomies of structure and culture by looking at the interplay of structure (global, regional, national, and local) along with strategies, actions, and meanings (framing, identity, power relations) (Meyer, 2002; Whittier, 2002; Buechler, 2000).

It seems clear that all the emphases briefly considered here are important in thinking about the AGM: the identification of an opponent; the identification of a group in whose interests the movement struggles; the development of societal and/or institutional alternatives; the resource and identity-constructing possibilities in mobilization; organizational and personnel characteristics; and political opportunities and the part of other forces in the cultural and political field (Scott, 2001). And Scott raises a number of crucial questions that need to be addressed in thinking about any social movement: what social changes does this social movement reflect? What sorts of changes might it bring about? What are the barriers to people's involvement in such a movement? What must the movement do to achieve involvement and pursue its goals?

We cannot attempt answers to all of these questions here, but a few preliminary comments along some relevant dimensions are in order. First, the AGM might be analyzed in terms of changes in class co-ordinates, with neoliberal restructuring and the internationalization and growing power of capital. Conversely, the AGM might be read as a precarious articulation of a wide range of grievances from a variety of actors who are seeking very different types of social change. In this vein, Brooks

(2004) contends that the inclusive and democratic master frame of the movement renders it ineffective as an agent of social change – for instance, by not enabling the exclusion of violent factions. For this reason, analysts might maintain that the AGM will need to establish firmer organizational principles, formulate a coherent programme, and pursue change through recognized political channels. More generally, the possible course of the movement might be affected by a whole range of factors – its ideology, its organizational features, the resources it is able to command, and the institutional context in which it operates (Scott, 2001). In terms of the context of operation, for instance, it might be argued that we have moved decisively away from possibilities that included the seizure of state power (revolution) towards a Gramscian long war of position, a more cultural and informational modality of social transformation (Foran, 2003; Goodwin, 2003).

It might also be argued that the events of September 11 have altered the terrain significantly, with the AGM connected by opponents to terrorism and anti-Americanism, resulting in a 'chilling effect' that is deepened by the post-9/11 enhancement of security and surveillance measures by states leading to what is arguably the 'criminalization of politics' (Panitch, 2002: 24). Some might feel that the movement faces dangers of absorption or incorporation into mainstream decision making institutions (Veltmeyer, 2004). There are, furthermore, a range of potential impacts that the movement might have – for instance, innovations in values (perhaps a general animus towards MNCs), organizational influences on other social movements, further challenges to the power of nation-states, the generation of a 'thicker' global consciousness around a range of issues such as Southern debt, environmental degradation, or pressure towards greater democratization and accountability within transnational institutions. On this last issue, for example, it might be argued that already the AGM has altered the agenda of institutions such as the World Bank and the WTO, who must now at least pay lip-service to issues such as poverty, the environment, and labour rights. This is a mere taste of the kinds of analytical implications social movement theory has for the AGM, and we will take up some of these issues in more detail below.

The emergence and eclipse of the socialist movement

A common emphasis for both enthusiasts and detractors of the AGM is the connection of the movement to socialism. Thus, in the words of Malcolm Wallop, a former US Senator from Wyoming, 'It's necessary to look at the endgame of these anti-globalist groups – a utopian, pollution-free, socialist world – and decide whether to fight for your business or let the radicals destroy it, issue by issue'. In a more positive vein, Bygrave (2002) asks, 'So is "global justice" [the aim of the alternative globalization movement] the socialism that dare not speak its name?' Because of the widespread sense of the resonances between the AGM and the socialist movement, we will in this section discuss, very schematically, the emergence and subsequent decline of socialism as a movement for social change, and in a later section we will analyze continuities and ruptures between these two movements.

It is often argued that the mass of people in Central and Western Europe took their place on the political stage during the revolutions of 1848. After this time, too, mass parties increasingly came to be central factors in political life. Such parties, characterized by ideologies, organizational structures, and characteristic modes of action (Gross, 1974), more and more became the vital feature of political landscapes in developed social orders. 1848 – the year of Marx and Engels's *Communist Manifesto* – is, in addition, seen as a crucial date in the genesis of the socialist movement.

Box 5.1   European Revolutions of 1848

Following the French Revolutionary and Napoleonic Era (1789–1815), the dynastic monarchies of Europe had been restored. However, the ideals of liberalism, constitutionalism, and nationalism were spreading widely and influencing populist challenges to traditional government authority. The years 1845–47 brought extensive famine, economic depression and high unemployment to much of Europe, prompting a radicalization of political attitudes amongst the lower and working classes. By early 1848 growing social unrest spilled over into revolutions across the continent. In France, socialists organized throughout Paris in order to secure the 'right of labour' to every citizen and the King, Louis Philippe, abdicated the throne following riots. In the German states, barricades were raised in a number of cities, including Berlin, to reinforce demands for social liberalization and a new national parliament was formed. In Italy, there were widespread uprisings against Austrian and Spanish rule and calls for national unification. And throughout the Hapsburg domains (Austria, Hungary, and Bohemia) national groups engaged in armed revolt for independence. These revolutionary movements soon collapsed, however, due to a combination of military success by royalist forces, political dealings by moderate reformers, and disagreements between different socialist, nationalist, and liberal groups. Nevertheless, the 'Springtime of the Peoples' led to the introduction of parliamentary governments, constitutional rights, and the extension of suffrage throughout much of Europe, thereby bringing millions of people into political life.

From this point, working class and socialist parties increasingly came to act as important political forces within a number of countries. These parties sought the conquest of state power and, following this, the socialization of the means of production. The most prominent national socialist organization in the late nineteenth and early twentieth centuries was the German Social Democratic Party (SPD), the 'jewel in the crown' of the international socialist movement in this period. Within Germany, the SPD came to form a culture within a culture, a state within a state, with a large membership, a host of prominent public intellectuals, and with cultural and sporting organizations, newspapers, and clubs attached to it (Ryder, 1967).

It is important to make note of the high degree of internationalism within the socialist movement. Marx had been a key organizer within the International Workingmen's Association, the First International (1864–76), which created an alliance of national labour unions and leftist political groups advocating, for instance, the goal of reducing the working day. This internationalism was especially marked in the period of the Second Socialist International (1889–1916). Intellectuals and parties within the various countries had contact with those in other countries, exchanging ideas, writing for each other's papers, and attempting to organize the socialist movement across state borders. This internationalism was clear in the response of the socialist parties to the growing threat of world war, as the big powers strove to extend and maintain their influence in the 'age of imperialism'. These socialist parties insisted, after Marx, that the interests of the working class transcended national borders, and that nationalism was merely bourgeois ideology. Further, because any world war would be a merely capitalist war (a struggle for raw materials, zones of influence, and the creation of new markets and consumers), socialist parties advocated transforming the war into a revolution in every country between workers and capitalists. However, with the outbreak of hostilities the nationalist elements within these parties and the 'war fever' of the period came to the fore and the Second International collapsed. The First World War created a profound crisis for international socialism, and eventually issued in a crucial fissure in the movement.

In Russia, towards the end of the war, the Bolshevik Party led by Vladimir Lenin mobilized the Russian people around slogans such as 'peace, land, and bread' and 'all power to the soviets' and seized power, inaugurating the first communist revolution in history. After this time, the socialist movement was split into radical, communist and more moderate social democratic wings. For many critics, the Russian communists had succeeded only in inaugurating a new form of domination over working people, a society far from the classless, stateless, democratic order imagined by Marx. According to some of these critics, a new class, centred on the party apparatus, had emerged and acted as a capitalist class, effectively owning and controlling the means of production and exploiting and dominating the workers. This new order was regarded by many not as communist but, instead, as 'state capitalist'. Increasingly, the Soviet Union, and other communist regimes formed after the Second World War, became less attractive to those on the Left as societal alternatives to capitalism. In the West, meanwhile, the social democratic parties became ever more moderate, especially after achieving power, promoting what might be called a 'social capitalism' of extensive state involvement in the economy and redistribution policies.

It has been widely argued that the Eastern European revolutions of 1989–91 signalled both the end of really existing socialism and the bankruptcy of social democracy. The communist countries had become increasingly less impressive economically, and there was widespread internal cynicism and dissent against communist rule. Social democracy, on the other hand, had become caught in the crisis of Keynesianism from the 1970s (Pierson, 1995), and the post-1968 critique of the state and party politics. More generally, from this point, socialism appeared to face a number of fundamental challenges: the collapse of faith in economic planning, the state, and political parties; scepticism about the mission of the working class, especially in the face of an alleged fragmentation of that class (with the rise of the middle class) and with the emergence of the 'new social movements'; and the growing prominence of individualism, consumerism, and life-style concerns. As André Gorz (1994: vii) announced, 'As a system, socialism is dead. As a movement and an organized political force, it is on its last legs. All the goals it once pronounced are out of date. The social forces which bear it along are disappearing'. And, in parallel fashion, from the 1970s Marxism as an intellectual force appeared to be in trouble, apparently unable to compete intellectually with new theories that were more subtle and more modest about what human beings could know theoretically and do politically.

Commentary around the crisis of socialism, particularly after the revolutions of 1989–91, has tended to be of the order of Fukuyama's notion of our arrival at the end of history. For Fukuyama (1992), as previously noted, in place of the old ideological battles between capitalism and the socialist alternative, there had emerged a 'remarkable consensus' around free market capitalism in the economic sphere and liberal, representative democracy in the political sphere. The vital point for Fukuyama is that we cannot any longer imagine a world other than the liberal capitalism of the West. Not only was this sort of argument echoed in mainstream media triumphalism around the period of the collapse of communism, but even among the Left many also read the events in a similar way. Thus, Fred Halliday (in Lane, 1996: 189) concluded that the collapse of really existing socialism meant 'nothing less than a defeat for the Communist project as it has been known in the twentieth century and a triumph of the capitalist'.

However, what Holmes (in Outhwaite and Ray, 2005: 120) has called the period of 'happy globalization' – the period of the early 1990s during which globalization was often viewed as a future promising progress, growth, and increasing harmony and equalization – was punctuated by a series of events that cast doubt on the smooth triumph of capitalism and the end of socialist contestation. It is necessary, before turning to what is perhaps socialism's re-emergence in the AGM, to seek some understanding of socialism's apparent eclipse.

According to Immanuel Wallerstein (2003), we are living through a period of transition that has witnessed the disappearance of the trajectories of both the French Revolution (the notions of progress and of the rationality of humanity) and the Russian Revolution (the notions of solidarity and equality). The collapse of this trajectory has brought significant transformations in what Wallerstein calls 'anti-systemic movements'. This term encapsulates the challenges to the world capitalist system by communist, social democratic, and nationalist movements. These movements dominated the politics of social change from the nineteenth century up to the 1970s, sharing a number of features in common: for instance, hoping for fundamental social change yet split about strategic questions; ending up state-focussed and embroiled in debates about reform versus revolution; and all, eventually, becoming embedded in and constrained by the interstate system, upon achieving power. After what Wallerstein calls the 'world revolution of 1968', these anti-systemic movements lost legitimacy, along with the state. Since that time, there has been a so-far-unsuccessful search for a better kind of anti-systemic movement – from third worldism, to the 'new social movements', to human rights organizations – that would lead to a more democratic, egalitarian world.

We would agree with Wallerstein here, but add that what appears to happen from the 1960s is that 'socialist orthodoxy' falls into a profound crisis, economically, politically, and culturally-intellectually. In sum, socialist orthodoxy – in its two modalities of social democracy and Leninism – was a project of state capitalism, a form of capitalism operated by the single party-state. This orthodoxy holds that parties, rather than the mass of people, are the major political movers. These parties are able to represent the subordinate class and, with the aid of that class, take power in order to run capitalism on the basis of the state, developing the forces of production, managing capitalism and seeking to eradicate its problems through planning, and hoping to secure greater wealth and status for the people (see, for instance, Boggs, 1995). This conception of party-led progressive social change increasingly lost legitimacy, and for a time socialism as a whole was implicated in the crisis of socialist orthodoxy. However, there have been other vital currents of socialism that are not implicated in the troubles of social democracy and Leninism (for instance, anarchism and left communism), and it is these currents that appear to be rekindled within the AGM. Thus it is clear that, as Beilharz (1994) notes, socialism has continued to have life, at least at cultural and ethical levels, in the still resonant appeals to social justice, equality, community, and in the elevation of social values over the values of profit making and growth. We will now turn to the emergence of the AGM, looking at the challenges to the 'remarkable consensus' of the postcommunist period and at the movement's affinities with socialism.

The emergence of the alternative globalization movement

The alternative globalization movement has been given many names: the global movement for social justice, the anti-corporate movement, the civil society movement, the global justice movement, the citizens' movement for world democracy, the anti-neoliberal movement, the anti-capitalist movement, and, most prominently, the anti-globalization movement. In particularly, this last label, 'anti-globalization', has been the one that has stuck. We think, however, that 'anti-globalization' is a misleading description, as many within the movement do not oppose globalization *per se*, but the particular version of globalization that currently dominates. Here, many participants would distinguish current 'globalization from above' from a possible and perhaps emerging 'globalization from below'. For this reason, the name 'alternative-globalization' seems a much more accurate and promising starting point.

Although the AGM became clearly visible as an important collective actor in the late 1990s, most spectacularly after the 'battle of Seattle' of 1999, its roots can be traced to a much earlier period. According to Katsiaficas (2004), for instance, the AGM has important origins in the resistance within the developing world to free market structural adjustment policies pushed by the World Bank and the International Monetary Fund since the 1980s. Since 1976, there have been at least 100 protests globally against IMF and World Bank policies (Znet. nd). The origins of the AGM are also often tied to the environmental movement from the 1980s, which drew attention to the way in which the aspirations to economic growth and profitability were casting an increasing shadow over the viability of life on the planet. And environmentalists were widely mobilized in the mid-1990s by prominent WTO rulings against environmental protection measures. Importantly, too, after a long period in which labour organizations were widely viewed as nationalized (functioning as integral features of nation-states), as capital became more internationalized after the 1970s a new labour internationalism grew (Munck, 2002). Thus, organized labour increasingly concerned itself with global issues such as the campaign against apartheid; and during the 1990s, for instance, American organizations the National Labour Committee and Global Exchange coordinated prominent and successful campaigns against corporations such as Gap who were subcontracting to manufacturers in the third world charged with union busting, providing unsafe work environments, and utilizing child and forced labour (Munck, 2002; Anderson *et al.*, 2000).

For Alex Callinicos (2003), the more recent coalescence of the AGM can be traced most centrally to a number of important events and struggles: the North American Free Trade Agreement, NAFTA, beginning in January 1994; the Zapatista rebellion of 1994, sparked, among other things, by NAFTA; the spread of NGOs through the 1990s, many of them contesting the effects of neoliberal restructuring; mobilization around the issue of third world debt; the East Asian crisis of 1997; and instances of large-scale resistance to neoliberalism – for example, the French public sector strikes of 1995, in response to plans for a widespread reform of the welfare system. We will now examine some of these central moments, in the process citing certain organizations and thinkers as a way of drawing out some of the key emphases of the AGM.

The Zapatista movement in Mexico is frequently taken to be an exemplary in terms of the AGM, and has been viewed, in terms of its values, goals, and strategies, as a 'postmodern' political movement (Burbach, 1994). The Zapatista rebellion began on January 1, 1994, the first day of the North American Free Trade Agreement (NAFTA), when 3,000 members of the Zapatista National Army (the EZLN), took control of a number of municipalities in the Southern Mexican state of

Chiapas (Castells, 2000). The Mexican army soon forced the Zapatistas to withdraw into the forest, a ceasefire was declared and a process of negotiation initiated, and since this time there has been a long running stand-off in the region (Cleaver, 1994; Collier and Collier, 2003). This stand-off has left the Zapatistas in control over large areas (autonomous zones), where local life has been organized according to the principle of self-management, and the rebellion has had significant impacts across Mexico – electoral reform, greater recognition of indigenous rights, the invigoration of Mexican civil society, and the decline in the hegemony of the Institutional Revolutionary Party (PRI) (Collier and Collier, 2003).

Most of the Zapatistas are Indian peasants (10 per cent of the Mexican population), and their rebellion has been presented as part of a 500 year struggle against colonization and the marginalization of the indigenous population (Castells, 2000). The more recent roots of the movement are to be found in transformations that have taken place in the region over the past 30 years. Chiapas is a wealthy state, with hydroelectric power production, petroleum exploitation, and corn and coffee production, but about three-quarters of its peoples are malnourished (Burbach, 1994). From the 1970s, there has been an intensification of social polarization in the region, with the growth of the cattle industry, the monopolization of land, the displacement of traditional crops through an increasing orientation of agriculture towards export, and the uprooting of peasants through the building of dams and the search for petroleum (Burbach, 1994). These processes resulted in resistance and violent state responses. For many of these peasants, NAFTA – and the threat of a reduction of subsidies for corn production and the elimination of price protection on coffee – and neoliberal policies in general spelled a 'death sentence' for their livelihoods (Castells, 2000). In Zapatista communiqués neoliberalism is clearly the adversary, with the Zapatistas initiating in 1996 the First Encounter for Humanity and Against Neoliberalism (Marcos, 1996; Seoane and Taddei, 2002). And while the EZLN is fighting for recognition of Indian and peasant rights, there is more than an echo of socialism in their communiqués.

The Zapatistas have proved to be not only popular in Mexico but extraordinarily successful and influential globally. Key here is their communication strategy – Castells (2000), for instance, describes this strategy as the first informational guerrilla movement. When commercial media refused to transmit Zapatista communiqués, dispatches went to Usenet groups around the world (Russell, 2001). There are today over 45,000 Zapatista-related websites in 26 countries, and the

Box 5.2   The Zapatistas and Global/Local Rebellion

The Zapatistas have embraced the creative use of local and transnational electronic media, especially the Internet, in order to disseminate their ideas and objectives and encourage grassroots mobilization. The Zapatistas have thus gained global visibility, reflected in their desire to link local, national, regional and global social struggles, particularly against the combined economic-political forces of neoliberal globalization. Several recent communiqués posted in their website (www.ezlnaldf.org/index.php) clearly express the Zapatista's political ideals:

Sixth Declaration of the Selva Lacandona (II) June 2005–
... And so the capitalism of today is not the same as before, when the rich were content with exploiting the workers in their own countries, but now they are on a path which is called Neoliberal Globalization. This globalization means that they no longer control the workers in one or several countries, but the capitalists are trying to dominate everything all over the world. ... And neoliberalism is the idea that capitalism is free to dominate the entire world, and so tough, you have to resign yourself and conform and not make a fuss, in other words, not rebel. ... But it is not so easy for neoliberal globalization, because the exploited of each country become discontented, and they will not say well, too bad, instead they rebel. And those who remain and who are in the way resist, and they don't allow themselves to be eliminated. And that is why we see, all over the world, those who are being screwed over making resistances, not putting up with it, in other words, they rebel, and not just in one country but wherever they abound. And so, as there is a neoliberal globalization, there is a globalization of rebellion. ... And we see this all over the world, and now our heart learns that we are not alone.

Sixth Declaration of the Selva Lacandona (III) June 2005–
... What we want in the world is to tell all of those who are resisting and fighting in their own ways and in their own countries, that you are not alone, that we, the zapatistas, even though we are very small, are supporting you, and we are going to look at how to help you in your struggles and to speak to you in order to learn, because what we have, in fact, learned is to learn. ... This is our word which we declare: In the world, we are going to join together more with the resistance struggles against neoliberalism and for humanity. And we are going to support, even if it's but little, those struggles. And we are going to exchange, with mutual respect, experiences, histories, ideas, dreams. In Mexico, we are going to travel all over the country, through the ruins left by the neoliberal wars and through those resistances which, entrenched, are flourishing in those ruins. We are going to seek, and to find, those who love these lands and these skies even as much as we do. ...We are going for democracy, liberty and justice for those of us who have been denied it.

writings of the Zapatista's nominal leader, Subcomandante Marcos, are available in at least 14 languages. The Zapatistas were, in this way, able to attract a great deal of attention and bring international journalists and members of NGOs into the region, making it hard for the Mexican government to engage in repressive measures, and bringing into focus issues of political corruption and social exclusion, forcing the government to negotiate (Castells, 2000). In this way the Zapatistas have been able to bring a local struggle to global attention, to reach the centre with their 'peripheral vision' (Russell, 2001). They have very skilfully connected their struggle to those taking place elsewhere, in sentiments such as Marcos's slogan 'we are you': 'Marcos is gay in San Francisco, black in South Africa, an Asian in Europe, an anarchist in Spain, a Palestinian in Israel, a Jew in Germany, a gypsy in Poland, a Mohawk in Quebec, a single woman on the metro at 10 p.m., a peasant without land, an unemployed worker and, of course, a Zapatista in the mountains'. Collier and Collier (2003) conclude that the Zapatistas, despite their meagre resources, have managed to win the media battle.

Despite the importance of the romantic mystique around the persona of Subcomandante Marcos, the Zapatistas are also seen as exemplary in breaking from older socialist emphases on leaders, parties, and socialist organization. A middle class urban intellectual committed to Marxism, Marcos (2001) insists that he was soon forced to abandon his plans to lead the peasants in the region and to abandon the vanguardist ideology of Marxist orthodoxy. Marcos thus denies that he is the leader of the movement, with the EZLN instead taking their orders from the Clandestine Revolutionary Indigenous Committee, which is made up of delegates from the local communities (Irish Mexico Group, 2001). The following quote gives some sense of the radically democratic and decentralizing organizational practice of the Zapatistas – a key matter to which we will return:

> We do not want others, more or less of the right, centre or left, to decide for us. We want to participate directly in the decisions which concern us, to control those who govern us, without regard to their political affiliation, and oblige them to 'rule by obeying'. We do not struggle to take power, we struggle for democracy, liberty, and justice. … It is not our arms which make us radical; it is the new political practice which we propose and in which we are immersed with thousands of men and women in Mexico and the world: the construction of a political practice which does not seek the taking of power but the organization of society. Intellectuals and political

leadership, of all sizes, of the ultraright, of the right, the center, of the left and the ultraleft, national and international criticize our proposal. We are so radical that we do not fit in the parameters of 'modern political science'. We are not bragging ... we are pointing out the facts (in Irish Mexico Group, 2001).

The Brazilian Landless Workers Movement, the MST, also deserves mention here. Sader (2005) notes that because of the extremity of restructuring since the 1980s and ensuing crises in the continent, Latin America has been the main focus for resistance to neoliberalism, with the emergence of Leftist governments and the flowering of social movements. Since the movement began in 1985, the MST have helped over 350,000 families to win titles to over 15 million acres of land, following MST occupations of unused land (MST, 2003; Stedile, 2002). In addition, the MST has helped create literacy programmes, over 60 food co-operatives, and a number of small agricultural industries (MST, 2003). The extreme polarization of wealth in Brazil is a central issue for the MST, and the organization views itself as promoting democracy and protecting the food sovereignty of ordinary people – in their opposition to GM seeds and in their commitment to redistribution – against the neoliberal programme and the interests of international capital (Stedile, 2002).

Sader (2005) points out that many of the social movements that have emerged in Latin America are led by peasants and indigenous people and, more generally, both of these broad social categories have been highly active and visible within the AGM. To take the case of peasants, it is often said that peasants have been neglected or worse by much of the organized Left. Via Campesina is an international farmers organization formed in 1992 in order to fight against neoliberalism and in defence of sustainable agriculture and food sovereignty, that is, the right to produce food on one's own territory. José Bové, a central figure in France's radical farmers' union, the Peasants' Confederation (a member of the Via Campesina coalition), has contested this marginality, and has attained a global reputation as a combative and charismatic defender of peasant interests. Bové has served jail sentences for his roles in the destruction of a McDonald's restaurant and the uprooting of genetically modified crops (Agence France Presse, 2003). Peasants, Bové (2001) argues, are exploited by banks, by companies who buy their produce, and by firms who sell them agricultural products. Bové opposes the dominant intensive farming model, the destruction of local production by dumping, attempts to patent living things, genetic modification, and poor quality food production that is, at present, dominating the world (Bové, 2001). Bové (2001) is particularly critical of the way in which free trade has become globalization's driving force, he insists countries have the right to produce the food they need and desire in the area in which they live, and he views the current period as marked by the dangerous autonomization of the economic at the expense of the political, of regulation, and of the public interest.

We have seen, thus far, that contestation of neoliberalism and concern over the effects of an overriding emphasis on free trade are crucial nodes in AGM discourse. These concerns have since 1999 issued in a number of very significant protests against institutions such as the WTO, the IMF and World Bank, the G8, the World Economic Forum, and against free trade agreements and regional bodies seen as promoting a free trade agenda. As mentioned, a key juncture in the crystallization of the AGM was the 1999 'battle of Seattle', the confrontations that erupted during the WTO's Third Ministerial Conference. During this conference a significantly international and highly variegated protest of between 40,000–50,000 protestors representing over 700 groups forced an early close to the meetings (Steger, 2002). On the first day of the conference, protestors sought to use non-violent direct action to shut down the meeting (Steger, 2002). Police moved in, using tear gas, batons, and rubber bullets, and soon a civil emergency was declared and a curfew imposed. Matters then became more extreme and National Guard units were called in, with over 600 arrests in all (Steger, 2002). Since Seattle, a number of similarly large and sometimes violent contestations have taken place across the world: for instance – February 2000, Davos, Switzerland (WEF); April 2000, Washington (IMF/World Bank); June 2000, Millau (trial of José Bové); May 2000, Chang Mai, Thailand (Asian Development Bank); September 2000, Melbourne, Australia (Asia-Pacific Summit of the WEF); September 2000, Prague (IMF/World Bank); October 2000, Seoul, Korea (Asia-EU Summit); December 2000, Nice, France (EU Summit); April 2001, Quebec City (Free Trade Agreement of the Americas); June 2001, Gothenburg, Sweden (EU Summit); July 2001, Genoa, Italy (G8); March 2002, Barcelona, Spain (EU Summit); September 2002, Washington, USA (IMF/World Bank); September 2003, Cancun, Mexico (WTO); July 2005, Edinburgh, Scotland (G8).

Many of these protests centred on the activities of the WTO, the IMF, and the World Bank. These institutions are seen as pushing the free trade and neoliberal agenda, often viewed as working primarily in the interests of investors and MNCs in the North. Focus on the Global South is a Bangkok-based research, analysis, and advocacy programme focussed on North-South issues (Steger, 2005). Walden Bello is a central figure within this organization, opposing corporate-driven globalization, which he views as increasing poverty and inequality, and oppressive economic and political institutions (Focus, 2005). Much of Bello's analysis of globalization has been focussed on international organizations such as the IMF, World Bank, and WTO. For instance, Bello (2004b: 59) sees the WTO as 'an opaque, unrepresentative and undemocratic organization driven by a free-trade ideology which ... has generated only greater poverty and inequality ...[T]he WTO is not an independent body but a representative of American state and corporate interests'. Bello (2004a) seeks what he calls 'deglobalization', a process of both deconstruction – a drastic reduction of the power of MNCs, the political and military hegemony of states that protect them, the Bretton Woods institutions and the WTO, and greater control of capital movements – and reconstruction – re-empowerment of the local and national, with ordinary people as active participants, within the framework of an alternative system of global governance.

Bello (2004a) is also concerned with the implications of the power of global financial markets, especially in the face of the ruinous impact of the 1997 East Asian financial crisis. ATTAC, an acronym for the Association for the Tobin Tax for the Aid of Citizens, was created in 1998 under the auspices of the French paper *Le Monde Diplomatique* by Barnard Cassen and Ignatio Ramonet, as a response to the Asian Crisis (Tormey, 2004). Originally, ATTAC was a relatively homogenous group (Tormey, 2004), seeking: 'to reconquer space lost by democracy to the sphere of finance; to oppose any new abandonment of national sovereignty on the pretext of the "rights" of investors and merchants; to create a democratic space at the global level' (ATTAC, nd). In ATTAC's view, 'Financial globalization increases economic insecurity and social inequalities. It bypasses and undermines popular decision-making, democratic institutions, and sovereign states responsible for the general interest. In their place, it substitutes a purely speculative logic that expresses nothing more than the interests of MNCs and financial markets'. The original aim was to lobby for the adoption of the so-called 'Tobin Tax', a tax on financial investments that aims to guard against purely speculative and short-term investments that can be profoundly destabilizing to countries. The money brought in by this tax might then be utilized to 'help struggle against social inequalities, promote public education and health in poor countries, and for food security and sustainable development' (ATTAC, nd). ATTAC is today an umbrella organization for a range of groups and individuals, with groups in all EU countries and 80,000 members worldwide (Cassen, 2004). ATTAC's aims have broadened to focus on issues such as cancellation of Southern debt and reform or abolition of the WTO (ATTAC, nd). Cassen (2004: 170) views ATTAC's fundamental aim as an educative one – to 'decontaminate people's minds. Our heads have been stuffed with neoliberalism. ... We have to be able to start thinking freely again, which means believing that something can be done ... it means that we are not condemned to neoliberalism. ... So our task is to persuade the largest number of people possible of the viability of such alternatives, and prepare the ground for a Gramscian hegemony that would allow different policies to be realized'.

ATTAC also played a role in the establishment of the World Social Forum (WSF). The WSF was conceived as a counterweight to the World Economic Forum (WEF). Since 1971, CEOs of large MNCs, political leaders, and academics have met at Davos, Switzerland to chart the global economic agenda under the banner of the WEF. This agenda, critics argue, is one that functions in the interests of elites and at the expense of ordinary people. As a counter to the WEF, the first WSF was held in January 2001 in the city of Porto Alegre, Brazil, and saw the participation of approximately 20,000 people (of whom 4,702 were registered delegates) representing over 500 national and international organizations from more than 100 countries. The second WSF held in January–February 2002 was an even larger event, with 15,000 registered delegates and a total of between 50,000 and 80,000 people from 131 countries. The 2004 WSF gathering in Mumbai, India, attracted 100,000 delegates, and at Porto Alegre in January 2005 – at which the 'Porto Alegre Manifesto' was produced (see below) – nearly 150,000 people took part.

The WSF meetings have been a highly diverse collection of groups, with a wide range of concerns and social alternatives. As Seoane and Taddei (2002: 100) describe the first WSF:

> activist intellectuals and intellectual activists shared ideas on the need to ensure the public character of humankind's goods, shielding them from the logic of the market; the construction of sustainable cities and habitats; the urgency of a fair redistribution of wealth and how to achieve it; the dimensions of the political, economic and military hegemony exercised by the USA and the structure of world power; the continuing validity of the concept of imperialism

and the idea of socialism ...; gender equality; democratization of power; the guaranteed right to information and democratization of the media; the need to regulate international capital movements; the future of the nation-state; and other issues.

Within the WSF, there are those, for example, who contend that a reform of the WTO and the World Bank and IMF is possible, and there are those who believe that reforming them is impossible and that a more basic and systemic change is necessary. There are those who propose dialogue, and others who see confrontation as the only credible option (Hardt, 2002). There were also national liberation tendencies and those who opposed national solutions for democratic, non-sovereign globalization (Hardt, 2002). Despite this diversity, the WSF is centrally contesting neoliberal globalization, and arguing against the undemocratic and unaccountable power of international institutions. In its insistence that 'another world is possible', the WSF is viewed as creating spaces for the discussion of alternatives, for exchanging experiences, and for strengthening alliances between social movements, progressive organizations, and NGOs.

It is already clear that for the large part of those within the movement, current globalization favours financial and commercial elites, at the expense of the mass of people (especially in the South). Implicit here is a critique of the present unaccountable power and practices of MNCs. Not only are these MNCs, as mentioned in Chapter 3, seen as wielding power without accompanying social responsibility – resulting in environmental destruction and violation of labour rights, for instance – but AGM activists also frequently draw attention to issues of privatization and commodification. One of the most prominent alternative globalization writers is Naomi Klein, whose book *No Logo* (2000) became something of an alternative globalization manifesto. In *No Logo*, Klein argues that today, the brand – Coke, McDonald's, Gap, Microsoft, Starbucks – has overtaken the product itself and become emblematic of an entire way of life. That is, Nike, for example, is not simply about sportswear, but is connected to a life-style, to dreams, and to fantasy. Klein sees this tendency as a manifestation of spreading commodification, a process in which a price is put on everything. Beneath the images and fantasies contained in brands are the realities of unaccountable corporate power. For Klein (2002), the corporate-led globalization of the present is associated with the image of the fence: 'barriers created by privatization that separate people from public resources like land and water, and restricting them from crossing borders and voicing dissent'.

Meanwhile, globalization means that vital fences – for example, keeping advertising out of schools – are under attack by corporate forces. According to Klein (2002), 'Every protected public space has been cracked open, only to be re-enclosed by the market', so that the 'fences that protect the public interest seem to be fast disappearing, while the ones that restrict our liberty keep multiplying'. Klein sees the possibility, though, of a reversal of this process in a growing movement of people around the world to 'reclaim the commons':

> People are reclaiming bits of nature and of culture, and saying 'this is going to be public space'. American students are kicking ads out of the classrooms. European environmentalists and ravers are throwing parties at busy intersections. Landless Thai peasants are planting organic vegetables on over-irrigated golf courses. Bolivian workers are reversing the privatization of their water supply. Outfits like Napster have been creating a kind of commons on the internet where kids can swap music with each other, rather than buying it from multinational record companies.

We are at a point now where it is important to summarize some of the diverse issues raised here. First, it needs to be underscored that the AGM is a complex 'movement of movements'. There are a variety of organizations connected to the movement – including prominent groups such as Focus on the Global South, ATTAC, Jubilee 2000/ Movement International, Peoples' Global Action, Global Exchange, Third World Network, and the WSF. Similarly, there are a wide range of concerns and social and institutional alternatives being pursued within the movement. Thus, no tidy map of the AGM can be produced in such a small space. We do think, though, that key concerns can be enumerated here:

- The AGM views its main adversary as neoliberal led globalization.
- This globalization works, in the main, on behalf of commercial and financial elites. In particular, it often functions in the interests of MNCs, who gain greater and greater power and are free of the burden of social concerns. Those within the movement might, for example, call for MNCs to be accountable to public needs and scrutiny (Global Exchange), opposing the 'disembedding' of capital from wider social relations (Kiely, 2004).
- International institutions such as the WTO, IMF, and World Bank are powerful promoters of this form of globalization, and are unde-

mocratic and unaccountable to the majority of people in the world. These organizations need to be either profoundly restructured or abolished.

- In addition, the IMF and World Bank are centrally implicated in the gigantic and devastating debt accumulated by many poorer countries, and have used these debts as leverage to push through neoliberal policies, making these nations even more vulnerable. Cancellation of Southern debt is thus often high on the agenda for those within the AGM.
- More generally, the overweening emphasis on free trade gives far too much autonomy to economic emphases such as growth and profitability. Such autonomization of the economic means that the environment, labour rights, and the issue of poverty, for instance, suffer or are neglected. In this vein, some within the AGM would prioritize 'fair trade' over free trade.
- The obsession with free trade is also leading to spreading and deepening commodification, the opposition to which is captured in the popular slogan, 'the world is not for sale'.
- Neoliberal globalization has particularly iniquitous consequences for certain categories of people – for instance, women or indigenous peoples.
- Global financial markets are dangerously uncontrolled and largely speculative, providing little real benefits to societies or ordinary people.
- Many within the movement view globalization as centrally linked to imperialism and militarism, and seek both greater local/regional/ national self-determination and the dissolution of the military-industrial complex (Callinicos, 2003).
- In the face of the multidimensional impacts of neoliberal-led globalization, the AGM appeals to democracy, to people power, and to 'globalization from below'.

This schematic list should be enough to at least trouble some of the common misrepresentations of the core of the movement, and we will say a word or two about this before moving on. As we have already said, we find the media-imposed label 'anti-globalization' inadequate, given that many participants are clearly not opposed to world interconnectedness *per se*. There is contained in this label, too, and in much of the discourse around the movement, connotations of the AGM as merely reactionary and backward-looking, threatening the immense and supposedly obvious benefits of globalization, and as marginal and perhaps even violent. It is true, for a start, that protests in Seattle and elsewhere have included Right-wing opponents of globalization. Such groupings are typically concerned with issues such as immigration, foreigners controlling national wealth, the activities of footloose corporations, the power of international finance (sometimes connected to the paranoid fantasy of an international Jewish conspiracy), and the threat of 'world government' (Castells, 2000; Steger, 2002). Examples of such Right-wing anti-globalization figures include Pat Buchanan (founder of The American Cause organization) in the US and Jean Marie Le Pen (leader of the National Front political party) in France. We will not focus any further on this brand of the critique of globalization, since it is a minute part of the movement and quite out of step with the major emphases on global justice, democracy, and solidarity within what is clearly a Left-wing movement.

Representations of the AGM have frequently portrayed participants as deluded, marginal, and primitivist. Bhagwati (2002: 2), for instance, argues that 'The opposition [to globalization] stems more from nostalgia and sterile theory than from economic realities'. Along these lines, protesters are often described, for example, as 'causists [sic] and all-purpose agitators', 'the terminally aggrieved', a 'travelling circus' of anarchists, selfish protectionists indifferent to the fate of the world's poor (Bygrave, 2002; Klein, 2002), or, in Thomas Friedman's words, 'a Noah's ark of flat-earth advocates, protectionist trade unions and yuppies looking for the 1960s fix' (in Steger, 2002). More disturbing are recent attempts to link the AGM to anti-Americanism and/or terrorism – for instance, the following from Canada's *National Post*: 'Like terrorists, the anti-globalization movement is disdainful of democratic institutions. ... Terrorism, if not so heinous as what we witnessed last week, has always been part of the protesters' game plan' (in Panitch, 2002: 13). The preceding survey and the discussion that follows should dispel these simplified and highly politicized representations.

Alternative globalization as postmodern socialism?

We have already noted that no exhaustive map of the AGM is feasible. As we have said, the period of 'happy globalization', during which a dominant imaginary posited the final death of socialism, gave way to the clear rise of the AGM and, in our opinion, the emergence of what might be described as a 'postmodern socialism' (Beilharz, 1994, 2005). We will then, at this point, note some of the resonances between socialism broadly and the AGM. We will also consider some central dilemmas within the movement, and, finally, we will comment upon two issues that appear to differentiate this form of socialism from the older socialist orthodoxy.

For a start, a glance at the key concerns of the AGM listed above indicates clear affinities between the AGM and socialism broadly understood. These include: a common cosmopolitanism or at least internationalism; a common opposition to the prioritization and autonomization of the economic; a common concern with the effects of spreading commodification; a common commitment to participation, justice, equality, and democracy; a common concern with imperialism and militarism; and, within sections of both movements, a common emphasis on notions of national or local autonomy and self-determination. Having noted these affinities, there are immediately key nodes of differentiation between the two movements as well. We could, schematically, say that while socialism's adversary is capitalism and it speaks on behalf of those exploited and/or dominated by capitalism – first and foremost, the working class – in the case of the AGM, the principal adversary is, above all, neoliberal globalization, and it speaks on behalf of a plurality of social groups suffering at the hands of this form of globalization.

As a way of exploring this position further, we will now focus on some central dilemmas within the AGM, which in many cases look close to dilemmas within the broad socialist movement. Seoane and Taddei (2002) contend that there are four pressing sets of dimensions of differentiation within the broad AGM. First, there is a debate over tactical questions – non-violent direct action versus more traditional mobilizations. Here, some see the real movement as happening 'on the streets', directly, and are fearful that NGOs are being drawn into the project of global governance by 'integrative participation' (see, for instance, Drainville, 2004; Veltmeyer, 2004). Second, there is the debate between a policy of reform within the system versus a policy of 'rupture' and 'disempowerment'. Third, there is the question of the relationship between social and political dimensions – the relationship, in other words, between the social movements, political parties, and the state. And, fourth, there are questions over the redistribution of wealth – regulatory proposals versus a fundamental questioning of property relations. We could add some further dilemmas to this list: fifth, a question about the site of resistance and alternative institution-building – proposals that prioritize the local versus those that accent the global; sixth, a differentiation with respect to the vision of a future order, which is, on the one side, local, small-scale, less technologically-driven versus more industrializing and modernizing visions of societal/global alternatives; seventh, there are interpretative questions about the centre of gravity of the AGM – the South as the pivotal part of the movement (for instance, Bello, 2004a) versus the North (see, for instance, Buttel and Gould, 2004).

Not all of these dilemmas can be addressed here. What we want to do instead is focus more closely on the question of the resonances between alternative globalization and socialism around questions of reform versus revolution and at modes of organizing and new modalities of action within the movement.

First, then, the question of reform versus revolution. This is broadly a question of how to achieve significant social change: can we work within the system, reorienting institutions to address problems of contemporary globalization, or is a more fundamental rupture required? This question seems to repeat a crucial problem formulated within the classical socialist movement and a central division between the social democrats and the communists. To see how this issue plays itself out within the AGM, we will compare attempts to reinvigorate social democracy as a response to globalization with the more radical alternatives presented by Hardt and Negri.

Anthony Giddens's (2000, 2003b) notion of the 'third way' reinvigoration of social democracy has been widely influential – for instance, on British Prime Minister Tony Blair – and much debated. It is also crucially linked to globalization (as well as other issues such as growing individualism and risk). Giddens argues that socialism's economic programme has now been discredited, and we cannot get beyond the need for free markets. However, he also insists that neoliberalism cannot adequately deal with the urgent issues that we face today. Giddens reads globalization as a potentially emancipatory matrix – for instance, in the democratizing trends of new information and communication technology and in the invigoration of a cosmopolitan public sphere (Lewandowski, 2003). Here, the third way puts emphasis on new orientations such as an active civil society in partnership with government, a mixed economy, positive welfare, a social investment state, equality with diversity, and equality as inclusion. The nation-state remains important as a stabilizing force against fragmentation but, in addition, new cosmopolitan institutions are required for the regulation of the world economy and for the control of ecological risks and global inequality.

David Held provides a more detailed analysis of the tasks facing a reinvigorated social democracy, promoting a cosmopolitan or global social democracy. Cosmopolitanism, as we saw in Chapter 4, imagines citizenship as potentially extended to world citizenship, as opposed to an internationalism that begins with states and then seeks the formation of an international society of states (Archibugi, 2002). States remain important, for Held (2003), but sovereignty is being reshaped, for instance, by the emergence of global civil society. And the global problems we collectively face call for collaborative, global action. Because the radical alternative globalization position tends to be oriented to the local, it is insufficient to deal with deepening and expanding world interconnectedness. Therefore, social democracy's essential values, Held (2003) argues, remain a crucial set of foundations – the rule of law, political equality, democratic politics, social justice, social solidarity and community, and economic efficiency – which can and must be extended globally. Reform, Held contends, is the best way to proceed because we are not starting from scratch: we can build on the achievements of multilateralism and the spread of cosmopolitan values, such as human rights, since 1945 (Held and McGrew, 2002). In this vein, Held's suggestions include: reform of the UN Security Council; the establishment of global institutions to deal with poverty and welfare as counterweights to institutions such as the WTO and the IMF; the clear rule of law in international relations; greater roles for developing countries in global financial regulation; and the reduction of debt burdens and increasing aid for developing nations (Held, 2003). Held's overall aims are for greater transparency, accountability, and democracy in global governance, greater equity in global economic distribution, and the provision of global public goods (Held and McGrew, 2002).

In contrast, the more radical strands of the AGM would reject the likelihood or benefit of such ameliorative strategies and would view the third way platform as far too much of a concession to neoliberalism. Tormey (2004) notes that these radicals in the movement are made up of Marxists, libertarian Marxists, autonomists, anarchists, and radical environmentalists. These currents, especially the libertarian Marxists, autonomists, and anarchists, Tormey (2004) argues, tend to share the following goals: the repoliticization of economic affairs, the reempowerment of people, the relocalization of power, and the repopularization of decision making. In order to illustrate the more radical strand of the AGM we will focus on the work of Antonio Negri and Michael Hardt, which emerges from the tradition of autonomism.

We have already examined, in Chapter 4, Hardt and Negri's (2000) analysis of the transformation in sovereignty towards what they call

Empire. The other side of that transformation, for them, is a new revolutionary subject, what they refer to as 'the multitude'. For Negri and Hardt, while we are witnessing the consolidation of this new Empire, we are also simultaneously seeing the growth of the multitude, the increasingly networked masses of citizens throughout the world who are responsible, through their resistant efforts, for the transformation towards Empire, but are also capable of constructing a counter-Empire, an alternative political organization of global flows and exchanges – a new socialism, in short.

Negri and Hardt's work, as mentioned, emerges from a radical neo or postMarxist tradition that, against socialist orthodoxy, highlights the creativity and centrality of the mass of people, that is radically democratic and decentralist, is deeply sceptical of the vanguardism and

---

Box 5.3   Autonomism, Negri and Hardt

Autonomism or Autonomist Marxism is a leftist political theory and movement that emerged in Italy in the 1960s as a variant on Workerism or Workerist communism. While Workerism emphasizes the central role of the working class and its emancipation through assuming organizational control of the workplace, Autonomism adopts a broader perspective that includes both waged and unwaged 'workers' (students, homemakers, beneficiaries) within the broad class of those capable of resisting capitalism. In particular, Autonomism encourages the self-organization of various social groups and movements independent of a central party structure. Antonio Negri (b. 1933), an Italian political theorist, was a key proponent of Autonomism in the 1960s and '70s. While a political science professor at the University of Padua, Negri aligned himself with radical leftists and advocated armed insurrection. He was arrested after the kidnapping and murder of former Prime Minister Aldo Moro by the militant Red Brigades, even though he had no demonstrable connection to the group. While in prison Negri was elected to the Italian Parliament as a member of the Radical Party, which entitled him to leave prison. Shortly thereafter he fled to France where he lived and taught for 14 years. In 1997 Negri returned to Italy, served the remainder of his prison sentence, and was released in 2003. Since then Negri has developed his theoretical stance in light of globalization, most significantly in collaboration with Michael Hardt (b. 1960), an American professor of comparative literature at Duke University. Hardt wrote his doctoral dissertation under Negri, and their subsequent collaborative works have sought to diagnose new global forms of sovereignty and the potentials for global democracy which resonate with the emancipatory spirit of Autonomism. In addition to his books co-authored with Hardt – *Labour of Dionysus* (1994), *Empire* (2000) and *Multitude* (2004) – Negri's recent works include *Time for Revolution* (2003) and *The Politics of Subversion* (2005).

substitutionism of socialist orthodoxy, and is much more open, theoretically and tactically, than is the mainstream of socialism (Tormey, 2004). Part of the openness of this current lies in its conceptualization of the subject of social change (Tormey, 2004). This new revolutionary subject, the multitude, is visible in a range of events and struggles – from Tiananmen Square in 1989, to the 1992 LA riots, to the uprisings in Chiapas in 1994, to the French industrial strikes of 1995, to the Palestinian Intifada. Unlike a conception of collective social subjects like the working class or the people, the multitude is not one but is made up of a set of singularities (Hardt and Negri, 2004). Hardt and Negri claim that such diverse struggles are crucially linked, that they go beyond the older class struggles, and that they offer central challenges to Empire as a whole: 'First, each struggle, though firmly rooted in local conditions, leaps immediately to the global level and attacks the imperial constitution in its generality. Second, all the struggles destroy the traditional distinction between economic and political struggles. The struggles are at once economic, political, and cultural – and hence they are biopolitical struggles, struggles over the form of life' (Hardt and Negri, 2000: 56). Empire, then, can be attacked from any point, and there is a certain unity to these struggles – for instance, in that in these plural forms of resistance we see the construction of new modes of life and community.

Rejecting the orthodox socialist construction of societal blueprints, Hardt and Negri (2000) do mention three important issues nonetheless for galvanizing resistance to Empire. The first is the demand for global citizenship – a demand in line with the current changes entailed by globalization: this is the multitudes' power to reappropriate control over space. The second issue is the demand for a social wage for all, since the whole of the people together produce and reproduce social life together. The third issue is the right to reappropriation. This is first and foremost the right to the reappropriation of the means of production, a classical socialist demand. But what is also involved in this new informational, postmodern world is free access to and control over knowledge, information, communication, and affects. In their later work, *Multitude* (2004), for Hardt and Negri what is most important and common amongst the struggles of the multitude is the desire for democracy, which also represents a fundamental critique of private property: 'the autonomy of the multitude and its capacity for economic, political, and social self-organization take away any role for sovereignty' (2004: 340). On this basis, they argue, 'The legal justification of private property is undermined by the common, social nature of production' (2004: 187).

Hardt and Negri's work has attracted a large amount of critical commentary. A good deal of this has centred on what is viewed as a 'revolutionary delirium' at work in their writings. The optimism of their work is seen as quite unrealistic before the enormous tasks at hand. Thus, Balakrishnan (2000) accuses Hardt and Negri of 'a millenarian erasure of the distinction between the armed and the unarmed, the powerful and the abjectly powerless', and Nairn (2005) views their work as a 'rehabilitation of spiritualism' that refuses to realistically assess a complex and ambiguous conjuncture and avoids specifying concretely what could and should be done towards a more just global order. There is, we believe, some justification to these objections. However, the work has justly been described as a *Communist Manifesto* for our period, a spirited political exercise in persuasion and a revival of utopian possibilities. In this way, the work is an important antidote to the many critical analyses of current globalization that point only to the growing power of capital and the relentless string of defeats suffered by democracy and ordinary people. In addition, the notion of the multitude chimes well with some of what is perhaps distinctive in the alternative globalization movement in contrast to socialist orthodoxy. We will now explore further two of these distinctive facets of the movement – organizational questions and new modalities of action.

For socialist orthodoxy of both social democratic and Leninist varieties, the key agent of revolution is the working class, or sometimes the peasantry. However, this agent cannot act alone. It needs to be represented by a socialist party who are able to know the goals of the movement, to lead, to show by exemplary action, and to take power on behalf of the working class. Socialist orthodoxy, then, as Robinson and Tormey (2005) argue, attaches great weight to party, programme, and state in progressive social change. Early in the history of the socialist movement this conception of socialist politics was challenged by anarchists and Left or libertarian communists, and these challenges reappeared with some force in the 1960s, especially during the events of May 1968 (see Box 5.4). These more marginal socialist currents were concerned that socialism would be conquered by the state, that the party might substitute for the mass of people or the working class, and they viewed such emphases as potentially issuing in new forms of domination and exploitation. Instead, ordinary people and their self-organization and direct (rather than representative) democracy were underscored as the vital characteristics of socialist politics.

The reappearance of this critique of the orthodox socialist politics of party, programme, and state from the 'world revolution of 1968' led, in

---

Box 5.4   May of '68

The late 1960s were characterized by a number of highly visible social movements, ranging from protests against the Vietnam War to activism in
support of the rights of racial and ethnic minorities and women. Across
North America and Europe, students were particularly active in movements
opposed to traditional morality and politics. In early May 1968, several universities in Paris (including the Sorbonne) were closed in response to student
protests and, when police occupied the universities, hundreds of students
were arrested. Shortly thereafter university and high school students and
teachers went on strike, and they were soon joined by many young workers.
Tens of thousands of strikers set up barricades throughout Paris, drawing a
swift and violent response from riot police. Further support for the strikers
was offered by the labour unions and the French Communist Party (PCF),
although the PCF was reluctant to lend support since it regarded many of
the strikers as 'anarchists'. More than a million people then marched
through Paris on 13 May in a general demonstration. In the following weeks
workers began occupying factories and by the end of May nearly ten million
of them were on strike. The strikers put forward a number of radical
demands, including the right to run their own factories as well as the dissolution of the existing government led by President Charles de Gaulle. While
de Gaulle dissolved the National Assembly and called for new parliamentary
elections in June, he also mobilized military units to quash the unrest,
banned a number of left-wing organizations, and ordered workers to return
to work under the threat of instituting a state of emergency and imposing
martial law. From this point the strikes and unrest began to recede, and de
Gaulle's party won a clear majority in the June elections. While the huge
demonstrations and strikes of May 1968 quickly dissipated, the revolutionary atmosphere inspired many social theorists, philosophers and activists
because of its unique characteristics. These include the fact that the rebellion
was not planned but arose from spontaneous actions, that it was not centrally co-ordinated by a vanguard party but operated according to a loose
network of groups acting in solidarity, and that it was not confined to the
working class in a conventional Marxist sense but involved the participation
of diverse groups united by the desire to challenge 'politics as usual' and
create a radically different society. The utopian spirit of May '68 is nicely
expressed in a slogan adopted during the rebellion: 'Be realistic, ask for the
impossible'.

---

particular, to a turn towards anarchist conceptions of social change.
The anarchist movement emerged in the nineteenth century around
the same time as Marxism but, generally, saw the state in a much less
ambiguously negative light and was much more sceptical about the
roles of leaders and organized politics. The anarchists tended to be critical of all forms of authority, refusing participation in electoral politics

and arguing instead for direct action, popular self-organization, and decentralization.

Because of the widespread AGM critique of the state, representation, leaders, and programmes ('not in our name'), and because of its aspirations for more direct democracy, decentralization, participation, and 'prefigurative politics' (living according to one's values), the movement does, in part at least, deserve the title of a 'new anarchism' (Epstein, 2001). Of particular relevance, here, is the contrast made by some analysts (Tormey, 2004; Cleaver, 1994, for instance) between the 'vertical' logic of orthodox socialist politics and the 'horizontal' organizational logic of this new anarchism. In a similar vein, poststructuralist thinkers Gilles Deleuze and Felix Guattari (1987) contrasted an 'arborescent' model of organization with a 'rhizomatic' model of organization. The arborescent model exemplifies a vertical or hierarchical logic, a tree-like structure with a central trunk and branches that always connect back to the centre. The rhizomatic model, on the other hand, embodies a horizontal logic represented by a 'perennial stem growing under the ground, shooting out roots in a random tangle' (Tormey, 2004).

Within the AGM, one finds both vertical and horizontal tendencies. The verticals – for instance, the British-based Socialist Workers' Party that dominates the group Globalize Resistance – tend to seek to leadership over the movement, and to contain and discipline them towards party and programmatic models of politics (Tormey, 2004). For many of these 'verticals', the problems with the alternative globalization movement at present include the lack of general strategy, the lack of a clear alternative vision, the inability to create new organizational forms and have significant policy impact, and its hostility and distance from the state, which leaves it politically impotent (for instance, see Vanaik, 2004; Sader, 2002; Callinicos, 2003; Panitch, 2002).

In contrast, we believe that the AGM's tendency towards horizontalism, its pluralism, and its uncontainability outside of the contention that 'another world is possible', is precisely what is of most interest and is most exciting about the movement. This aspect of the AGM reflects Morton's (2004: 162) claim that, 'Contemporary political agency is [today] seemingly more open-ended, plural and inclusive. Hence the need to move beyond notions of the conventional mass political party as the basis for organization within the framework of bourgeois representative democracy'. As Tormey (2004) notes, this horizontalism promises a return of people to politics and a move of politics to another stage beyond the traditional strategy of capturing state and party power.

If these decentred, plural, and anti-hierarchical tendencies are one dimension of what might be described as a 'postmodern politics' (Kiely, 2004), there are others too that again provide lines of demarcation from socialist orthodoxy. We will, in the remainder of this section, focus on the idea that we have seen emerging new characteristic means or tendencies in political practice or activism. One part of this is what has been called 'informational politics'. A frequently commented upon feature of the AGM is the way in which those within the movement have used new media – cell phones and the Internet, for instance – to monitor and spread news of the activities of governments and corporations, to co-ordinate protests and respond to police activities, to share information about methods of resistance, and to bypass corporate media in the name of decentralization, democracy, and participation. For example, the California-based Ruckus Society was formed in 1995 out of the environmental movement and has, since this time, broadened its concerns to human rights and the activities of the WTO (Sellers, 2001). The Ruckus Society uses video capacities on the Internet to train activists in non-violent direct action (Ruckus, 2003; Sellers, 2001). Informational politics are also at work in so-called 'hactivism', a form of virtual protest that seeks to disrupt the flow of information using new communication technologies. For instance, during the June 1999 international protests organized to coincide with the G7 summit in Cologne, Germany, there were more than 10,000 cyber-attacks on the computer systems of large corporations (Steger, 2005).

Another version of such informational politics is the collective of independent media organizations, Indymedia. Indymedia was formed in late November 1999 to cover the Seattle protests against the WTO and, as of 2002, there were over 80 Indymedia centres operating globally (Platon and Dueze, 2003). The Indymedia website received almost 1.5 million hits during the anti-WTO protests in Seattle; it received about 5 million hits during the Genoa G8 protests; and it generally gets around 100,000 hits a day (Indymedia, 2004). Indymedia seeks to provide democratic and non-corporate coverage of current affairs, using real time distribution of video, audio, text, and photos (Kidd, 2003). Many Indymedia organizers and participants share an alternative globalization position: 'The Seattle IMC and the growing Independent Media Centre Network represent a new and powerful emerging model that counters the trend toward the privatization of all public spaces by expanding our capacity to reclaim public airwaves and resources' (Kidd, 2003). In particular, such activism indicates the importance of media to politics today, and it tends to contain a solid critique of the type of coverage given, say, to issues of social justice, by the corporate media. Indymedia offers activists a chance to 'become the media', and ordinary citizens are able to publish their stories on the Indymedia newswire by following on-line instructions (Indymedia, 2004).

In general, many activists are seeing new democratic possibilities for activism and information-sharing opened up by new technology. Tormey (2004), for instance, notes the way in which the Internet makes marginal groups visible, enables the creation of activist networks, helps co-ordinate activity, provides alternative sources of information, and offers new forms of direct action. Here, again, we see the important emphases on decentralization, participation, and the notion of a reinvigoration of democracy so as to make it more direct, less distanced and alienated.

There is very often in this activism as well a highly sophisticated and playful approach to politics, which provides links to anarchist notions of 'prefigurative politics'. This can be illustrated by the example of 'culture jamming', a variety of political activism often linked with the AGM. Culture jamming is frequently traced to the work of the Left-wing artists and activists of the Situationist International, the SI (1957–72). The SI played a role in the Paris rebellion of 1968, when there appeared many Situationist-inspired slogans and collective attempts to institute forms of direct democracy. Guy Debord, the SI's leading theoretical light, designated the social order of the period a 'society of the spectacle', an order connected to the spread of media, advertising, and fashion that was turning people into passive spectators and consumers. The SI believed, though, that this world could be overturned and that people might creatively and actively transform their situations. Revolutionary art, Debord felt, had a place in this 'reversal of perspective'. A filmmaker, Debord's own artistic practice – what he called 'diversion' – saw him obtaining already existing images, editing them together, and then seeking to reverse the message (through a sound track), in a way that would expose the underlying reality of the society of the spectacle.

A variant of this diversion is visible in culture jamming, perhaps most prominently practiced by Adbusters. Adbusters are a Canadian-based global network of activists with environmental and anti-corporate links. One common Adbusters technique is the sophisticated alteration of corporate advertisements to reveal the hidden truth beneath the glossy surface of that product or organization (see Box 5.5). As Klein (2005:

Box 5.5 The Adbusters Technique

Adbusters' 'culture jamming' campaigns feature existing mass media images that have been altered in order to 'spoof' the ideas and icons of popular mass culture and subvert the image's original advertising intent. An example of this technique is the following image taken from the Adbusters website.

Courtesy of: www.adbusters.org

438) says culture jamming represents a rejection of the notion that marketing messages are passively absorbed in a one-way movement of information: 'A good jam … is an X-ray of the subconscious of a campaign, uncovering not an opposite meaning but the deeper truth hidden beneath the layers of advertising euphemisms'. Adbusters are also involved in organizing campaigns such as 'buy nothing day' and 'TV turnoff week'.

This sophisticated and humorous approach to activism, and the concern with the reconfiguration of daily life, can be seen across much of the AGM. Graeber (2002), for instance, notes the important features of festival, street theatre, and humour within the movement, visible in sub-groupings such as the revolutionary anarchist clown bloc, or in some of the chants heard at demonstrations – for example, 'Democracy? Ha, Ha, Ha', 'The pizza united can never be defeated', and 'Three word chant! Three word chant!'. For de Goede (2005: 381), 'ambiguity, laughter and making strange can be important political practices in their own right ... which might constitute important transformations of people's experiences of money and finance'. Too often, says de Goede (2005: 381), dissent is understood 'in romantic and masculine terms, as heroic rebellions against authority, exemplified by demonstrating masses, striking workers, brick-throwing students and fasting dissidents'. Humour and 'carnivalesque dissent' are not superficial or impotent gestures but instead can 'shake the discursive foundations of modern financial rationality' (*ibid.*), demonstrating the 'contingency and vulnerability of financial power' (382), and overcoming fear and intimidation. The Yes Men exemplify this sort of playful activism, as well as the informational accent of 'postmodern politics'. The Yes Men are activists who, in 1999, set up a parody of the WTO website and were subsequently asked to conferences as WTO spokespeople, where they delivered policy proposals mocking and exposing the general thrust of the WTO – for example, suggesting the use of a giant phallus for administering electric shocks to sweatshop employees, or that global hunger could be addressed by having the poor eat hamburgers and then recycle them up to ten times (Yes Men, nd).

Concluding comments and reflections on utopia: 'another world is possible'

There are a number of important issues raised by this rather brief survey of the AGM. In terms of the direction of the movement, we believe that the 'horizontal' mode is encouraging and important, reflecting significant contestation around the meaning of democracy, and providing a different modality of politics for a transformed world. Nevertheless, this does not mean that there are not strategic questions to be asked towards increasing the effectiveness of the movement. Wallerstein (2003), for instance, contends that to become a genuinely anti-systemic alternative, the AGM needs to address four issues. First, a process of open debate and dialogue is needed around the transition the movement is seeking. Second, the movement cannot ignore short-term defensive action, including electoral action, in contrast to an older revolutionary tradition that rigidly separated itself from official political involvement in the present in favour of hopes for a total revolution in the future. Third, the movement needs somehow to establish middle-range goals as well. Here, Wallerstein suggests progressive decommodification (with performance and survival rather than profits as goals) against neoliberal attempts to commodify everything. Fourth, the movement needs to develop the substantive meaning of its long-term emphases.

Wallerstein's fourth emphasis is intended to accent the revival of a critical utopian dimension, what he calls 'utopistics'. In our view, this last suggestion must be given the kind of serious consideration that the other issues tend to receive. In this regard, while the openness of and excitement generated by the World Social Forum's insistence that 'another world is possible' may be viewed as enough, it is still perhaps seen as less pressing than some other dimensions of the AGM. This insistence in itself, though, is an important utopian moment. We believe that one of the most unfortunate aspects of the period of 'happy globalization' or 'the end of history' was the apparent evacuation from the popular imaginary of any sort of utopian dimension. For some, the demise of utopia was an extremely positive thing because utopias, in this view, are in essence religious and irrational, projecting the possibility of perfect future harmony, transparency, and order, thereby fleeing dangerously from the complex realities of modern life and modern people. The inevitable failure of such unrealistic aims, it is often argued, leads inexorably first to disillusionment then to coercion and totalitarianism. From this perspective, the apparent triumph of liberal modesty about what we can know and do would be viewed as an important victory.

For others, the loss of the utopian dimension would be a tragedy, meaning an end to thinking deeply about what makes politics meaningful in human life and a closing down of democracy's potential. Thus, Perry Anderson (2004) laments the general suspension of utopia since the mid-1970s, which has produced a 'remorseless closure of space'. Similarly, Bourdieu (1998) spoke of the spread of a 'banker's fatalism' across the world, and Castoriadis (1997a, 1997b, 2004) was concerned that the postmodern present was threatening to fall back into what he called 'heteronomy'. Castoriadis's argument was that *autonomy*, the radical political move away from tradition, wherein the social order was viewed as established outside of the activities and imaginations of human beings acting collectively, had appeared twice in history – first with Greek Antiquity and then again in the modern period. This autonomy signified the realization that human beings were collectively responsible for the institutions they had created, with the radical accompanying thought that, therefore, we could collectively take up and transform these institutions again. For this reason autonomy requires the ability to think both in and through the present, to imagine a better future – what Camus (1991: 121) called a 'relative utopia' – that can be realistically constructed from the contradictory conditions of the current global system. Here the utopian impulse remains strong, although shorn of any messianism (found in both Marxist and capitalist ideologies) bent on perfecting the world in an absolute sense, that is, according to a single and final 'blueprint', and thereby ushering in the supposedly inevitable 'end' of history.

In both pro- and anti-globalization arguments, there is frequently a desperate sense that the system is moving all by itself, that we can do nothing to alter its inexorable unfolding. Thus, Thomas Friedman (1999) contends that no one is to blame for globalization and its failures, no one can control its dynamic, and therefore we need to submit to its dictates and learn to love it. From a very different ideological pole, Bauman (1999a) notes the widespread sense of globalization's unstoppability, likening our contemporary experience to that of passengers in a plane who discover that the pilot's cabin is empty. Such senses of globalization's self-propelling dynamic are, to our minds, the very opposite of the autonomy Castoriadis speaks of. It means a closing down of the utopian imagination, and this in turn is devastating to democracy, which surely should be precisely about the sort of unlimited and unending critique and questioning that Castoriadis points to as a central modern achievement. This reinvigoration of the utopian dimension means a return to one of the crucial dimensions of critical theory – 'thinking beyond' the politics of the present while acutely aware of the demands and limits that the present places upon us – and the message we wish this book to send: that the utopian heartbeat can and must still be detected in our globalizing world.

Further reading

Aaronson, S. A. *Taking to the Streets: The Lost History of Public Efforts to Shape Globalization* (Ann Arbor: University of Michigan Press, 2002).

Burbach, R. and Danaher, K. (eds) *Globalize This! The Battle Against the World Trade Organization* (Monroe: Common Courage Press, 2000)

Egan, D. 'Constructing Globalization: Capital, State, and Social Movements', *New Political Science*, 23 (2001) 559–64.

Fotopoulos, T. 'The End of Traditional Anti-systemic Movements and the Need for a New Type of Anti-systemic Movement Today', *Democracy & Nature*, 7 (2001) 415–55.

Gills, B. K. (ed.) *Globalization and the Politics of Resistance* (Basingstoke: Palgrave Macmillan, 2000).

Guidry, J. A., Kennedy, M. D. and Zald, M. N. (eds) *Globalizations and Social Movements: Culture, Power, and the Transnational Public Sphere* (Ann Arbor: University of Michigan Press, 1999).

Hubbard, G. and Miller, D. (eds) *Arguments Against G8* (London: Pluto, 2005).
Kiely, R. 'Globalization: From Domination to Resistance', *Third World Quarterly*, 21 (1999) 1059–70.
Luke, T. W. 'Globalization, Popular Resistance and Postmodernity', *Democracy & Nature*, 7 (2001) 317–29.
Martinez-Torres, M. E. 'Civil Society, the Internet, and the Zapatistas', *Peace Review*, 13 (2001) 347–55.

Bibliography

Abernethy, D. B. *The Dynamics of Global Dominance: European Overseas Empires, 1415–1980* (New Haven: Yale University Press, 2000).

Adbusters 'The Media Foundation' (www.adbusters.org/information/foundation/, nd).

Adorno, T. W. *The Culture Industry: Selected Essays on Mass Culture* (London: Routledge, 1991).

Agence France-Presse 'French Anti-Globalization Leader José Bové Jailed' (www.commondreams.org/headlines03/0622-02.htm, 22 June 2003).

Agger, B. *Speeding Up Fast Capitalism: Cultures, Jobs, Families, Schools, Bodies* (Boulder: Paradigm Publishers, 2004).

Al-Azmeh, A. *Islams and Modernity* (London: Verso, 1993).

Al-Azmeh, A. 'Conversation With Aziz Al-Azmeh on Islamism and Modernism' (www.iran-bulletin.org/interview/AZMEH_1.html, 1997).

Al-Azmeh, A. 'Postmodern Obscurantism and "The Muslim Question"', *JSRI*, 5 (2003) 21–46.

Albert, M. 'A Q & A on the WTO, IMF, World Bank, and Activism' (www.zmag.org/ZMag/articles/jan2000albert.htm, 2000).

Alexander, C. J. and Pal, L. A. (eds) *Digital Democracy: Policy and Politics in the Wired World* (Oxford: Oxford University Press, 1998).

Ali, T. *The Clash of Fundamentalisms* (London: Verso, 2002).

Allen, J. 'Fordism and Modern Industry', in J. Allen, P. Braham, and P. Lewis (eds), *Political and Economic Forms of Modernity* (Cambridge: Polity, 2001).

Alter, P. *Nationalism and After* (London: Edward Arnold, 1989).

Anderson, P. *Considerations on Western Marxism* (London: New Left Books, 1976).

Anderson, P. *In the Tracks of Historical Materialism* (London: New Left Books, 1983).

Anderson, P. *The Origins of Postmodernity* (London: Verso, 1999).

Anderson, P. 'Renewals', *New Left Review*, 1 (2000) 5–24.

Anderson, P. 'Internationalism: A Breviary', *New Left Review*, 14 (2002) 5–25.

Anderson, P. 'The River of Time', *New Left Review*, 26 (2004) 67–77.

Anderson, S. and Cavanagh, J. 'Top 200: The Rise of Global Corporate Power' (wwwglobalpolicy.org/socecon/tncs/top200.htm, 2000).

Anderson, S., Cavanagh, J., and Lee, T. *Field Guide to the Global Economy* (New York: The New Press, 2000).

Annan, K. *In Larger Freedom: Towards Development, Security, and Human Rights for All*, A/59/2005, 21 March 2005.

Appadurai, A. 'Disjuncture and Difference in the Global Cultural Economy', in M. Featherstone (ed.), *Global Culture: Nationalism, Globalization and Modernity* (London: Sage, 1990).

Archibugi, D. 'Demos and Cosmopolis', *New Left Review*, 13 (2002) 24–38.

Archibugi, D. 'Cosmopolitical Democracy', in D. Archibugi (ed.), *Debating Cosmopolitics* (London: Verso, 2003).

Arjomand, S. A. 'Social Theory and the Changing World: Mass Democracy, Development, Modernization and Globalization', *International Sociology*, 19 (2004) 321–53.

Arnason, J. P. 'Nationalism, Globalization and Modernity', in M. Featherstone (ed.), *Global Culture: Nationalism, Globalization and Modernity* (London: Sage, 1990).

Arrighi, G. 'The African Crisis: World Systemic and Regional Aspects', *New Left Review*, 15 (2002) 5–36.

Arrighi, G. 'Hegemony Unravelling, Part I', *New Left Review*, 32 (2005a) 23–80.

Arrighi, G. 'Hegemony Unravelling, Part II', *New Left Review*, 33 (2005b) 83–116.

Arrighi, G., Barr, K., and Hisaeda, S. 'The Transformation of the Business Enterprise', in G. Arrighi and B. Silver (eds), *Chaos and Governance in the Modern World System* (Minneapolis: University of Minnesota Press, 1999).

Arrighi, G., Hui, P., Ray, K., and Reifer, T. E. 'Geopolitics and High Finance', in G. Arrighi and B. Silver (eds), *Chaos and Governance in the Modern World System* (Minneapolis: University of Minnesota Press, 1999).

Arrighi, G. and Silver, B. (eds) *Chaos and Governance in the Modern World System* (Minneapolis: University of Minnesota Press, 1999).

Athreya, B. 'Trade is a Women's Issue' (wwwglobalpolicy.org/socecon/inequal/labor/2003/0220women.htm, 2003).

ATTAC 'Platform of the International Movement ATTAC' (www.attac.org/contact/indexpfen.htm, nd).

ATTAC 'Trade is a Women's Issue' (www.globalpolicy.org/socecon/inequal/labor/2003/0220women.htm, 2003).

Axford, B. *The Global System: Economics, Politics and Culture* (New York: St Martin's Press, 1995).

Badiou, A. *Infinite Thought: Truth and the Return to Philosophy* (London: Continuum, 2004a).

Badiou, A. 'Behind the Scarfed Law, There is Fear', *Le Monde* (www.islamonline.net/English/in_depth/hijab/2004–03/artcile_04.shtml, 2004b).

Bagdikian, B. *The Media Monopoly* (Boston: Beacon, 1997).

Balakrishnan, G. 'Hardt and Negri's Empire', *New Left Review*, 5 (2000) 142–48.

Barber, B. R. *Jihad Versus McWorld: How Globalism and Tribalism are Reshaping the World* (New York Ballantine Books, 1996).

Barrett, M. *The Politics of Truth: From Marx to Foucault* (Cambridge: Polity, 1991).

Baudrillard, J. *Simulations* (New York: Semiotext(e), 1983).

Baudrillard, J. *The Gulf War Did Not Take Place* (Bloomington: Indiana University Press, 1995).

Bauman, Z. *Work, Consumerism, and the New Poor* (Buckingham: Open University Press, 1998).

Bauman, Z. *Globalization: The Human Consequences* (Cambridge: Polity, 1999a).

Bauman, Z. 'Postmodernity, or Living With Ambivalence', in A. Elliott (ed.), *The Blackwell Reader in Contemporary Social Theory* (Oxford: Blackwell, 1999b).

Bauman, Z. *In Search of Politics* (Cambridge: Polity, 1999c).

Bauman, Z. 'Identity in the Globalizing World', in E. Ben-Rafael and Y. Sternberg (eds), *Identity, Culture and Globalization* (Boston: Brill, 2001).

Bauman, Z. 'Reconnaisance Wars of the Planetary Frontierland', *Theory, Culture and Society*, 19 (2002) 81–90.

BBC 'Headscarves in the Headlines' (http://news.bbc.co/1world/europe/ 346163.stm, 10 February 2004).

Beck, U. *The Reinvention of Politics: Rethinking Modernity in the Global Social Order* (Cambridge: Polity, 1997).

Beck, U. *World Risk Society* (Cambridge: Polity, 1999).

Beck, U. 'Living Your Own Life in a Runaway World: Individualization, Globalization and Politics', in W. Hutton and A. Giddens (eds), *Global Capitalism* (New York: New Press, 2000).

Beck, U. 'The Terrorist Threat: World Risk Society Revisited', *Theory, Culture and Society*, 19 (2002), 39–55.

Beilharz, P. *Postmodern Socialism: Romanticism, City and State* (Melbourne: Melbourne University Press, 1994).

Beilharz, P. 'Postmodern Socialism Revisited', in P. Hayden and C. el-Ojeili (eds), *Confronting Globalization: Humanity, Justice and the Renewal of Politics* (London: Palgrave Macmillan, 2005).

Beilharz, P. *et al.* 'The Globalization of Nothing: A Review Symposium of George Ritzer, *The Globalization of Nothing*', *Thesis Eleven*, 76 (2004) 103–14.

Bell, D. *The Coming of Post-Industrial Society: A Venture in Social Forecasting* (New York: Basic Books, 1999).

Bello, W., Bullard, N., and Malhotra, K. *Global Finance: New Thinking on Regulating Speculative Capital Markets* (London: Zed, 2000).

Bello, W. *Deglobalization: Ideas for a New World Economy* (London: Zed, 2004a).

Bello, W. 'The Global South', in T. Mertes (ed.), *A Movement of Movements: Is Another World Really Possible?* (London: Zed, 2004b).

Bendle, M. F. 'The Crisis of "Identity" in High Modernity', *British Journal of Sociology*, 53 (2002) 1–18.

Berman, M. *All That is Solid Melts into Air: The Experience of Modernity* (London: Verso, 1983).

Bertens, H. 'The Postmodern *Weltanschauung* and its Relation to Modernism', in J. Natoli and L. Hutcheson (eds), *A Postmodern Reader* (Albany: State University of New York Press, 1993).

Betz, H. G. 'The Growing Threat of the Extreme Right', in P. H. Merkl and L. Weinberg (eds), *Right-Wing Extremism in the Twenty-First Century* (London: Frank Cass, 2003).

Bhagwati, J. 'Coping With Antiglobalization: A Trilogy of Discontents', *Foreign Affairs*, 81 (2002) 2–7.

Blair, T. 'The Threat of Global Terrorism' (www.opinionjournal.com/extra/ ?id=110004783, 2004).

Blanford, N. 'Bleak Arab Progress Report', *Christian Science Monitor* (www.globalpolicy.org/socecon/develop/2003/1021arabhdr.htm, October 21, 2003).

Bobbio, N. *The Age of Rights* (Cambridge: Polity, 1996).

Boggs, C. *The Socialist Tradition: From Crisis to Decline* (London: Routledge, 1995).

Bourdieu, P. 'A Reasoned Utopia and Economic Fatalism', *New Left Review*, 227 (1998) 125–30.

Bové, J. 'A Farmers' International?', *New Left Review*, 12 (2001) 89–101.

Bradshaw, M. and Stenning, A. (eds) *East Central Europe and the Former Soviet Union: The Post-Socialist States* (Essex: Pearson, 2004).

Braeckman, C. 'New York and Kigali', *New Left Review*, 9 (2001) 141–7.

Brehony, K. J. and Rassool, N (eds). *Nationalism Old and New* (London: Macmillan, 1999).

Brennan, A. J. 'Environmental Problems of the World: Global Warming and Biodiversity', in P. A. O'Hara (ed.), *Global Political Economy and the Wealth of Nations: Performance, Institutions, Problems and Policies* (London: Routledge, 2004).

Brenner, M. 'Daughters of France, Daughters of Allah', *Vanity Fair* (www.vanity-fair.com/commentary/content/articles/051117roco04a, 2004).

Brooks, D. C. 'Faction in Movement: The Impact of Inclusivity on the Anti-Globalization Movement', *Social Science Quarterly*, 85 (2004) 559–77.

Brown, C. '"Turtles all the Way Down": Antifoundationalism, Critical Theory and International Relations', *Millennium*, 23 (1994) 213–36.

Buechler, S. M. *Social Movements in Advanced Capitalism: The Political Economy and Cultural Construction of Social Activism* (Oxford: Oxford University Press, 2000).

Buick, A. and Crump, J. *State Capitalism: The Wages System Under New Management* (London: Macmillan, 1986).

Bull, H. *The Anarchical Society: A Study of Order in World Politics* (London: Macmillan, 1977).

Bullock, A. and Trombley, S. (eds) *The New Fontana Dictionary of Modern Thought*, 3rd edn (London: HarperCollins, 1999).

Burbach, R. 'Roots of the Postmodern Rebellion in Chiapas', *New Left Review*, 205 (1994) 113–24.

Burton, M. and Nesiba, R. 'Transnational Financial Institutions, Global Financial Flows and the International Monetary Fund', in P. A. O'Hara (ed.), *Global Political Economy and the Wealth of Nations: Performance, Institutions, Problems and Policies* (London: Routledge, 2004).

Butler, J. 'Merely Cultural', *New Left Review*, 227 (1998) 33–44.

Buttel, F. H. and Gould, K. A. 'Global Social Movement(s) at the Crossroads: Some Observations on the Trajectory of the Anti-Corporate Globalization Movement', *Journal of World-System Research*, X (2004) 37–66.

Bygrave, M. 'Where Did all the Protesters Go?', *The Observer* (www.observer.co.uk/comment/story/0,6903,754862,00.html, 2002)

Calhoun, C. (ed.) *Dictionary of the Social Sciences.* (Oxford: Oxford University Press, 2002).

Callinicos, A. and Harman, C. *The Changing Working Class: Essays on Class Structure Today* (London: Bookmarks, 1987).

Callinicos, A. *Against Postmodernism* (Cambridge: Polity, 1989).

Callinicos, A. *An Anti-Capitalist Manifesto* (Cambridge: Polity, 2003).

Camus, A. *Between Hell and Reason: Essays from the Resistance Newspaper 'Combat', 1944–1947* (Hanover: Wesleyan University Press, 1991).

Cassen, B. 'Inventing ATTAC', in T. Mertes (ed.), *A Movement of Movements: Is Another World Really Possible?* (London: Verso, 2004).

Castells, M. *The Information Age: Economy, Society and Culture – The Rise of the Network Society* (Oxford: Blackwell, 1996).

Castells, M. *The Information Age: Economy, Society and Culture – End of Millennium* (Oxford: Blackwell, 1998).

Castells, M. *The Information Age: Economy, Society and Culture – The Power of Identity* (Oxford: Blackwell, 2000).

Castoriadis, C. *The Castoriadis Reader* (Cambridge: Blackwell, 1997a).

Castoriadis, C. *The World in Fragments: Writings on Politics, Society, Psychoanalysis, and the Imagination* (Stanford: Stanford University Press, 1997b).

Castoriadis, C. 'The Rising Tide of Insignificancy (The Big Sleep)' (www.not-bored.org/RTI.pdf, 2004).

Castoriadis, C. 'Figures of the Thinkable' (www.notbored.org/FTPK.pdf, 2005).

Cater, E. 'Consuming Spaces: Global Tourism', in J. Allen and C. Hamnett (eds), *A Shrinking World?* (Oxford: Oxford University Press, 1995).

Catholic Agency for Overseas Development. 'Don't Make Poor Nations "Pay" for Debt Cancellation' (wwwglobalpolicy.org/socecon/develop/debt/2004/0914debtcancel.htm, 2004).

Cetina, K. K. and Preda, A. (eds) *The Sociology of Financial Markets* (Oxford: Oxford University Press, 2005).

Chalaby, J. K. 'Television for a New Global Order: Transnational Television Networks and the Formation of Global Systems', *The International Journal for Communication Studies*, 65 (2003) 457–72.

Chirot, D. *Social Change in the Modern Era* (San Diego: Harcourt Brace Jovanovich, 1986).

Chomsky, N. *The Culture of Terrorism* (Montreal: Black Rose Books, 1988).

Chomsky, N. *Hegemony or Survival: America's Quest for Global Dominance* (New York: Henry Holt, 2003).

Chomsky, N. *Imperial Ambitions: Conversations With Noam Chomsky on the Post 9/11 World* (London: Hamish Hamilton, 2005).

Chossudovsky, M. *The Globalization of Poverty and the New World* Order, 2nd edn (Ontario: Global Outlook, 2003).

Clark, W. C. 'Environmental Globalization', in J. S. Nye and J. D. Donahue (eds), *Governance in a Globalizing World* (Washington, DC: Brookings Institution Press, 2000).

Cleaver, H. 'Introduction' (http://lanic.utexas.edu/project/Zapatistas/INTRO.TXT, 1994).

Cleaver, T. *Understanding the World Economy*, 2nd edn (London: Routledge, 2002).

Cobb, R. 'Behind the Veil' (http://inthefray.com/html/article.php?sid=482&mode=thread&order=0, 2004).

Cochrane, A. and Pain, K. 'A Globalizing Society?', in D. Held (ed.), *A Globalising World? Culture, Economics, Politics* (London: Routledge, 2000).

Cohen, R. and Kennedy, P. M. *Global Sociology* (Basingstoke: Palgrave Macmillan, 2000).

Cohn, T. H. *Global Political Economy: Theory and Practice*, 2nd edn (New York: Longman, 2003).

Coicaud, J. M. *Legitimacy and Politics: A Contribution to the Study of Political Right and Political Responsibility* (Cambridge: Cambridge University Press, 2002).

Collier, G. A. and Collier, J. F. 'The Zapatista Rebellion in the Context of Globalization', in J. Foran (ed.), *The Future of Revolutions: Rethinking Radical Change in the Age of Globalization* (London: Zed, 2003).

Commission on Global Governance. *Our Global Neighbourhood: The Report of the Commission on Global Governance* (Oxford: Oxford University Press, 1995).

Crouch, C. *Post-Democracy* (Cambridge: Polity, 2004).

Dahlberg, L. 'Extending the Public Sphere through Cyberspace: The Case of Minnesota E-Democracy', *First Monday*, 6 (www.firstmonday.org/issues/issue6_3/dahlberg/, 2001).

Davies, P. and Lynch, D. *The Routledge Companion to Fascism and the Far Right* (London: Routledge, 2002).

Davis, M. 'Planet of Slums', *New Left Review*, 26 (2004) 5–34.

Debrix, F. 'Tricky Business: Challenging Risk Theory and its Vision of a Better Global Future', in P. Hayden and C. el-Ojeili (eds), *Confronting Globalization: Humanity, Justice and the Renewal of Politics* (Basingstoke: Palgrave Macmillan, 2005).

de Goede, M. 'Carnival of Money: Politics of Dissent in an Era of Globalizing Finance', in L. Amoore (ed.), *The Global Resistance Reader* (London: Routledge, 2005).

Delanty, G. *Citizenship in a Global Age: Society, Culture, Politics* (Buckingham: Open University Press, 2000).

Deleuze, G. and Guattari, F. *A Thousand Plateaus: Capitalism and Schizophrenia* (Minneapolis: University of Minnesota Press, 1987).

Derrida, J. 'Interview with Richard Beardsworth', *Journal of Nietzsche Studies*, 7 (1994) 7–66.

Derrida, J. 'Politics and Friendship: A Discussion With Jacques Derrida' (www.sussex.ac.uk/Units/frenchthought/derrida.htm, 1997).

Diamond, L. 'Toward Democratic Consolidation', in L. Diamond and M. F. Plattner (eds), *The Global Resurgence of Democracy*, 2nd edn (Baltimore: Johns Hopkins University Press, 1996).

Dirlik, A. *The Post-colonial Aura: Third World Criticism in the Age of Global Capitalism* (Boulder: Westview, 1997).

Doorne, S. 'Tourism: The Culture of Capital', in J. McConchie, D. Winchester, and R. Willis (eds), *Dynamic Wellington: A Contemporary Synthesis and Expanation of Wellington* (Wellington: Institute of Geography, 2000).

Drainville, A. C. *Contesting Globalization: Space and Place in the World Economy* (London: Routledge, 2004).

Dunaway, W. A. 'Ethnic Conflict in the Modern World-System: the Dialectics of Counter-Hegemonic Resistance in an Age of Transition', *Journal of World-Systems Research*, 9 (2003) 3–34.

Dutt, A. K. 'Uneven Development, Convergence and North-South Interaction', in P. A. O'Hara (ed.), *Global Political Economy and the Wealth of Nations: Performance, Institutions, Problems and Policies* (London: Routledge, 2004).

Eagleton, T. *Ideology* (London: Verso, 1991).

Eatwell, R. 'Ten Theories of the Extreme Right', in P. H. Merkl and L. Weinberg (eds), *Right-Wing Extremism in the Twenty-First Century* (London: Frank Cass, 2003).

Economist 'Toxic but Containable' (www.economist.com/displayStory.cfm?story_id= 1100205, April 25 2002).

Economist 'The Headscarf, A Muslim Symbol Turned into Political Dynamite', *The Economist*, 369 (2003) 41.

Elliott, L. 'The Lost Decade' (wwwglobalpolicy.org/socecon/un/2003/0709lost.htm, 2003).

Energy Information Administration 'Executive Summary: Summary of the Kyoto Report' (www.eia.doe.gov/oiaf/kyoto/execsum.html, 2002).

Epstein, B. 'Anarchism and the Anti-Globalization Movement', *Monthly Review*, 53 (2001) 1–14.

Epstein, S. 'Nationalism and Globalization in Korean Underground Music: Our Nation Volume One', in R. Starrs (ed.), *Asian Nationalism in an Age of Globalization* (Surrey: Japan Library, 2001).

EZLN 'Closing Words of the EZLN at the Intercontinental Encounter – Second Declaration of La Realidad' (www.struggle.ws/mexico/ezln/1996/ccri_encount_aug.html, 1999).

Falk, R. A. *On Humane Governance: Toward a New Global Politics* (Cambridge: Polity, 1995).

Faux, J. and Mishel, L. 'Inequality and the Global Economy', in W. Hutton and A. Giddens (eds), *Global Capitalism* (New York: New Press, 2000).

Featherstone, M. (ed.) *Global Culture: Nationalism, Globalization and Modernity* (London: Sage, 1990).

Featherstone, M. Lash, S., and Robertson, R. (eds) *Global Modernities* (London: Sage, 1995).

Feher, F. and Heller, A. *Eastern Left, Western Left: Totalitarianism, Freedom and Democracy* (Cambridge: Polity 1987).

Focus on the Global South 'About Us' (www.focusweb.org/main.html, 2005).

Foran, J. (ed.) *The Future of Revolutions: Rethinking Radical Change in the Age of Globalization* (London: Zed, 2003).

Fotopoulos, T. *Towards an Inclusive Democracy: The Crisis of the Growth Economy and the Need for a New Liberatory Project* (London: Cassell, 1997).

Fotopoulos, T. 'Kyoto and Other Tales' (www.inclusivedemocracy.org/journal/newsletter/kyoto.htm, 2005).

Franck, T. *Nation Against Nation* (New York: Oxford University Press, 1985).

Frank, A. G. *Sociology of Development and Underdevelopment of Sociology* (London: Pluto Press, 1971).

Friedman, J. 'Indigenous Struggle and the Discrete Charm of the Bourgeoisie', *Journal of World-Systems Research*, 5 (1999) 391–411.

Friedman, J. 'Globalization, Class, and Culture in Global Systems', *Journal of World-Systems Research*, 6 (2000) 636–56.

Friedman, T. *The Lexus and the Olive Tree* (London: HarperCollins, 1999).

Friedman, T. 'It's a Flat World, After All', *The New York Times*, 3 April 2005.

Frynas, J. G. 'The Oil Industry in Nigeria: Conflict Between Oil Companies and Local People', in J. G. Frynas and S. Pegg (eds), *Transnational Corporations and Human Rights* (Basingstoke: Palgrave Macmillan, 2003).

Fukuyama, F. *The End of History and the Last Man* (London: Penguin, 1992).

Gandhi, L. *Post-Colonial Theory: A Critical introduction* (St. Leonards, N.S.W: Allen and Unwin, 1998).

George, S. 'A Short History of Neoliberalism' (wwwglobalpolicy.org/globaliz/econ/histneol.htm, 1999).

Giddens, A. *The Consequences of Modernity* (Palo Alto: Stanford University Press, 1990).

Giddens, A. *Modernity and Self-Identity* (Palo Alto: Stanford University Press, 1991).

Giddens, A. *Runaway World* (London: Profile Books, 1999).

Giddens, A. *The Third Way* (Cambridge: Polity: 2000).

Giddens, A. 'An Interview With Anthony Giddens', *Journal of Consumer Culture*, 3 (2003a) 387–99.

Giddens, A. (ed.) *The Progressive Manifesto* (Cambridge: Polity: 2003b).

Giddens, A. 'French Headscarf Ban Against Interests of Women', *Global Viewpoint* (www.digitalnpq.org/global_services/global%20viewpoint/01-05-04.html, 2004).

Giddens, A. 'Giddens and the "G" Word: An Interview With Anthony Giddens', *Global Media and Communication* 1 (2005) 63–77.

Gilroy, P. 'Diaspora and the Detours of Identity', in K. Woodward (ed.), *Identity and Difference* (London: Sage, 1999).

Glendon, M. A. *A World Made New: Eleanor Roosevelt and the Universal Declaration of Human Rights* (New York: Random House, 2001).

Global Exchange 'About Us' (www.globalexchange.org.html, 2004).

Global Policy Forum 'Timing the Spread of Technologies' (www.globalpolicy.org/globaliz/charts/techsp1.htm, 1999).

Global Policy Forum 'Average GDP Per Capita in 20 High Income Countries and 20 Low Income Countries' (wwwglobalpolicy.org/socecon/tables/gdpdeftab.htm, 2000).

Global Policy Forum 'Internet Users, 1996–2002' (www.globalpolicy.org/globaliz/charts/internet.htm, 2003).

Globalise Resistance 'What Globalise Resistance Stands For' (www.resist.org.uk/about/standfor.php, 2003).

Goldsmith, E. 'Profits of Doom' (www.edwardgoldsmith.com/page141.html, 1999).

Goldsmith, E. 'Can the Environment Survive the Global Economy?' (www.edwardgoldsmith.com/page47.html, 2001a).

Goldsmith, E. 'The Last Word – A Personal Commentary' (www.edwardgoldsmith.com/page60.html, 2001b)

Goodwin, J. 'The Renewal of Socialism and the Decline of Revolution', in J. Foran (ed.), *The Future of Revolutions: Rethinking Radical Change in the Age of Globalization* (London: Zed, 2003).

Gorz, A. *Capitalism, Socialism and Ecology* (London: Verso, 1994).

Gourevitch, P. *We Wish to Inform You That Tomorrow We Will Be Killed with Our Families: Stories from Rwanda* (New York: Farrar, Straus and Giroux, 1998).

Gowan, P. 'Neoliberal Cosmopolitanism', *New Left Review*, 11 (2001) 79–93.

Gowan, P. 'US: UN', *New Left Review*, 24 (2003) 5–28.

Graduate Institute of International Studies. *Small Arms Survey 2002* (Oxford: Oxford University Press, 2002).

Graeber, D. 'The New Anarchists', *New Left Review*, 13 (2002), pp. 61–73.

Green, D. G. *The New Right: The Counter-Revolution in Political, Economic and Social Thought* (Sussex: Wheatsheaf Books, 1987).

Grimwade, N. *International Trade: New Patterns of Trade, Production and Investment*, 2nd edn (New York: Routledge, 2000).

Gross, F. *The Revolutionary Party: Essays in the Politics of Socialism* (London: Greenwood Press, 1974).

Guardian 'The IMF' (www.guardian.co.uk/globalisation/story/0,7369,548410,00.html, 7 September 2001a).

Guardian 'The World Bank' (www.guardian.co.uk/globalisation/story/0,6512,546797,00.html, 4 September 2001b).

Guardian 'Special Report: Europe's Far Right' (www.guardian.co.uk/gall/0,8542,711990,00.html, 2004).

Habermas, J. *The Theory of Communicative Action* (Boston: Beacon Press, 1981).

Habermas, J. *The Philosophical Discourse of Modernity: Twelve Lectures* (Cambridge, MA: MIT, 1987).

Habermas, J. 'Fundamentalism and Terror: A Dialogue With Jürgen Habermas' (www.press.uchicago.edu/Misc/Chicago/066649.html, 2003).

Hall, J. 'Globalization and Nationalism', *Thesis Eleven*, 63 (2000) 63–79.

Hall, S. Held, D., and McGrew, A. (eds). *Modernity and its Futures* (Cambridge: Polity, 2001).

Hamilton, P. 'The Enlightenment and the Birth of Social Science', in S. Hall and B. Gieben (eds), *Formations of Modernity* (Cambridge: Polity, 1999).

Hardt, M. 'Porto Alegre: Today's Bundung?', *New Left Review*, 14 (2002) 112–19.

Hardt, M. and Negri, A. *Labour of Dionysus: Critique of the State-Form* (Minneapolis: University of Minnesota Press, 1994).

Hardt, M. and Negri, A. *Empire* (Cambridge, MA: Harvard University Press, 2000).

Hardt, M. and Negri, A. *Multitude: War and Democracy in the Age of Empire* (New York: Penguin, 2004).

Harvey, D. *The Condition of Postmodernity: An Enquiry into the Origins of Cultural Change* (Oxford: Blackwell, 1989).

Hayden, P. and el-Ojeili, C. (eds) *Confronting Globalization: Humanity, Justice and the Renewal of Politics* (Basingstoke: Palgrave Macmillan, 2005).

Hechter, M. 'Nationalism and Rationality', *Journal of World-Systems Research*, 6 (2000) 308–29.

Hedley, R. A. *Running Out of Control: Dilemmas of Globalization* (Bloomfield, CT: Kumarian Press, 2002).

Heelas, P. 'Introduction: Detraditionalization and its Rivals', in P. Heelas, S. Lash, and P. M. Morris, *Detraditionalization: Critical Reflections on Authority and Identity* (Oxford: Blackwell, 1996).

Heelas, P., Lash, S., and Morris, P. M. *Detraditionalization: Critical Reflections on Authority and Identity* (Oxford: Blackwell, 1996).

Held, D. *Democracy and the Global Order* (Cambridge: Polity, 1995).

Held, D. 'Realism Versus Cosmopolitanism: A Debate Between Barry Buzan and David Held' (www.polity.co.uk/global/realism.htm, 1996).

Held, D. (ed.) *A Globalising World? Culture, Economics, Politics* (London: Routledge, 2000).

Held, D. 'Global Social Democracy', in A. Giddens (ed.), *The Progressive Manifesto* (Cambridge: Polity, 2003).

Held, D. 'Introduction to Critical Theory', in D. Rasmussen and J. Swindal (eds), *Critical Theory: Volume I – Historical Perspectives* (London: Sage, 2004a).

Held, D. *Global Covenant: The Social Democratic Alternative to the Washington Consensus* (Cambridge: Polity, 2004b).

Held, D. and McGrew, A. *Globalization/Anti-Globalization* (Cambridge: Polity, 2002).

Held, D., McGrew, A., Goldblatt, D., and Perraton, J. *Global Transformations: Politics, Economics and Culture* (Cambridge: Polity, 1999).

Herman, E. S. and Chomsky, N. *Manufacturing Consent: The Political Economy of the Mass Media* (New York: Pantheon, 1988).

Hesmondhalgh, D. *The Culture Industries* (London: Sage, 2002).

Hindess, B. *Politics and Class Analysis* (Oxford: Oxford University Press, 1987).

Hirst, P. and Thompson, G. *Globalization in Question: The International Economy and the Possibility of Governance* (Cambridge: Polity, 1996).

Hirst, P. and Thompson, G. 'The Future of Globalization', *Cooperation and Conflict: Journal of the Nordic International Studies Association*, 37 (2002) 247–65.

Hobsbawm, E. J. *The Age of Revolution, 1789–1848* (New York: Mentor, 1962).

Hobsbawm, E. J. *Age of Extremes: The Short Twentieth Century, 1914–1991* (London: Michael Joseph, 1994).

Hobsbawm, E. J. *The Age of Capital, 1848–1875* (London: Weidenfeld and Nicolson, 1995a).

Hobsbawm, E. J. *The Age of Empire, 1875–1914* (London: Weidenfeld and Nicolson, 1995b).

Hoffman, M. 'Critical Theory and the Inter–Paradigm Debate', *Millennium*, 16 (1987) 232–49.

Holton, R. 'Globalization's Cultural Consequences', *Annals*, 570 (2000) 140–52.

Hoogvelt, A. M. *The Sociology of Developing Societies*, 2nd edn (London: Macmillan, 1978).

Horkheimer, M. *Critical Theory: Selected Essays* (New York: Continuum, 1995).

Horkheimer, M. and Adorno, T. *Dialectic of Enlightenment* (New York: Continuum, 1989).

Horschelmann, K. 'The Social Consequences of Transformation', in M. Bradshaw and A. Stenning (eds), *East Central Europe and the Former Soviet Union: The Post-Socialist States* (Essex: Pearson, 2004).

Hout, W. 'A Global Economy, Polycentric World or System of Nation-States?', in P. A. O'Hara (ed.), *Global Political Economy and the Wealth of Nations: Performance, Institutions, Problems and Policies* (London: Routledge, 2004).

How, A. *Critical Theory* (Basingstoke: Palgrave Macmillan, 2002).

Huber, E. and Stephens, J. D. *Development and Crisis of the Welfare State: Parties and Policies in Global Markets* (Chicago: University of Chicago Press, 2001).

Hulme, D. and Turner, M. *Sociology and Development: Theories, Policies and Practices* (London: Harvester Wheatsheaf, 1990).

Huntington, S. P. 'The Clash of Civilizations, *Foreign Affairs*, 72 (1993) 22–49.

Huntington, S. P. *The Clash of Civilizations and the Remaking of World Order* (New York: Simon and Shuster, 1996).

Huntington, S. 'The Age of Muslim Wars', *Newsweek* (December 2001) 6–15.

Hutchinson, J. *Modern Nationalism* (London: Fontana, 1994).

Hutton, W. and Giddens, A. (eds) *Global Capitalism* (New York: New Press, 2000). Ignatieff, M. *Empire Lite: Nation-Building in Bosnia, Kosovo and Afghanistan* (London: Vintage 2003).

Indymedia 'Frequently Asked Questions' (www.docs.indymedia.org/view/Global/FrequentlyAskedQuestionsEn, 2004).

International Labour Organization *Labour Practices in the Footwear, Leather, Textiles and Clothing Industries* (Geneva: ILO, 2000).

International Labour Organization *Women and Men in the Informal Economy: A Statistical Picture* (Geneva: ILO, 2002).

International Labour Organization *Global Employment Trends 2004* (Geneva: ILO, 2004).

International Labour Organization *A Global Alliance against Forced Labour* (Geneva: ILO, 2005).

International Monetary Fund 'Colombia: Letter of Intent, Memorandum of Economic Policy and Technical Memorandum of Understanding 2002' (www.imf.org/external/np/loi/2002/col/01/index.htm, 2002).

Irish Mexico Group 'Chiapas Revealed' (http://flag.blackened.net/revolt/mexico/pdf/revealed1.html, 2001).

Jackson, L. 'Nationality, Citizenship and Identity, in M. Bradshaw and A. Stenning (eds), *East Central Europe and the Former Soviet Union: The Post-Socialist States* (Essex: Pearson, 2004).

Jameson, F. 'Postmodernism, Or, The Cultural Logic of Late Capitalism', *New Left Review*, 146 (1984) 52–92.

Jameson, F. *Postmodernism, or, the Cultural Logic of Late Capitalism* (Durham: Duke University Press, 1991).

Jameson, F. 'Globalization and Political Strategy', *New Left Review*, 4 (2000) 49–68.

Jameson, F. *A Singular Modernity: Essay on the Ontology of the Present* (London: Verso, 2002).

Jauch, H. 'Export Processing Zones and the Quest for Sustainable Development: A South African Perspective', *Environment and Urbanization*, 14 (2002) 101–14.

Johnson, R. 'Defending Ways of Life: The (Anti-) Terrorist Rhetorics of Bush and Blair', *Theory, Culture and Society*, 19 (2002) 211–31.

Joll, J. *Europe Since 1870: An International History* (London: Penguin, 1978).

Kaldor, M. *New and Old Wars: Organized Violence in a Global Era* (Cambridge: Polity, 1999).

Kaldor, M. 'Global Terrorism', in A. Giddens (ed.), *The Progressive Manifesto* (Cambridge: Polity, 2003).

Kaldor, M., Anheier, H., and Glasius, M. (eds) *Global Civil Society* (London: Sage, 2004).

Kapitan, T. 'The Terrorism of "Terrorism"', in J. P. Sterba (ed.), *Terrorism and International Justice* (Oxford: Oxford University Press, 2003).

Katsiaficas, G. *Confronting Capitalism: Dispatches From a Global Movement* (Brooklyn: Soft Skull Press, 2004).

Keane, J. *Global Civil Society?* (Cambridge: Cambridge University Press, 2003).

Kellner, D. 'Media Culture and the Triumph of the Spectacle' (www.uta.edu/huma/agger/fastcapitalism/1_1kellner.htm, 2004).

Kennedy, P. 'Global Challenges in the Beginning of the Twenty-First Century', in P. Kennedy, D. Messner, and F. Nuschler (eds), *Global Trends and Global Governance* (London: Pluto, 2002).

Kennedy, P., Messner, D., and Nuschler, F. (eds) *Global Trends and Global Governance* (London: Pluto, 2002).

Khor, M. *Rethinking Globalization: Critical Issues and Policy Choices* (London: Zed, 2001).

Kidd, D. 'Indymedia.org: A New Communications Commons', in M. McCaughey and M. Ayers (eds), *Cyberactivism: Online Activism in Theory and Practice* (New York: Routledge, 2003).

Kiely, R. 'Neo-liberal Globalization Meets Global Resistance: The Significance of "Anti-Globalization" Protest', in S. Dasgupta (ed.), *The Changing Face of Globalization* (London: Sage, 2004).

Klein, N. *No Logo* (New York: HarperCollins, 2000).

Klein, N. 'The Unknown Icon', *The Guardian* (www.gaurdian.co.uk/Columnists/Column/0,5673,446977,00.html, 3 March 2001).

Klein, N. *Fences and Windows: Dispatches From the Front Lines of the Globalization Debate* (London: Flamingo, 2002).

Klein, N. 'Culture Jamming: Ads Under Attack', in L. Amoore (ed.), *The Global Resistance Reader* (London: Routledge, 2005).

Krueger, A. B. 'UN Aims to Cut Poverty in Half as Experts Wonder How to Measure it' (www.globalpolicy.org/socecon/develop/2005/0203measuring.htm, 2005).

Kumar, K. *From Post-Industrial to Post-Modern Society: New Theories of the Contemporary World* (Oxford: Blackwell, 1995).

Kuper, A. and Kuper, J. (eds) *The Social Sciences Encyclopaedia*, 2nd edn (London: Routledge, 1996).

Kuttner, R. 'The Role of Governments in the Global Economy', in W. Hutton and A. Giddens (eds), *Global Capitalism* (New York: New Press, 2000).

Kyoto Protocol Facts and Figures (http://www.cop3.org/facts_and_figures.htm, nd).

Lane, D. *The Rise and Fall of State Socialism: Industrial Society and the Socialist State* (Cambridge: Polity, 1996).

Langhorne, R. *The Coming of Globalization* (Basingstoke: Palgrave Macmillan, 2001).

Lash, S. and Urry, J. *The End of Organized Capitalism* (Cambridge: Polity, 1987).

Lechner, F. J. 2000. "Global Fundamentalism", in F. J. Lechner and J. Boli (eds), *The Globalization Reader* (Oxford: Blackwell, 2000).

Lechte, J. *Key Contemporary Concepts: From Abjection to Zeno's Paradox* (London: Sage, 2003).

Lefort, C. *Democracy and Political Theory* (Cambridge: Polity, 1988).

Legrain, P. *Open World: The Truth About Globalization* (London: Abacus, 2002).

Lemert, C. *Social Theory: The Multicultural and Classical Readings* (Boulder: Westview, 1998).

Lenin, V. I. *Imperialism, The Highest Stage of Capitalism* (Peking: Foreign Language Press, 1970).

Lewandowski, J. D. 'Disembedded Democracy? Globalization and the "Third Way"', *European Journal of Social Theory*, 6 (2003) 115–31.

Liagouras, G. 'The Political Economy of Post-Industrial Capitalism', *Thesis Eleven*, 81 (2005) 20–35.

Linklater, A. *The Transformation of Political Community* (Cambridge: Polity, 1998).

Lipschutz, R. D. and Meyer, J. *Global Civil Society and Global Environmental Governance* (Albany: SUNY Press, 1996).

Long, N. *An Introduction to the Sociology of Rural Development* (London: Tavistock, 1977).

Lucie-Smith, E. *Art in the Eighties* (Oxford: Phaidon, 1990).

Lukic, R. and Brint, M. (eds) *Culture, Politics, and Nationalism in the Age of Globalization* (Aldershot: Ashgate, 2001).

Luxemburg, R. *Rosa Luxemburg Speaks* (New York: Pathfinder, 1970).

Lyon, D. *Surveillance after September 11* (Cambridge: Polity, 2003).

Lyotard, J. F. *The Postmodern Condition: A Report on Knowledge* (Manchester, Manchester University Press, 1984).

Mackay, H. 'The Globalization of Culture?', in D. Held (ed.), *A Globalizing World? Culture, Economics, Politics* (London: Routledge, 2000).

Mackay, H. *Investigating the Information Society* (London: Routledge, 2001).

Mackay, H. 'New Media and Time-Space Reconfiguration', in T. Jordan and S. Pile (eds), *Social Change* (Oxford: Blackwell, 2002).

Mackay, H., Maples, W., and Reynolds, P. *Social Science in Action: Investigating the Information Society* (Milton Keynes: Open University Press, 2001).

Mahajan, R. *Full Spectrum Dominance: US Power in Iraq and Beyond* (New York: Seven Stories Press, 2003).

Malesevic, S. and Haugaard, M. (eds) *Making Sense of Collectivity: Ethnicity, Nationalism, and Globalization* (London: Pluto, 2003).

Mann, M. 'Globalization and September 11', *New Left Review*, 12 (2001) 51–72.

Marangos, J. 'Transformation to a Market Economy in Eastern Europe, the Former Soviet Union and Asia', in P. A. O'Hara (ed.), *Global Political Economy and the Wealth of Nations: Performance, Institutions, Problems and Policies* (London: Routledge, 2004).

Marcos, Subcommandante 'Closing Words of the EZLN at the Intercontinental Encounter – Second Declaration of La Realidad' (www.struggle.ws/mexico/ezln/1996/ccri_encount_aug.html, 1996).

Marcos, Subcomandante 'The Punch Card and the Hour Glass', *New Left Review*, 9 (2001) 69–79.

Marcuse, H. *One-Dimensional Man: Studies in the Ideology of Advanced Industrial Society* (Boston: Beacon Press, 1964).

Marcuse, H. *Studies in Critical Philosophy* (Boston: Beacon Press, 1973).

Marshall, P. *Demanding the Impossible: A History of Anarchism* (London: Fontana, 1994).

Martin, H. P. and Schumann, H. *The Global Trap: Globalization and the Assault on Democracy and Prosperity* (New York: Zed, 1998).

Martin, P. 'The Moral Case for Globalization', in F. J. Lechner and J. Boli (eds), *The Globalization Reader* (Oxford: Blackwell, 2000).

Marx, K. *Karl Marx: Selected Writings*, (ed.) D. McLellan (Oxford: Oxford University Press, 1987).

McAuley, C. A. 'The Demise of Bolshevism and the Rebirth of Zapatismo: Revolutionary Options in a Post-Soviet World', in J. Foran (ed.), *The Future of Revolutions: Rethinking Radical Change in the Age of Globalization* (London: Zed, 2003).

McGrew, A. 'Power Shift: From National Government to Global Governance?', in D. Held (ed.), *A Globalising World? Culture, Economics, Politics* (London: Routledge, 2000).

McLelland, D. 'The Achievement Motive in Economic Growth', in G. D. Ness (ed.), *The Sociology of Economic Development: A Reader* (New York: Harper and Row, 1970).

McLennan, G. 'The New Positivity', in J. Eldridge *et al.*, *For Sociology: Legacies and Prospects* (Durham: Sociology Press, 2000).

Merkl, P. H. 'Stronger than Ever', in P. H. Merkl and L. Weinberg (eds), *Right-Wing Extremism in the Twenty-First Century* (London: Frank Cass, 2003).

Meyer, D. S., Whittier, N., and Bobnett, B. (eds) *Social Movements: Identity, Culture, and the State* (Oxford: Oxford University Press, 2002).

Moretti, F. 'Planet Hollywood', *New Left Review*, 9 (2001) 90–101.

Morsink, J. *The Universal Declaration of Human Rights: Origins, Drafting, and Intent* (Philadelphia: University of Pennsylvania Press, 1999).

Morton, A. D. 'The Antiglobalization Movement: Juggernaut or Jalopy?', in H. Veltmeyer (ed.), *Globalization and Antiglobalization: Dynamics of Change in the New World Order* (Aldershot: Ashgate, 2004).

Mount, G. 'A "World of Tribes"', in G. Fry and J. O'Hagan (eds), *Contending Images of World Politics* (London: Palgrave Macmillan, 2000).

Mouzelis, N. 'Modernity: A Non-European Conceptualization', *British Journal of Sociology*, 50 (1999) 141–59.

Movimento dos Trabalhadores Rurais Sem Terra 'Landless Workers' Movement' (www.mstbrazil.org/, 2003).

Mueller, C. M. 'Building Social Movement Theory', in A. D. Morris and C. M. Mueller (eds), *Frontiers in Social Movement Theory* (New Haven: Yale University Press, 1992).

Munck, R. *Globalisation and Labour: The New 'Great Transformation'* (London: Zed Books, 2002).

Murden, S. W. *Islam, the Middle East, and the New Global Hegemony* (Boulder: Lynne Rienner, 2002).

Nader, R. 'Interview', *Globalization and Human Rights* (New York: PBS Video and Globalivision, 1998).

Nairn, T. 'Make for the Boondocks', *London Review of Books*, 27 (www.lrb.co.uk/v27/n09/nair01_.html, 2005).

National Labor Committee 'Industrial Embroidery' (www.nlcnet.org/campaigns/ca03/industrial/industrial.pdf, 2003).

Nederveen Pieterse, J. *Globalization and Culture: Global Melange* (Lanham: Rowman and Littlefield, 2004).

Negri, A. *Time for Revolution* (New York: Continuum, 2003).

Negri, A. *The Politics of Subversion: A Manifesto for the Twenty-First Century* (Cambridge: Polity, 2005).

Neill, A. 'National Culture and the New Museology', in A. Smith and L. Wevers (eds), *On Display: New Essays in Cultural Studies* (Wellington: Victoria University Press, 2004).

New Internationalist *Issue 329* (www.newint.org/issue329/facts.htm, November 2000).

New Internationalist *Issue 337* (www.newint.orgIssue337/facts.htm, August 2001).

New Internationalist *Issue 355* (www.newint.org/issue355/facts.htm, April 2003a).

New Internationalist *Issue 362* (www.newint.org/issue362/facts.htm, November 2003b).

New Internationalist *Issue 365* (www.newint.org/issue365/facts.htm, March 2004a).

New Internationalist *Issue 374* (www.newint.org/issue374/facts.htm, December 2004b).

Nye, J. S. *Power in the Global Information Age: From Realism to Globalization* (London: Routledge, 2004).

OECD 'Standardized Unemployment Rates' (www.oecd.org/document/15/0,2340,en_2825_293564_1873295_1_1_1_1,00. html#sur, 2005).

O'Hara, P. A (ed.) *Global Political Economy and the Wealth of Nations: Performance, Institutions, Problems and Policies* (London: Routledge, 2004).

Ohmae, K. 'The End of the Nation State', in F. J. Lechner and J. Boli (eds), *The Globalization Reader* (Oxford: Blackwell, 2000).

Osterhammel, J. and Petersson, N. P. *Globalization: A Short History* (Princeton: Princeton University Press, 2003).

Outhwaite, W. and Ray, L. *Social Theory and Postcommunism* (Oxford: Blackwell, 2005).

Oxfam *Trading Away Our Rights: Women Working in Global Supply Chains* (www.oxfam.org/eng/pdfs/report_042008_labor.pdf, 2004a).

Oxfam 'Guns or Growth? Assessing the Impact of Arms Sales on Sustainable Development – A Summary' (wwwglobalpolicy.org/socecon/develop/2004/06oxfamarms.htm, 2004b).

Ozkirimli, U. *Theories of Nationalism: A Critical Introduction* (New York: St Martin's Press, 2000).

Page, R. M. 'Globalization and Social Welfare', in V. George and R. M. Page (eds), *Global Social Problems* (Cambridge: Polity, 2004).

Panitch, L. 'Violence as a Tool of Order and Change: The War on Terrorism and the Antiglobalization Movement', *Monthly Review*, 54 (2002) 12–32.

Patin, V. 'Will Market Forces Rule?', *UNESCO Courier*, 52 (1999) 35–6.

Peoples' Global Action 'Peoples' Global Action Manifesto' (www.nadir.org/nadir/initiativ/agp/en/pgainfos/manifesto.htm, 1998).

Perrons, D. *Globalization and Social Change: People and Places in a Divided World* (London: Routledge, 2004).

Petras, J. and Veltmeyer, H. *Globalization Unmasked: Imperialism in the 21st Century* (New York: Zed, 2001).

Pettit, P. *Republicanism: A Theory of Freedom and Government* (Oxford: Oxford University Press, 1997).

Pierson, C. *Socialism After Communism: The New Market Socialism* (Cambridge: Polity, 1995).

Platon, S. and Dueze, M. 'Indymedia Journalism: A Radical Way of Making, Selecting and Sharing News?', *Journalism*, 4 (2003) 336–55.

Pojman, L. P. 'The Moral Response to Terrorism and Cosmopolitanism', in J. P. Sterba (ed.), *Terrorism and International Justice* (Oxford: Oxford University Press, 2003).

Power, S. *'A Problem From Hell': America and the Age of Genocide* (New York: Basic Books, 2002).

Puri, J. *Encountering Nationalism* (Oxford: Blackwell, 2004).

Ramsdale, P. *International Flows of Selected Cultural Goods, 1980–98* (Paris: UNESCO, 2000).

Rapley, J. *Globalization and Inequality: Neoliberalism's Downward Spiral* (Boulder: Lynne Reinner, 2004).

Rasmussen, D. and Swindal, J. (eds) *Critical Theory, Volume I: Historical Perspectives* (London: Sage, 2004).

Reuters 'What is the Kyoto Protocol?' (www.alertnet.org/thenews/newsdesk/L07590569.htm, 2005).

Risse, T., Ropp, S. C., and Sikkink, K. (eds) *The Power of Human Rights: International Norms and Domestic Change* (Cambridge: Cambridge University Press, 1999.

Ritzer, G. 'The McDonaldization of Society', in A. Giddens (ed.), *Sociology*, rev. edn (Cambridge: Polity, 2001).

Ritzer, G. *The Globalization of Nothing* (Thousand Oaks, CA: Pine Forge, 2004).

Robertson, R. 'Glocalization: Time-Space and Homogeneity-Heterogeneity, in M. Featherstone, S. Lash, and R. Robertson (eds), *Global Modernities* (London: Sage, 1995).

Robertson, R. 'Globalization Theory 2000+: Major Problematics', in G. Ritzer and B. Smart (eds), *Handbook of Social Theory* (London: Sage, 2003).

Robertson, R. T. *The Three Waves of Globalization: A History of a Developing Global Consciousness* (London: Zed, 2003).

Robinson, A. and Tormey, S. 'The Conflicting Logics of Transformative Politics', in P. Hayden and C. el-Ojeili (eds), *Confronting Globalization: Humanity, Justice and the Renewal of Politics* (Basingstoke: Palgrave Macmillan, 2005).

Robinson, M. 'Is Cultural Tourism on the Right Track?', *UNESCO Courier*, 52 (1999) 27.

Rodda, C. 'The World Trade Organisation (WTO)' (www.crl.dircon.co.uk/TB/4/WTO.htm, 2001).

Rojeck, C. and Turner, B. S. (eds) *Forget Baudrillard?* (London: Routledge, 1993).

Rosenberg, J. *The Follies of Globalization Theory: Polemical Essays* (London: Verso, 2000).

Roxburgh, A. *Preachers of Hate: The Rise of the Far Right* (London: Gibson Square Books, 2002).

Ruckus Society. 'About Ruckus' (www.ruckus.org/about/mission.html, 2003).

Ruggie, J. G. 'Taking Embedded Liberalism Global: the Corporate Connection', in D. Held and M. Koenig-Archibugi (eds), *Taming Globalization: Frontiers of Governance* (Cambridge: Polity, 2003).

Russell, A. 'The Zapatistas Online: Shifting the Discourse of Globalization', *Gazette*, 63 (2001) 399–413.

Ryder, A. J. *The German Revolution of 1918: A Study of German Socialism in War and Revolt* (Cambridge: Cambridge University Press, 1967).

Sader, E. 'Beyond Civil Society: The Left After Porto Alegre', *New Left Review*, 17 (2002) 87–99.

Sader, E. 'Taking Lula's Measure', *New Left Review*, 33 (2005) 58–80.

Said, E. W. *Orientalism* (London: Penguin, 1978).

Said, E. W. *Covering Islam: How the Media and Experts Determine How We See the Rest of the World* (London: Routledge and Kegan Paul, 1981).

Said, E. W. *Culture and Imperialism* (London: Vintage, 1993).

Said, E. W. *Representations of the Intellectual: The 1993 Reith Lectures* (London: Vintage, 1994).

Said, E. W. *Reflections of Exile: And Other Literary and Cultural Essays* (London: Granta, 2001).

Sane, P. 'Poverty, the Next Frontier in the Struggle for Human Rights' (www-globalpolicy.org/socecon/develop/2004/1209sanepoverty.htm, 2004).

Santana, K. 'MTV Goes to Asia' (www.globalpolicy.org/globaliz/cultural/2003/0812mtv.htm, 2003).

Sassen, S. 'Urban Economies and Fading Distances', *Megacities Lectures* (www.megacities.n1/lectrue_sassen.htm, 1998).

Sassen, S. *The Global City* (Princeton: Princeton University Press, 1999).

Sassen, S. 'From Globalization and its Discontents', in G. Bridge and S. Watson (eds), *The Blackwell City Reader* (Oxford: Blackwell, 2002).

Sassen, S. 'The Embeddedness of Electronic Markets: The Case of Global Capital Markets', in K. K. Cetina and A. Preda (eds), *The Sociology of Financial Markets* (Oxford: Oxford University Press, 2005).

Sassoon, D. 'On Cultural Markets', *New Left Review*, 17 (2002) 113–26.

Sayyid, B. *A Fundamental Fear: Eurocentrism and the Emergence of Islamism* (London: Zed, 1997).

Schirato, T. and Webb, J. *Understanding Globalization* (London: Sage, 2003).

Scholte, J. A. 'Beyond the Buzzword: Towards a Critical Theory of Globalization', in E. Kofman and G. Young (eds), *Globalization: Theory and Practice* (London: Pinter, 1996).

Scholte, J. A. *Globalization: A Critical Introduction* (Basingstoke: Palgrave Macmillan, 2000).

Schroeder, R. 'Rethinking Nationalism in the Context of Globalization', in K. J. Brehony and N. Rassool (eds), *Nationalisms Old and New* (Basingstoke: Palgrave Macmillan, 1999).

Scott, A. 'Political Culture and Social Movements', in J. Allen, P. Braham, and P. Lewis (eds), *Political and Economic Forms of Modernity* (Cambridge: Polity, 2001).

Scraton, P. (ed.) *Beyond September 11: An Anthology of Dissent* (London: Pluto, 2002).

Scruton, R. *The West and the Rest: Globalization and the Terrorist Threat* (Wilmington: ISI Books, 2002).

Sellers, J. 'Raising a Ruckus', *New Left Review*, 10 (2001) 71–85.

Seoane, J. and Taddei, E. 'From Seattle to Porto Alegre: The Anti-Neoliberal Globalization Movement', *Current Sociology*, 50 (2002) 99–122.

Shalom, S. R. 'The State of the World' (www.zmag.org/CrisesCurEvts/Globalism/14shalom.htm, 1999).

Shiva, V. 'The World on the Edge', in W. Hutton and A. Giddens (eds), *Global Capitalism* (New York: New Press, 2000).

Short, J. R. *Global Dimensions: Space, Place and the Contemporary World* (London: Reaktion Books, 2001).

Silver, B. and Slater, E. 'The Social Origins of World Hegemonies', in G. Arrighi and B. Silver (eds), *Chaos and Governance in the Modern World System* (Minneapolis: University of Minnesota Press, 1999).

Sim, S. *Irony and Crisis: A Critical History of Postmodern Culture* (Cambridge: Icon, 2002).

Sim, S. *Fundamentalist World: The New Dark Age of Dogma* (Cambridge: Icon, 2004).

Simonis, U. E. and Bruhl, T. 'World Ecology – Structures and Trends', in P. Kennedy, D. Messner, and F. Nuschler (eds), *Global Trends and Global Governance* (London: Pluto, 2002).

Singer, P. *One World: The Ethics of Globalization* (New Haven: Yale University Press, 2002).

SIPRI *SIPRI Yearbook 2003: Armaments, Disarmament and International Security* (Oxford: Oxford University Press, 2003).

Smart, B. *Modern Controversies, Postmodern Conditions* (London: Routledge, 1992).

Smart, B. *Postmodernity* (London: Routledge, 1993).

Smart. B. *Economy, Culture and Society: A Sociological Critique of Neo-Liberalism* (Buckingham: Open University Press, 2003).

Smith, A. D. 'Towards a Global Culture?', in M. Featherstone (ed.), *Global Culture: Nationalism, Globalization and Modernity* (London: Sage, 1990).

Socialist Worker 'Another World is Possible' (www.socialistworker.org/2001/374/374_01_Genoa.shtml, 2001).

Soros, G. *On Globalization* (New York: Public Affairs, 2002).

Spivak, G. C. 'Can the Subaltern Speak?', in C. Nelson and L. Grossberg (eds), *Marxism and the Interpretation of Culture* (Urbana: University of Illinois Press, 1988).

Stedile, J. P. 'Landless Battalions: The Sem Terra Movement of Brazil', *New Left Review*, 15 (2002) 76–104.

Steger, M. *Globalism: The New Market Ideology* (Lanham: Rowman and Littlefield, 2002).

Steger, M. *Globalization: A Very Short Introduction* (Oxford: Oxford University Press, 2003).

Steger, M. *Globalism: Market Ideology Meets Terrorism*, 2nd edn (Lanham: Rowman and Littlefield, 2005).

Stehr, N. 'Modern Societies as Knowledge Societies', in G. Ritzer and B. Smart (eds), *Handbook of Social Theory* (London: Sage, 2003).

Sterba, J. P. (ed.) *Terrorism and International Justice* (Oxford: Oxford University Press, 2003).

Stiglitz, J. 'The Hospital that Makes you Sicker – Interview With Joseph Stiglitz', *New Internationalist*, 365 (2004) 14–16.

Suri, S. 'What Just One Company Can Do to the World' (wwwglobalpolicy.org/socecon/tncs/2004/0129exxonclimate.htm, 2004).

Taylor, P. M. *Global Communication, International Affairs and the Media Since 1945* (London: Routledge, 1997).

Terray, E. 'Headscarf Hysteria', *New Left Review*, 26 (2004) 118–27.

Therborn, G. 'Globalizations: Dimensions, Historical Waves, Regional Effects, Normative Governance', *International Sociology*, 15 (2000) 151–79.

Therborn, G. 'Into the 21st Century', *New Left Review*, 10 (2001) 87–110.

Thompson, K. (ed.) *Media and Cultural Regulation* (London: Sage, 1997).

Thompson, W. *Global Expansion: Britain and its Empire, 1870–1914* (London: Pluto, 1999).

Tilly, C. *Social Movements, 1768–2004* (Boulder: Paradigm, 2004).

Tomlinson, J. *Globalization and Culture* (Chicago: University of Chicago Press, 1999).

Tormey, S. 'Against "Representation": Deleuze, Zapatismo and the Search for the Post-Political Subject' (http://homepage.ntlworld.com/simon.tormey/articles/representation.pdf, 2003).

Tormey, S. *Anti-Capitalism: A Beginner's Guide* (Oxford: Oneworld, 2004).

Torres, R. *Towards a Socially Sustainable World Economy: An Analysis of the Social Pillars of Globalization* (Geneva: ILO, 2001).

Trocchi, A. *Cain's Book* (London: Jupiter Books, 1966).

United Nations Children's Fund 'One in Twelve of the World's Children are Forced into Child Labour' (wwwglobalpolicy.org/socecon/inequal/labor/2005/0218unicef.htm, 2005).

United Nations Chronicle 'Under the Gun – Controlling Illegal Firearms Trade' (www.findarticles.com/p/articles/mi_m1309/is_1_38/ai_80497124, 2001).

United Nations Development Programme *Human Development Report 1999* (Oxford: Oxford University Press, 1999).

United Nations Development Programme *Human Development Report 2000* (Oxford: Oxford University Press, 2000).

United Nations Development Programme *Human Development Report 2003* (Oxford: Oxford University Press, 2003).

United Nations Development Programme *Human Development Report 2004* (Oxford: Oxford University Press, 2004).

United Nations Development Programme *Human Development Report 2005* (Oxford: Oxford University Press, 2005).

United Nations Educational, Scientific, and Cultural Organization *World Culture Report: Cultural Diversity, Conflict and Pluralism* (Paris: UNESCO Publishing, 2000).

United Nations Educational, Scientific, and Cultural Organization '25 Questions on Culture, Trade and Globalisation' (http://portal.unesco.org/culture/en/ev.php-URL_ID=2461&URL_DO=DO_TOPIC&URL_SECTION=-512.html, 2004).

United Nations Educational, Scientific, and Cultural Organization 'Cultural Tourism' (http://portal.unesco.org/culture/en/ev.php-URL_ID=11408&URL_DO=DO_TOPIC&URL_SECTION=201.html, 2005).

United Nations Human Settlement Programme *The Challenge of Slums: Global Report on Human Settlements* (London: Earthscan Publications and UN-Habitat, 2003).

United Nations Office on Drugs and Crime *World Drug Report* (www.unodc.org/unodc/en/world_drug_report.html, 2005a).

United Nations Office on Drugs and Crime 'Trafficking in Human Beings' www.unodc.org/unodc/en/trafficking_human_beings.html, 2005b).

United Nations Secretary General *In Larger Freedom: Towards Development, Security, and Human Rights for All* (http://www.un.org/largerfreedom/contents.htm, 2005).

Urry, J. 'Globalization and Citizenship', *Journal of World-Systems Research*, V (1999) 311–24.

Valentine, G. *Social Geographies: Space and Society* (New York: Prentice Hall, 2001).

Vanaik, A. 'Rendezvous at Mumbai', *New Left Review*, 26 (2004) 53–65.

Veltmeyer, H. (ed.) Globalization and Antiglobalization: Dynamics of Change in the New World Order (Aldershot: Ashgate, 2004).

Verdery, K. 'Nationalism, Postsocialism, and Space in Eastern Europe – Nationalism Re-examined', *Social Research*, 63 (1996) 77–95.

Via Campesina. 'La Via Campesina: International Peasant Movement' (http://viacampesina.org/en/index.php, 2005).

Viner, K. 'Hand-To-Brand-Combat: A Profile of Naomi Klein', *The Guardian* (www.commondreams.org/views/092300-103.htm, 23 September 2000).

Vogler, J. and Imber, M. (eds) *The Environment and International Relations* (London: Routledge, 1996).

Volcker, P. A. 'The Sea of Global Finance', in W. Hutton and A. Giddens (eds), *Global Capitalism* (New York: New Press, 2000).

Wade, R. 'The Ringmaster of Doha', *New Left Review*, 25 (2004) 146–52.

Walby, S. 'The Myth of the Nation-State: Theorizing Society and Polities in a Global Era', *Sociology*, 37 (2003), 529–46.

Wallach, L. and Woodall, P. *Whose Trade Organization? A Comprehensive Guide to the WTO* (New York: The New Press, 2004).

Wallerstein, I. 'New Revolts Against the System', *New Left Review*, 18 (2002) 29–39.

Wallerstein, I. *The Decline of American Power: The U.S. in a Chaotic World* (New York: The New Press, 2003).

Wallerstein, I. *World-Systems Analysis: An Introduction* (Durham: Duke University Press, 2005).

Warren, B. 'Imperialism and Capitalist Industrialization', *New Left Review*, 81 (1973) 3–44.

Waters, M. *Globalization*, 2nd edn (London: Routledge, 1999).

Webster, A. *Introduction to the Sociology of Development*, 2nd edn (London: Macmillan, 1990).

Webster, F. 'A New Politics?', in F. Webster (ed.), *Culture and Politics in the Information Age: A New Politics?* (London: Routledge, 2001).

Webster, F. *Theories of the Information Society* (London: Routledge, 2002).

Whittaker, D. J. *United Nations in the Contemporary World* (London: Routledge, 1997).

Whittier, N. 'Meaning and Structure in Social Movements', in D. S. Meyer, N. Whittier, and B. Bobnett (eds), *Social Movements: Identity, Culture, and the State* (Oxford: Oxford University Press, 2002).

Woods, N. (ed.) *The Political Economy of Globalization* (New York: St Martin's Press, 2000).

Woodward, K. (ed.) *Identity and Difference* (London: Sage, 1999).

World Economic Forum *Voice of the People Survey: Gallup International* (www.voice-of-the-people.net/ContentFiles/docs/VoP_Trust_Survey.pdf, 2002).

World Social Forum 'Charter of Principles' (www.wsfindia.org/charter.php, 2004).

World Tourism Organization 'International Tourist Arrivals' (www.world-tourism.org/facts/tmt.html, 2005).

Worldwatch Institute *Vital Signs* (London: Earthscan Publications, 1999).

Worldwatch Institute *Vital Signs: The Environmental Trends that are Shaping Our Future, 2000–2001* (London: Earthscan Publications, 2001).

Worldwatch Institute *State of the World 2002* (New York: Norton, 2002).

Worldwatch Institute *State of the World: Progress Towards a Sustainable Society* (London: Earthscan Publications, 2003).

Worldwatch Institute *State of the World 2004* (New York: Norton, 2004).

Worldwatch Institute 'Poverty, Disease, Environmental Decline are True "Axis of Evil"' (wwwglobalpolicy.org/socecon/develop/2005/0112stateoftheworld.htm, 2005).

Yearly, S. 'Dirty Connections: Transnational Pollution', in J. Allen and C. Hamnett (eds), *A Shrinking World?* (Oxford: Oxford University Press, 1995).

Yes Men, 'WTO' (www.theyesmen.org/hijinks/wto.shtml, nd).

Yuen, E., Burton-Rose, D., and Katsiaficas, G. *Confronting Capitalism: Dispatches From a Global Movement* (Brooklyn: Soft Skull Press, 2004).

Žižek, S. 'Multiculturalism, or, the Cultural Logic of Multinational Capitalism', *New Left Review*, 225 (1997) 28–51.

Žižek, S. 'Why we all Love to Hate Haider', *New Left Review*, 2 (2000) 37–45.

Žižek, S. 'Against Human Rights', *New Left Review*, 34 (2005) 115–31.

Znet 'Global Watch/Protests' (www.zmag.org/GlobalWatch/DiverseDemos.html, nd).

Zook, M. A. 'Old Hierarchies or New Networks of Centrality? The Global Geography of the Internet Content Market', *American Behavioural Scientist*, 44 (2001) 1679–96.

Index